JUSTICE MALALA is one of South Africa's most well-known political commentators. He was founding editor of *ThisDay* newspaper, publisher of the *Sowetan* and *Sunday World*, and *Sunday Times* correspondent in London and New York. He has been published internationally and writes weekly columns in *The Times* and the *Financial Mail*. He presents a weekly TV talk show, *The Justice Factor*.

JUSTICE MALALA

We have now begun our descent

*How to Stop South Africa
Losing its Way*

Jonathan Ball Publishers
Johannesburg & Cape Town

© Text, Justice Malala, 2015

Published in South Africa in 2015 by
JONATHAN BALL PUBLISHERS
A division of Media24 Limited
PO Box 33977
Jeppestown
2043

This limited edition printed twice in 2015

ISBN 978-1-86842-679-9
ebook ISBN 978-1-86842-680-5

Every effort has been made to trace the copyright holders and to obtain their permission for the use of copyright material. The publishers apologise for any errors or omissions and would be grateful to be notified of any corrections that should be incorporated in future editions of this book.

Twitter: www.twitter.com/JonathanBallPub
Facebook: www.facebook.com/JonathanBallPublishers
Blog: http://jonathanball.bookslive.co.za/

Author photograph by Gallo Images/Daily Dispatch/Alan Eason
Cover by Michiel Botha
Design and typesetting by Nazli Jacobs
Printed and bound by Mega Digital (Pty) Ltd

Set in Palatino

Contents

Prologue

I am angry. I am furious. Because I never thought it would happen to us. I never thought we would be having such a conversation. Not us, not the rainbow nation that defied doomsayers and suckled and nurtured a fragile democracy into life for its children. I never thought it would happen to us, this relentless decline, the flirtation with a leap over the cliff.

How could it? How can it? We are the children of Nelson Mandela, after all. We are the country that gave birth to the first liberation movement on the African continent, the African National Congress (ANC).[1] We wrote the world's most admired Constitution,[2] a document held up as an example by progressive forces around the globe.

It would never happen to us, I said, as I tucked into a bowl of pepper soup in Lagos, Nigeria, in 2004, surrounded by some of the most astute Nigerians of my generation. At our table of eight were bankers, editors, accountants and a government official. I spoke confidently of my faith in my people, in my country, and in my country's leaders, to break the narrative of Africa as a continent of post-colonial plunder, poverty, dictatorship and war.

They laughed. They laughed good-naturedly, as if I was a child, as if I was yet to learn the ways of the world. They all laughed, all of them, without exception.

That sweltering afternoon in Lagos, when I joshed with my colleagues and told them South Africa would never descend into the anarchy and decrepitude and chaos that made me love and hate their city, came back to me on the evening of 12 February 2015. South Africa's democracy was being stolen, and the slow decline we had suffered over the previous seven years was coming to a head.

The young firebrand Julius Malema, leader of the Economic Freedom Fighters (EFF) and former president of the ANC Youth League, had made it clear in the run-up to the State of the Nation Address, to be delivered by President Jacob Zuma, that he would demand that the President answer to the charge of theft.[3] Zuma's administration had, over the previous six years, spent R246 million in public money on improvements to the President's vast house in his home village of Nkandla, in rural KwaZulu-Natal.

The Public Protector, Thuli Madonsela, had been scathing in her findings about the house. Her report found that Zuma had dispro-portionately benefited from the upgrades; that the work on his home was 'exorbitant'; that he had failed to stop the spiralling costs; and that he had allowed the building of a visitors' centre, cattle kraal and chicken run, swimming pool and amphitheatre under the guise of 'security upgrades', which these were clearly not.[4]

This was what Malema was challenging Zuma about in Parliament. Both the EFF and the rest of the opposition wanted Zuma to pay back the money he owed to South Africans for the building of this gaudy palace in the midst of the poverty and despair of Nkandla.

As the respected economist Nazmeera Moola has pointed out, the Nkandla Local Municipality 'has 114 416 people living within its juris-diction. Only 32 per cent of the 22 463 dwellings in the municipality are classified as "formal". Only 16.7 per cent have piped water inside their dwelling, 8.1 per cent have toilets connected to a sewerage system and 7.8 per cent have their garbage collected by the council.'[5]

Here, in this sea of poverty, is where our government spends R246 million on one man. It reminds me of the Zairean kleptocrat, Mobutu Sese Seko. At the height of his excesses in the 1980s, Mobutu built an airport next to his palace at Gbadolite with a runway long enough to accommodate the Concorde, so he could hop over to Paris for a quick shop.[6]

And so Malema arrived at a tense Parliament in Cape Town, having declared his intention to ensure that Zuma answer what can be distilled into this simple question: 'When will the President pay back the money spent on non-essential security items at his Nkandla home?'

A security blanket had been thrown over proceedings, with every single person who made it into the parliamentary precinct on the day subjected to pre-screening by intelligence services and rigorous security checks.[7] At the start of proceedings, mysterious men and women in white shirts were seen outside the parliamentary chamber. No official would say who they were and why they were there. You would have thought South Africa had received credible information about a threatened terrorist attack, but the threat was that an opposition politician wanted to ask the sitting head of state a question. Just one question.

When proceedings were supposed to start, journalists realised that their mobile devices were jammed and they could not transmit messages to the outside world. The journalists and opposition parties began shouting: 'Bring back the signal!'[8] After several exchanges with irate opposition MPs, the Speaker of the National Assembly, Baleka Mbete, informed the chamber that the signal had been unscrambled. This was essentially an admission that the signal had been purposefully scrambled in the first place. Who ordered this? Why? The Minister of State Security was later to say that the cellphone signal had been jammed by mistake.[9] If that was the case, how could it be unscrambled so quickly? Why was it unscrambled after he, David Mahlobo, had received a note from Deputy President Cyril Ramaphosa and then left the chamber?

After that there was an argument when Malema's party insisted that Zuma answer the question of when he would pay back the money spent on Nkandla. That was when Mbete ordered the mysterious figures in white shirts and black trousers to enter the room. Using their fists liberally, they removed the EFF MPs from the chamber. Several of the EFF MPs, including Malema, were bleeding. A female EFF MP suffered a broken jaw and spent days in hospital.[10]

This was the South African Parliament, where our revered Constitution – authored by men and women led by Cyril Ramaphosa, one of the men now sitting in the National Assembly – was adopted in 1997. In a speech at the adoption ceremony for the Constitution, symbolically held in Sharpeville, Gauteng, where 69 South Africans were murdered by apartheid police in March 1960, Ramaphosa had said: 'Here, at Sharpeville, in Vereeniging, both powerful symbols of past relationships between South Africans, we are making a break with the past. A break with the pain, a break with betrayal. We are starting a new chapter.

'Today marks the legal transition to a Constitution that represents the will of the overwhelming majority of the people of this country. It's one law for one nation, a document that commits not only the government but every single one of us to the values that have been disregarded in the past – to human rights, fair, decent treatment for all, to democracy and government that is accountable to the people, to tolerance of our differences and appreciation of our common humanity.'[11]

The events in Parliament on that day in February 2015 were the furthest we have ever been from that beautiful statement. Accountability, openness, democracy – all lay in tatters. South Africa's democracy was being compromised in defence of one man: a leader around whom swirled allegations of corruption, lack of values, lethargy and failure to govern properly.

That was when I knew that South Africa had begun its descent into what my lunch colleagues in Lagos had joked about with me. In the years since 2009, when Jacob Gedleyihlekisa Zuma ascended to the presidency of South Africa, we have gone backwards on every conceivable front. We are losing our way. The principles embodied by our founding fathers are under siege; the poor are treated with disdain; the powerful and politically connected are looting the coffers of the state; while the masses of our people are becoming increasingly desperate and have only government handouts to thank for their survival.

Under Nelson Mandela and Thabo Mbeki, government debt was reduced from the disgraceful apartheid levels (52 per cent of GDP in

1994) to less than 30 per cent of GDP. Under Zuma it has ratcheted up dramatically to 45.9 per cent.[12] Unemployment is ticking up, while economic growth has deteriorated sharply since 2009. Statistics South Africa's quarterly labour force survey found that the jobless rate rose to 26.4 per cent in the first three months of 2015 – the highest level in 11 years. In all, 8.7 million people are unemployed, if we include those who have given up looking for work.[13]

Gross domestic product grew by an annualised 1.3 per cent quarter-on-quarter in the first three months of 2015. That is worse than the miserable 1.5 per cent growth of 2014. Worse, though, is that GDP contracted an annualised 1.3 per cent from the first quarter of 2015. GDP growth has deteriorated steadily under Zuma: 3.6 per cent in 2011, 2.5 per cent in 2012, 1.9 per cent in 2013. The trend is set to continue up to 2017.[14]

Zuma was re-elected for a second term in May 2014, at exactly the same time as Indian Prime Minister Narendra Modi. At the time India's inflation was running at 9 per cent and economic growth had slowed to less than 5 per cent. When Modi celebrated a year in office in 2015, inflation was down to 5 per cent, and the International Monetary Fund was forecasting that India's economy would grow by 7.5 per cent in 2015. The same institution believes South Africa will struggle to achieve 2 per cent growth.

Unemployment is the single most dangerous issue facing South Africa today. It is creating a great mass of anger and frustration. As the young and hopeless watch Zuma and his cronies eat and ask for more from their mothers and fathers in taxes, rates, eTolls (highway tolls) and other charges, they begin to ask themselves: why, and for how long? Police minister Nathi Nhleko reported to Parliament in May 2015 that there were a staggering 14 700 incidents of unrest – community and service delivery protests – reported to the South African Police Service (SAPS) in the previous year.[15]

There will be howling from Zuma and his cronies at all these things I say. They will allege all sorts of things. They will accuse me – as they have accused every black person who dares to call them out on their looting – a coconut, a sellout, a tool of whites and of the West.

To them I say: it is black people, my people, that you are betraying. It is black people who are unemployed, whose taxes you steal, whose lives you condemn to hopelessness and despair. It is black people who suffer when the institutions of state are rendered useless and cowed. It is black people – who the Zuma administration claims to be working for – who bear the brunt of the failure of the police, the courts, the state, to deliver on their mandates. These people didn't fight and defeat apartheid for this. They didn't fight and defeat apartheid to see their leaders feed at the trough while thousands go to bed hungry and cold. If they did, then indeed I am a sellout. Then indeed every man and woman of conscience who stands up against the spread of corruption and the betrayal of the liberation ethos espoused by Mandela and others is a sellout.

Are we a failed state? No, not by a long shot. Are we a Syria or an Eritrea or a Libya? Not at all. We have a beautiful country, a peace that defies belief and a people committed to the democracy we have painstakingly built over 21 years. That is why we need to take heed of the warning lights that are flashing.

Failure, disaster and collapse can arrive very quickly. Sometimes it can take years of the drip-drip effect, of small things going wrong and being left unfixed. One day you look around and realise that everything is broken, that your country has been stolen. That is what I fear the Zuma presidency has been doing to South Africa since the man came to power in 2009.

The Zuma bus is taking us over the cliff. And if we stay quiet, if we don't point out the sharp decline that he has brought about, both in the quality of the ANC's leadership of society and in the quality of leadership in government, then we are laughing with the bus driver, the thief-in-chief from Nkandla.

What is going on? On the day the Public Protector comprehensively proved that a crime had been committed against the taxpayer over the building of Zuma's palatial home, and that he had benefited unduly from this crime, he gave a speech in which he did not even see fit to mention her findings.

You see, he is not ashamed at all. He is not ashamed that he is exposed, that he is naked, that the world is pointing and laughing at him – and at us. He has no shame. Without this sense of shame, this acknowledgement of wrongdoing, he will sit in office and continue as if nothing is wrong. I believe that, in his warped view, the only thing that would lead to his being removed from office would be a jail sentence.

We are sliding from our high ideals into a free-for-all in which politicians are a law unto themselves and accountability is a word used only for PowerPoint presentations. Not a single member of the ANC's national executive committee (NEC) is prepared to raise their hand and say to Zuma: thus far, and no further. In the NEC, the rot is now endemic.

It is, of course, easy to point fingers and accuse Zuma and his cronies of all sorts of things. The truth is, they are not the only guilty party here. We are guilty too.

South Africans deserve these leaders. We deserve a Zuma, because we have rewarded him for his scandals: Guptagate, Khwezigate, Malawigate, the spy tapes, Schabir Shaik …

The list of scandals is long. Yet we chose the man at the heart of them all. Not just once. Twice.

The depressing part is that Zuma and the 'leaders' he has surrounded himself with are busy subverting our institutions of accountability and turning them into paper tigers. By the time they leave – for they shall – they will have done us a huge amount of damage. Think about the many once-respected institutions that, over the Zuma years, have become nothing but shadows of their former selves, with mostly puppets at the helm: the National Prosecuting Authority (NPA), the Hawks, the South African Revenue Service (Sars). And what about the collapse of the Scorpions, the attempts to subvert the judiciary, the hijacking of the National Intelligence Agency and of course the disgraceful violation of Parliament in February 2015 when police hammered the EFF's MPs – despite the outcry when this happened for the first time in November 2014.

The problems we face are not insurmountable, though. Indeed, we are luckier than most in that our beautiful country can turn itself around quickly – if we move fast.

South Africa needs some serious, ethical, authentic, values-driven and dynamic leadership – from government, business and civil society – over the next few years. Without such leadership we shall lose a golden opportunity to take this country towards the prosperity, peace and pride that it sorely needs.

In the run-up to the 2009 elections many of us said that Zuma was not the right man for the job. He was compromised then, and his track record since 2009 proves that he is not the type of inclusive, principled or decisive leader that the country needs, and that our challenges demand. This is a challenge for the ANC to grapple with, but it is one that the electorate will decide for it if the party does not mend its ways. They will walk away from the party of Mandela sooner rather than later.

Zuma is a liability for the ANC. He is a liability for the country. He should do the right thing and go. He must go. South Africa cannot afford such a leader for the long, challenging period ahead to 2019, when the next general election will be held. I shudder to think of the damage we will have suffered by then.

The much-lauded former Minister in the Presidency, Trevor Manuel, and his impressive National Planning Commission produced a comprehensive set of recommendations, in the form of the National Development Plan (NDP), about how we can make South Africa a prosperous country, free of unemployment and homelessness, by 2030.[16] The commission's report will make many of us uncomfortable. Its analysis of our shortcomings is searing. Its honesty in pointing out our failures over the past 21 years is clinical and admirable, yet painful. Its proposals on how we get our education system, labour market, government and other spheres of society back to winning ways will require much hard work.

Key to all of it, however, is leadership. Since the NDP was adopted by

Cabinet, very little of it has been implemented. We need leadership to implement some of the extremely tough measures that are called for in the report.

The problem goes further than Zuma. Ordinary citizens will have to get out of the slump of dependency that so many of us have fallen into. Trade unions will have to stomach the idea that things have to change, and that the unemployed are as important as the employed. Principals and teachers will have to accept that supervision of schools will be stepped up. Business will have to accept that, without ethical leadership and participation in South Africa as a corporate citizen, the profit motive alone is just not good enough.

It is bitter medicine, but it is medicine that we have to take. Reading the NDP document, it is clear that we could become a prosperous country within a relatively short period of time. But we need resolve at leadership level, we need non-partisanship, and we need to understand that this is the crossroads.

We can choose to be decisive in our leadership and walk the road Manuel and his commission have mapped out for this country. Or we can fall into the lazy thinking, the woolly policies, the selfish gestures, of the Zuma school of leadership. That way leads to entropy, chaos and collapse.

The warning lights are flashing. We need to wake up and smell the coffee. We are going down.

This book is an attempt to point out how Jacob Zuma and his cronies have stolen our democracy. They have infected us with poor governance and poorer values. I hope this book can help us get our democracy back. It is an attempt to show how we can put the nightmare years behind us and begin the tough task of giving jobs, water, education, housing and dignity to our people. At the end of the day, this is the urgent task that Mandela and Tambo and many others – the founding fathers of our democracy – were all about.

In his first speech to Parliament in 1994, Mandela set out exactly what it was the ANC-led government would seek to achieve: 'My government's commitment to create a people-centred society of liberty binds us to the pursuit of the goals of freedom from want, freedom from hunger, freedom from deprivation, freedom from ignorance, freedom from suppression and freedom from fear.'[17]

This is what we all want. The Zuma years have been the polar opposite. As Zwelinzima Vavi, the former secretary-general of Cosatu and a former ally of Zuma, said in 2010: 'We're headed for a predator state where a powerful, corrupt and demagogic elite of political hyenas are increasingly using the state to get rich.'[18]

We are there now. We can still fix things before we hit rock bottom. But time is running out. We have now begun our descent.

PART ONE
The Way We Are Now

1
And So it Begins

'Yeah, every night it's the same old thing
Getting high, getting drunk, getting horny
At the Inn-Between, again.'
– Rodriguez, 'A Most Disgusting Song'

My brother Ernest is reading *Time* magazine. It is the year 1991, a bright, hot, clear April day. He is 14 years old. He comes over to me, lolling on the one sofa in our family home, a corrugated-iron shack, and asks for the meaning of a word he is unfamiliar with.

We play around with the word, *factotum*, which he likes the sound of, and make examples of sentences in which it appears. Then we have a short discussion about Angola's MPLA. *Movimento Popular de Libertação de Angola,* he tells me. That is what it stands for in Portuguese. I don't know how good a leader José Eduardo dos Santos is, which is what Ernest wants to know, as he has lately heard about the Angolan president.

Then his friend Ndembeni rides into our yard on his bicycle. Ndembeni is two years older than Ernest. They are fast friends. Ernest gets onto the handlebars of the bicycle and they ride off, free as a pair of birds.

Two hours later my cousin Dan Malala's son, also named Justice, comes running into our yard. He tells me that two teenagers have been hit by a bakkie down in Block A of our village of New Eersterus, just north of Pretoria, near where they live. He is not sure that it is Ernest and his friend. He says I must hurry.

I walk, in a daze, to the scene of the accident, a journey of 30 minutes. A large crowd has gathered. A man stands by the side of the road, holding his head in his hands. He is the driver.

It is Ernest who is lying on the side of the road. We put him in the back of the bakkie. I sit with him. I know he is dead, but we all pretend that there is hope. The driver, the man with his head in his hands, takes the wheel. An Indian doctor comes to the door at the hospital, Jubilee. He shakes his head.

'He is dead,' he says, his tone flat. Final.

Hospital orderlies take Ernest's body to the morgue.

Both of Ndembeni's legs are broken. He is in a coma for weeks. There are injuries to his head, his arms and his face. They did not see the bakkie coming. There is no police investigation.

The driver takes me back to our house. My mother is back from work at the nearby Catholic seminary. There are women sitting with her, surrounding her. They know. I tell them. They hold my mother down. Her weeping is silent. I don't know what to do, what to hold.

Ernest was special. Top of his class whenever he felt like it, he was already a political activist, attending South African Youth Congress and ANC Youth League meetings all over the country. When he returned from his first Young Pioneers (ANC Youth League members younger than 14) meeting just the year before he died, in 1990, he fell into memorising the ANC's guiding document, the Freedom Charter. It begins with the historic, unifying line, 'We, the People of South Africa, declare for all our country and the world to know: that South Africa belongs to all who live in it, black and white, and that no government can justly claim authority unless it is based on the will of all the people.'[1]

He committed the document to memory within a couple of days, and quoted it to anyone who would listen.

And so, when he died, the ANC in the village rallied to my family's cause. It was not just that my brother was a committed ANC member at just 14. My brother Eric had been an activist and was beaten and detained for months by the Bophuthatswana police in the 1980s. My younger sister was a fierce student activist. I had helped launch the local ANC and ANC Youth League branches in the village, becoming the first acting branch secretary-general of the unbanned ANC in 1990.

Local ANC leaders took refuge at my mother's house when they were on the run. Even when we had little food, they were guaranteed a plate of pap and relish at our house. Every week, political education sessions were held under my mother's roof until it became too dangerous to do so.

When my brother's coffin was lowered into his grave, an ANC flag went down with it. The black, green and gold was in our blood. The beautiful melody of 'Nkosi Sikelel' iAfrika', the ANC anthem that was later to become part of a spliced-together national anthem, rose up over the New Eersterus cemetery.

We were proud ANC members. That year, as the pain of my brother's passing began to mend, my comrades and I were entranced by a widely circulated paper written by an ANC intellectual, Albie Sachs, who later became a Constitutional Court judge and celebrated South African author.

Towards the end of the paper he made one of the most moving declarations I have ever read about what it meant, then, to be a member of the ANC. It was as if Sachs knew my heart, the very depths of my soul.

He wrote: 'We think we are the best (and we are), that is why we are in the ANC. We work hard to persuade the people of our country that we are the best (and we are succeeding). But this does not require us to force our views down the throats of others.

'On the contrary, we exercise true leadership by being non-hegemonic, by selflessly trying to create the widest unity of the oppressed and to encourage all forces of change, by showing the people that we are fighting not to impose a view upon them but to give them the right to choose the kind of society they want and the kind of government they want.

'We are not afraid of the ballot box, of open debate, of opposition. One fine day we will even have our Ian Smith equivalents protesting and grumbling about every change being made and looking back with nostalgia to the good old days of apartheid, but we will take them on at the hustings. In conditions of freedom, we have no doubt who will win, and if we should forfeit the trust of the people, then we deserve to lose.'[2]

It was such belief in the ANC and the possibility of a new order, a new progressive country, that made the release of Nelson Mandela and the unbanning of the ANC in February 1990 such seminal moments in our collective history. I was walking in the Johannesburg city centre on 2 February 1990 when a huge surge of people ran towards me. They were holding posters of the afternoon edition of the *Star* newspaper. President FW de Klerk had that morning announced that the government would release Nelson Mandela and unban the African National Congress and its allied organisations.

I joined the surging masses of people running through the streets of Johannesburg, laughing, hugging, weeping, running, crying. The country of our dreams had finally arrived. I arrived back home in Pretoria at midnight. My whole journey from Johannesburg, in three different taxis, had consisted of people hugging, singing freedom songs and dancing.

These were the thoughts and images racing through my mind at 3.41 am on Saturday 7 January 2012, a day before the celebrations to mark the centenary of the founding of the ANC. There was nothing revolutionary about the Cubaña restaurant-cum-nightclub in Bloemfontein, the sleepy city in the centre of South Africa where the ANC was born.

As the sun rose, the morning light revealed all the signs of the crass, conspicuous consumption that we have come to expect of the ANC, not the signs of the revolution the party had set out to achieve. The evidence of the night's partying looked more like a bacchanalian bankers' feast than a humble ANC celebration. Outside, the streets of Bloemfontein were clogged with Range Rovers, massive Mercedes-Benzes and BMWs.[3] Inside, ANC leaders enjoyed Moët et Chandon champagne in massive quantities. No one, it seemed, was interested in the fine South African sparkling wines available at far cheaper prices. This was not about enjoyment. It was about showing that you had arrived. It was not about good champagne. It was about showing that you could afford expensive stuff. It was about the label, the price tag, and not what was in the bottle.

The ANC's arrival in Bloemfontein in the Free State province – a place so racist under apartheid that people of Indian origin were not allowed to sleep there overnight – had attracted the party's elite from across the country. And if the ANC has succeeded at anything, it is at enriching a narrow black elite that is not afraid of flaunting its material wealth. In Mangaung, as the Bloemfontein metro area is called today, ANC leaders, hangers-on and others jostled to show each other and the poor masses how big their cars and their bank balances were. That is the measure of our success today.

At 4 am the music stopped. As Cubaña prepared to shut down, President Jacob Zuma's supporters started singing in praise of him. The songs started here, there and everywhere in the club. There was a variety of songs, including the man's infamous signature song, 'Awu Lethe uMshini Wami' (Bring Me My Machine Gun).

The singing was full of vim and bravado. The same vigour continued the next day with the speeches and public celebrations. Yet there was no doubt that the mighty ANC house was creaky and facing collapse. Noble and admirable as the ANC's 82 years of liberation struggle are, there was no doubt at those celebrations that 18 years of power had presented extraordinary challenges to the grand old lady of the continent's liberation movements.

In Mangaung, these challenges were writ large: societal poverty cheek by jowl with vulgar displays of affluence by party luminaries; institutional decay and creeping moral degeneration; allegations of corruption within party leadership and at the highest echelons of the state.

At the heart of the ANC's rotting corpse stood one man: its president, Jacob Zuma. When Zuma was rising to power in the late 2000s much was made of his middle name, Gedleyihlekisa (He who smiles while

23

crushing you).[4] There was another name the ANC rank and file liked to attach to him as he swatted aside one criminal charge or scandal after another: *Phunyuka bemphete!* This is a Zulu expression meaning 'the one who escapes [when there is no way out, every time]'. In a Western context, it is the equivalent of calling Zuma 'Houdini'.

Zuma is a man known for his gorgeous singing and for his dismissive giggle in response to difficult questions. Many think his lack of schooling – he has only five years of formal education to his name – means he is a fool. But a fool he is not. He makes gaffes every week, and has no idea what constitutionality means, but he is not a fool. He might not read, as has been alleged by intellectuals such as political analyst and academic Richard Calland,[5] but in the first five years of his administration he amply proved that he knows how to work the levers of power to ensure he never sees the interior of a court of law to answer the more than 750 instances of corruption levelled at him on 28 December 2007, which he has so far managed to evade.[6] This is a remarkable feat given that Schabir Shaik, his friend and benefactor, was convicted of bribing him. So the briber, as it were, went to jail while the man who accepted the bribes rose to the presidency.

Since he became the president of the ANC in 2007, Zuma has overseen the most concerted and successful assault on the independent institutions of South Africa since democracy dawned in 1994. The judiciary is today facing a major crisis of confidence because of cases involving him at the Constitutional Court. The minute he left Polokwane after winning the ANC presidency his lieutenants in Parliament ensured that the Scorpions investigative unit, which had investigated Zuma for taking bribes, was disbanded. It was quick, cruel and ruthless.

Over the past few years it has been the turn of the Office of the Public Protector – an independent constitutional body aimed at ensuring honesty and proper delivery of services by the state and its many arms. The profile of the Public Protector has been raised by the fearlessness of the incumbent, Thuli Madonsela, who has taken on the unauthorised expenditure of R246 million of taxpayers' money on Zuma's private residence in his rural KwaZulu-Natal village of Nkandla.

Madonsela has proposed that Zuma pay back some of the money used for what have been termed 'security upgrades' – including a cattle kraal, swimming pool and chicken coop – at his home. He has refused, and instead set up various investigations stuffed with cronies to exonerate him. The concerted, coordinated attacks from Parliament, the executive and various sections of the ANC on the Public Protector's office have turned Madonsela into possibly the most admired 'public servant' in South Africa today.

In late 2013 we had the extraordinary spectacle of our security cluster ministers – including the ministers of intelligence, police and defence – turning on the populace and declaring that publication of pictures of the taxpayer-funded Nkandla was illegal and the full might of the law would come down on those who dared to do so.[7] All this for one man: Jacob Gedleyihlekisa Zuma.

The man is not a fool. He has managed to turn the mighty ANC into a tool for his protection. Whatever he does, whether it is allowing his friends the Gupta family to blatantly make use of military installations[8] or pretending to know nothing of the monstrous, hideous compound being built for him for R246 million, the man has the party rushing to do his bidding.

And so we have to ask: which African National Congress is this? How can an organisation that refused to build a personality cult around Nelson Mandela allow itself to become a mere tool in the hands of Zuma? What kind of leaders does it have that they can cast aside the party's historical mission – to transform the lives of millions of poor black people and build a united, non-racial, prosperous and democratic country – and work as nothing more than gophers for Zuma?

Yet that is what the party's 86-member NEC does. The party's Members of Parliament (MPs) stand and introduce legislation that is aimed solely at protecting this one man. Six months after he was confronted by the EFF in Parliament, ANC MPs pushed through new parliamentary regulations to ensure that an MP could be kicked out of the National Assembly for making certain utterances.[9] Across the land, provincial party leaders hobble state machinery merely to protect and keep this one compromised leader out of jail and in power. Not only has he faced rape charges[10] but he has also impregnated the daughter of a friend,[11] and allegations abound that he has handed out plum posts to his mistresses at key parastatals such as South African Airways.[12]

It is an astounding sight, this. Once-proud leaders who served our nation in exile, in the United Democratic Front and in other anti-apartheid organisations and in trade unions now scrape and bow before this one man. From the great heights of leaders such as Nobel Peace Prize winner Albert Luthuli, the ANC no longer has leaders. It has zombies who mindlessly follow this one leader and do his bidding. It is quite extraordinary.

What has happened to the culture of debate and contestation that once permeated this movement? What happened to the pride that made this organisation stand up and expel people who muddied its name? How can this lot walk in the shoes of leaders such as Walter Sisulu, AP Mda, Anton Lembede and Pixley kaIsaka Seme?

So, as we look at the extraordinary lengths to which the current ANC 'leadership' has gone to defend a compromised embarrassment of a leader whose entire family seems to be infused by a shocking culture of entitlement (Zuma's brother Michael has admitted, on live radio, using his name to swing government contracts or tenders to benefactors who had promised him a house[13]), we have to ask: where is the African National Congress of my dreams, of my father's dreams, of my brother's and sister's dreams?

The answer is heartbreaking: the ANC is compromised, it is weak, it is lost. It has lost its moral compass and its leadership of society. The man at its head is a reflection of what the party is: ill disciplined, compromised, unprincipled. The fish rots from the head.

The desperation we see among the ANC's leaders is a reflection of

26

this. When a man as widely admired as Cyril Ramaphosa – the former trade union leader, architect of our Constitution and respected businessman who hitched his wagon to the Zuma camp in 2012 to become deputy president of the party and the country – has no argument to convince a disgruntled voter except to say 'the Boers will return'[14] if the voter doesn't cast his ballot for the ANC, then you know that this is a movement that is both intellectually and morally bankrupt. The emperor and his lieutenants have no clothes.

This is the way we will remember the reign of Zuma. We will remember it not for its achievements, but for the cowardice, callowness and bankruptcy of the leadership that he brought with him. We will remember them for their bowing and scraping and their destruction of a great liberation movement.

Yet even as we consider that the ANC has come to this, we must not be fooled into thinking that the narrative will be a straight line of decline and inevitable destruction over the next decade. The ANC has faced some serious challenges in the past, and has not just survived; it has emerged from some of its trials and tribulations even stronger. The departure of the so-called Africanists in 1958 after the adoption of the Freedom Charter – a document that asserted the ANC's non-racial character – was supposedly the death knell of the ANC. It was not. Exile, violence and dissent in its camps, the merciless tactics of the apartheid government, the imprisonment of its leaders – these are just some of the things the ANC has survived.

And yet, as I stood in Mangaung on 8 January 2012, with the many thoughts of the ANC swirling in my head, I could not be churlish. It was a gorgeous day. The ANC's history of struggle is something to be celebrated by all. Nothing makes me prouder than what those great men and women selflessly and bravely gave up for all of us – and the freedoms we enjoy and take for granted today. It is a glorious achievement, one alluded to by Nelson Mandela when he was sworn in as president of a free, united, democratic and non-racial South Africa in 1994: 'Let each know that for each the body, the mind and the soul have been freed to fulfil themselves. Never, never and never again shall it be that this beautiful land will again experience the oppression of one by another and suffer the indignity of being the skunk of the world.'

Then he concluded by saying: 'Let freedom reign. The sun shall never set on so glorious a human achievement.'[15]

What a glorious achievement indeed: black and white defying the odds to build an extraordinary, beautiful, divided and yet united entity whose existence many wouldn't have believed was possible.

Yet.

Yet, despite this, the truth is that this ANC is in trouble and faces terminal decline. More than 20 years in power have been challenging for the party. Its decline is taking South Africa down with it. The sheen and hope of the new South Africa is coming off. Why?

The most heated discussion points among those attending the Mangaung celebrations were about leadership. There is no doubt, even among his supporters, that Zuma is seen as an intellectual flyweight whose tenure in the Union Buildings has been a rudderless, scriptless farce. To see his picture beside those of his predecessors is jarring for many; he just has not displayed the intellectual rigour and exemplary, values-based leadership displayed by them.

Zuma's poor leadership is not his problem alone, though. Current ANC leaders campaigned for him and elected him. They got the leader they deserved, and by voting for the ANC in 2009 and in 2014 we, too, got the leader we deserved. If Zuma is a problem, the people who lined him up next to OR Tambo, Nelson Mandela and Albert Luthuli have a serious problem too.

Gwede Mantashe, the cantankerous ANC secretary-general, has bemoaned the fact that many of Africa's liberation movements are not just out of power but cannot even win a single seat in parliamentary elections.[16] Mantashe and his comrades know full well why this is so. It is because, when those organisations faced what the ANC faces today, they just continued the slide down into poor leadership and corruption.

Under Zuma, the ANC has become exactly that kind of organisation.

And so we have to ask: what will South Africa look like when Zuma bids us goodbye in 2019? The answer is pretty simple: the relentless and single-minded assault on the institutions of our democracy that he has overseen will leave us a country whose carefully constructed democracy is deeply compromised.

Given the intensity of the assault on the office of the Public Protector, the NPA, the judiciary and the independent media, it is possible that the country will be cowed and subjugated in five years. We won't be South Africa Inc; we will be Zuma Inc.

Imagine that the year is 2024. Our children will live in a country where the Public Protector's office is led by a yes man and the NPA rouses itself only to prosecute vocal opposition leaders such as the Democratic Alliance's Mmusi Maimane and the EFF's Julius Malema. The newspapers will look like our collapsed neighbour Zimbabwe's state-run press – full of stories congratulating the first lady on her cooked-up PhD and lauding the president's achievements as scientist of the year.[17] This is the country Zuma wants.

Meanwhile, everything that Zuma touches at state level falls apart. State finances are a mess. Unemployment is ticking up while economic growth is getting worse. State schools are terrible (a child died in a pit latrine early in 2014,[18] while female teachers have to give sex to get jobs in the Eastern Cape and KwaZulu-Natal[19]), the economy is on its knees and the monstrosity that is Nkandla is rubbed in our faces every day as ANC leaders defend Zuma from accountability and scrutiny on the issue.[20]

It is a measure of the ethical and moral vacuity of the man that Zuma tells us that corruption is a Western thing and that people who complain about Nkandla should also complain about George airport, which was once named after the apartheid monster PW Botha.[21] That is the level at which the president of Mandela's South Africa has chosen to pitch himself: if it was good enough for an apartheid leader,

29

then it is good enough for him. That is not a low; it is scraping the barrel of depravity, of ignorance.

What has South Africa done to deserve such ignominy? What have we done to become the laughing stock of the world, as the public intellectual Xolela Mangcu put it heartbreakingly and succinctly in a column when a Harvard University seminar he was attending descended into fits of laughter at the mere mention of our leader, Zuma?[22]

How do we give hope to the more than 8 million unemployed South Africans that the party of Mandela can turn itself around and fulfil its promise, when all they see is a leader and a party that seems hell-bent on enriching itself? What do we say to the many who see cronyism at play in the most brazen manner – Zuma's 25-year-old daughter, straight out of school, was given a plum job in 2014 for which she had neither the experience nor the credentials[23] – while nothing is done about it?

How did the hopeful South Africa of Nelson Mandela find itself so compromised and descending towards failure, despair and anarchy? Can the hopeful rainbow nation that astounded the world find its way back to restart its journey towards equality and prosperity?

Sadly, South Africa is quickly reverting to a patriarchal culture where the Big Man is never questioned, never confronted, never probed. I see it at events where all present have to stand when 'the President' enters, where we have to genuflect and treat our elected leaders as though we are in feudal times.

Worse, though, is that we have lost the ability to tell the emperor that he wears no clothes. Even when things are at their lowest ebb, it has become clear to me that our leaders surround themselves with sycophants who cannot find in themselves the self-belief, the courage, to point out the simple things. Our leaders like it, hence the obsequious yes men they continue to surround themselves with. The worst, and most painful, example of this was the failure of those around former President Thabo Mbeki to rein him in when he took it upon himself to become a spokesperson for a fringe grouping of scientists who propagated the idea that HIV infection does not cause Aids.[24]

First, Mbeki's own spokesperson and a friend – not just of mine but also of many journalists – believed in Mbeki's crazy ideas. Parks Mankahlana, a brilliant and charming young former ANC Youth League leader, refused to take anti-retroviral drugs.[25] I returned to South Africa just weeks before he died and saw him at his house in Midrand. He was thin, but he still believed. Weeks later he was dead.

A Harvard University study has estimated that Mbeki's deluded policies on Aids led to the deaths of more than 300 000 people.[26]

It should not have been so. It must never, ever, happen again. Those people – and we can have the debate about just how many people died because of those policies – did not die because the head of state held deplorable views on Aids. They died because only very few of us had the guts to stand up and speak out against Mbeki's madness. The blood is therefore not just on Mbeki's hands. It is also on the hands of the obsequious civil servants, ANC leaders and civil society activists who did not raise their voices, who did not speak when their voices were most needed.

That culture has to stop. We need to stop believing that shielding our leaders from the truth is respect. It is patently not. We disrespect our leaders by shielding them from the truth and by refusing to hold them to account. Ordinary South Africans face the truth of lack of infrastructure every day. Leaders should face similar truths every day, too.

What of the ANC? Can it be saved? Can the rot and decline affecting it be stopped?

There was a time when the ANC was the leader of society in matters intellectual and ethical. At decisive times in our history the ANC and a core of intellectuals in its leadership would process events and emerging trends and apply the party's history and moral and ethical compass, and emerge on the other side with hard, sometimes painful, but necessary positions.

This does not mean that the ANC was always the instigator of events. The party was caught flat-footed by the 1976 student uprising. However, it managed to thread a strong enough narrative for students fleeing South Africa to be attracted to it. It did not foresee the Cato Manor race riots of 1949, but it rose up intellectually and built alliances with progressive Indian organisations in the aftermath of those events.

This is an organisation that has through the decades been able to emerge as a leader of society by giving intellectual succour to its people when they needed it. At various points in the evolution of our country and our democracy, it has stepped in to be a bridge over our troubled waters.

Who wanted the Truth and Reconciliation Commission (TRC) of the 1990s? Not many, not even within the ANC. Yet the party coaxed a reluctant South Africa towards a breathtaking human achievement. Who was for the 'sunset clauses'? At a crucial time the ANC chose to give wide-ranging concessions to a morally vanquished white regime to get us to the 1994 elections. It was not easy. It took courage, intellectual application and strategic and tactical nous to achieve all these things. It was the ANC at its best. To quote the party's slogan: the ANC leads.

Not now. In all recent debates the party of Zuma has been nowhere to be seen. It was outflanked, outgunned, outmanoeuvred and hopelessly inadequate on how to deal with the wave of #RhodesMustFall statue protests across the country in early 2015. During the debates over the removal of the Rhodes statue at UCT, and others on campuses and in cities across South Africa, the best the ANC could offer was a sad, weak, entreaty for us to 'debate these issues'. It had nothing more to offer.

In KwaZulu-Natal, where xenophobic attacks rose sharply after Zulu King Goodwill Zwelithini said foreign nationals must pack up and go,[27] the ANC was paralysed. Instead of providing moral, ethical and intellectual leadership on this issue, the ANC kept schtum. Rather, it commented on the burning issue of the decision to buy seven Mercedes-Benz E-Class sedans for the King's wives. ANC provincial secretary Sihle Zikalala told *The Mercury* newspaper that the purchase was in fact a 'cost-cutting' measure for the royal household.[28]

The truth is that the ANC has forgotten its intellectual roots. Since 2007 it has become an organisation dedicated to protecting its leader, Zuma, at the expense of providing leadership on burning societal issues. Consider, for instance, the party's zeal in dealing with the Nkandla issue. Virtually every brain in the party has been engaged with spinning the looting of R246 million of taxpayer funds to build Zuma's house. Yet the party postponed its crucial national general council – scheduled for June 2015 but pushed out to October – because no one could be bothered to write up policy papers. That's the ANC under Zuma: morally bankrupt, ethically compromised and intellectually lazy.

There are consequences for this betrayal.

Populists, looters, securocrats, revisionists and all sorts of other miscreants have gleefully entered the space and are at play. South Africa, casting about for leadership, finds itself surrounded by mere noise and no substance. The cacophony rises while the real issues and challenges of our time – the tearing of our social fabric, the decline of our economy, the despair of the unemployed, the poor teaching in our schools – increase by the day.

Where are the ANC's intellectuals? Where is the ANC's leadership as these challenges increase? Too many have given up and are looting as much as they can while the going is good. Too many keep quiet while Zuma and his cronies introduce a chauvinistic, anti-intellectual, tribalist, xenophobic rhetoric to mask their looting of the fiscus.

The bottom line is that the ANC of my youth, the ANC that is hardwired into the minds of so many South Africans, and who still vote for it in their millions, is gone. Only a glimmer of it exists. Only its history exists.

The ANC's leadership, and its membership, has now been infected by a mob that is intent on feeding as much as possible before things blow up. They know that this is a game of diminishing returns, yet they cannot stop. When they raise their heads everyone else has their snout in the trough – and so they too fall in and eat. There is no one to stop the orgy of looting.

Our salvation lies in those who have chosen to walk away and begin working in civil society to effect change. Our salvation no longer lies with the ANC, for that ANC died in the kind of looting exemplified by the party's leaders in Mangaung when it celebrated its centenary.

2

How Did We Get Here?

'Then they came for me – and
there was no one left to speak for me.'
– Pastor Martin Niemöller

My friend Comfort Masike and I nearly miss the bus. It is the morning of 19 August 1989, and a big day for the Mass Democratic Movement, an umbrella of civic, youth, student and trade union organisations that have banded together to carry forward the banned ANC's call to render the apartheid system unworkable and make South Africa ungovernable.

Comfort was a mathematics prodigy and my best friend at the University of Cape Town (UCT). We were running late for the bus because we had been busy plastering our T-shirts with Black Students' Society stickers in preparation for the day's events.

After months of protesting across Cape Town in defiance of apartheid laws, 19 August had been set aside for activists to defy 'whites only' beaches at Strand and Bloubergstrand. The idea was to break what we called 'beach apartheid'. In Pretoria my friends were getting on 'whites only' municipal buses and refusing to get off.

The whole of South Africa was in defiance. Parks, beaches, toilets – anything that still carried the vestiges of apartheid was being challenged.

And so we got on the first, early, bus to Bloubergstrand beach. We were on the early bus because we were marshals, supposed to help with crowd control later on in the day. We had practised various responses to the police brutality that was meted out every time a Defiance Campaign event took place: lying down, exhorting people to stand still, and so forth.

We weren't great revolutionaries, Comfort and I. As marshals we were dropped off along the beachfront road to direct buses carrying other protesters to the meeting points further down. It was around 11 am when we were dropped off.

Ten minutes later, a yellow police van pulled up in front of us and three aggressive white officers jumped out, shouting that we were under arrest for incitement – we weren't inciting anyone, there was no one to incite – and bundled us into the back of the van. They drove us down the road and parked. Like us, they were the police's forward party. They stood awkwardly outside the van and stared at us, locked up inside.

'Why,' ventured one of them, finally, 'do you want to swim here? The beach at Mnandi [a local beach designated for use by blacks] is much better than this one. We gave you a better beach, why aren't you happy?'

'Would you like to swim at Mnandi?' asked Comfort.

'Yes,' said the policeman, young, perhaps five years older than my 19 years.

Comfort pointed at the barbed wire strung along the beach by the police to discourage that day's picnickers and marchers.

'Do you think anyone would put up fences like that to stop you from swimming at Mnandi?' he asked.

The police radio crackled. The van was needed elsewhere. Comfort never got his answer.

'Loop, moet nie terug kom nie' (Go, and never come back), said one of the older cops as they jumped into the van and rushed off, leaving us on the side of the road. We went onto the beach. Hours later, buses started arriving, and by afternoon more than 500 people had congregated. Then the police arrived, told the crowd that this was an illegal gathering, and asked us to disperse. Of course we didn't. The police laid into us with sjamboks to make us leave.

It was a scene of great barbarity. Although black protestors like me were hit, arrested and kicked around, I was interested to see that the police saved their venom for the white protesters. At one point I saw two young policemen beating a young white woman – in a strapless black dress, carrying a picnic basket – with such force and so repeatedly on her back that it was a sea of blood.

We ran helter-skelter, getting into buses and away from the police beatings. Comfort and I found ourselves in the Cape Town city centre at nightfall. We took a train back to the UCT campus in Rondebosch.

On the train were people from all over Cape Town, returning home from marches across the city. Some had been on beaches, while others had been to parks and other segregated amenities. We hugged strangers, shouted 'Amandla!' at some, and sang freedom songs.

Across the country, apartheid was creaking to a halt. The police could not enforce grand apartheid's ridiculous laws. The centre was not holding. Towards the end of that year, many political prisoners were released from jail. Nelson Mandela's fellow Rivonia trialists, including the man who recruited him into the ANC, Walter Sisulu, and his lifelong friend Ahmed Kathrada, walked out of Robben Island after 26 years in jail.

The streets were full of people, agitating, raising their voices. After being cowed for decades, South Africans were finally shaking their fists at authority openly and in their millions. In villages and townships, men and women were taking responsibility for schools and their own safety. South Africa had found its voice.

For the ten years between 1984 and 1994 South Africa was a country of people who participated, who were active and engaged with their society. There were many on the sidelines, of course. Yet there were many more who took their destiny into their own hands.

It is these activists, these engaged people, who have disappeared from South Africa today. For years now, as the hope of the new South Africa has taken on a decidedly lacklustre sheen, these people have not raised their voices and warned of the increasing corruption, crime, nepotism and sloth that has gripped the highest echelons of our government.

Countries become basket cases when good men and women check out of the system. They do their own thing, and do not get involved in the conversations and actions of the rest of the country. They live and let die.

Think of what happened to South Africa in 2008, when the first of what have now become regular electricity outages hit the country. Business and industry came to a standstill. Homes, schools and factories were without lights and in many cases water. The economy lost billions of rands.

We had a spike in generator sales then as people decided that they did not have confidence in the country's power supply system. They were saying goodbye to Eskom and to South Africa. They were checking out. They had given up on the system.

In September 2013, in Johannesburg, the economic hub of Africa, power was disrupted in parts of the West Rand and at least 10 northern Joburg suburbs after a few hundred City Power staff downed tools on a Wednesday afternoon. The workers were apparently unhappy about a new shift system being implemented by City Power. There are strong suspicions that they not only downed tools but also sabotaged the system to ensure maximum chaos.

The consequences of these workers' actions were huge. Schools had no electricity or water. Patients needing oxygen had to be evacuated from hospitals. One of the continent's biggest shopping centres, Cresta, was out of action for two days. A newspaper quoted Bramley Park resident Roy Wilson, who lives in a complex, saying his area had been without power for two days and he was the only one in the complex who had a generator. 'I am trying to help my neighbours charge their phones and boil water for a cup of tea,' he told reporters.[1]

How many people in the complex will be following in Wilson's footsteps and buying generators? How many across Joburg and South Africa, fearful of the fire next time, will do the same, have done so already?

The day they do so, they are in effect saying: 'I am tired of being held to ransom by government incompetence and workers' unreliability and criminality. I am checking out. I will rely on my own electricity supply.'

Think about what the same people who are opting out of the electricity grid have opted out of already. They no longer trust the police, so they pay security companies to look after them while they live behind electric fences and high walls. They do not trust the water supply, so they have sunk boreholes in their gardens. They do not trust state schools, so they send their children to private schools.

And they no longer comment on or follow the country's politics, because they feel powerless as monstrosities such as the R246-million Nkandla, private home of the president, are built while his friends, the Gupta family, fly their wedding guests into Waterkloof Air Force Base without any fear of censure. These people keep their heads down and make money.

This is the moment that is most brilliantly described by my friend Dele Olojede, the Pulitzer Prize-winning journalist. I have used his words before, but they return to me often when I reflect on the silence of South Africa's elites. Speaking of his native Nigeria in 2005, he said: 'We live in a Hobbesian jungle, where every man is for himself and the concept of the common good has become totally alien ...

'In such a state, there is no law that anyone is willing to obey. The state itself is considered illegitimate. Force and fraud are the two driving forces. Individuals arrange for their own security, their own electricity, their own water; every home is like a private local government. What we need we take, in complete disregard of any rules. Hobbes calls this chaotic free-for-all a state of war, the very heart of our darkness. It is an entirely unpredictable place, and everyone plans only for the short term.'[2]

In such a place, teachers refuse to send their own children to public schools. They have checked out. In such a place, out of the whole Cabinet, only health minister Aaron Motsoaledi goes to public hospitals.[3] The rest of our 37-member Cabinet have signed out. They cannot be expected to fight to make public services better. They don't care any more. They have checked out, and the poor will just have to deal with it.

What has happened to all these people? I see them in me, too, sometimes. You must understand that I am one of those crazy, news-obsessed people. The thud of the newspaper landing in the drive on a Sunday morning used to galvanise me into action as I rushed to pick it up and delve into the contents.

I shout at the television news. I stand close to the radio at the top of the hour to catch the news bulletin. I read the paper with nods of my head and uhmms and ahhs. I have become my late father. He used to do all these things (before television and Twitter, of course). He cared. Like so many other people who call into radio stations and write to newspapers, he knew that caring is the beginning of a good society. They care, and people who care want to change things. They want to make things better.

These are people who want to make their local school better, and so get engaged with the school governing body. These are people who want to make their streets safer, and so get engaged with the local policing forum.

What happens, though, when they are bombarded with unbearable corruption and crime?

I think about this because I, too, worry that I am changing. I don't rush to pick up my newspaper. I can skip the news. I don't shout back at inanities on television or Twitter. Nowadays, I too go through periods of not caring, or, even worse, I have become inured to the pain, corruption, poverty and crime around me. It scares me that I may think that the abnormalities in my country, the outrages of our politicians, are just what they are.

In July 2014 the *Mail & Guardian* published yet another story about the Zuma family. The President's 25-year-old daughter had just been promoted to a R1-million-a-year job in the office of Minister of Telecommunications Siyabonga Cwele.[4] I read the story with great equanimity, with nary a flutter of my heart. But I don't seem to care as

40

much as I used to any more. This is what the many scandals around Zuma have done to me and many others.

That poor Zuma child. She probably deserves the job and can probably do it pretty well. Truth is, though, what with the Gupta family and all the other scandals that are part of the Zuma train, my instinctive thought is this: that is just how they roll – nepotism, jobs for pals, corruption, tenders for friends. That is their game. I have become inured to the scandals of the Zuma family. I have stopped caring. If they are looting the state – as many say they are – then I have come to accept it as part of what South Africa is.

The *City Press* newspaper carried a story in July 2014 about the Cabinet's business connections, saying essentially that ministers are more businesspeople than servants of the people.[5] This I know. I have stopped caring. I stopped caring when the minerals minister intervened in the platinum strike without thinking that it would be proper to declare a conflict of interest due to his owning shares in a platinum mining company. I am not even shocked that the agriculture minister did not see anything wrong with paying his worker R26 a day while advocating for farmers to pay their workers upwards of R100 a day.

In July 2014 the death of four-year-old Taegrin Morris in a brutal car hijacking reminded us all of the horrors of violent crime. As his mother was hijacked, the child became entangled in the car safety belt. The hijacker drove off, with the boy flapping against the wheel of the car, outside, and being dragged on the tarmac. He was dragged behind the car for 3.4 kilometres. The hijacker did not stop even after being alerted to what was happening. My stomach turns to think about the little boy's agony, his horror, his pain.[6]

The truth is that Taegrin Morris died because we have become inured to violent crime in South Africa. In my neighbourhood, identified recently in the *Sunday Times* as a hijacking hot spot, hijackings happen extremely frequently. Hijacking never went away. It just became normal. We became inured to it. At around the time of the Taegrin Morris incident, a friend's daughter was hijacked and raped. She is one of the more than 66 000 women sexually assaulted every year.[7] We are not angry. We have become inured to horror.

I keep returning to the initiation schools that spring up every winter. Research says more than 500 young men have died in these schools since 2010.[8] Deputy Minister of Traditional Affairs Obed Bapela says many more have died.[9] Thousands more have had their penises chopped off by fraudulent initiation practitioners. Why aren't we outraged that so many kids have died and been maimed? Why is life so cheap?

What has happened here? We have become a people who have been made to accept that violence is okay, corruption is the usual way of doing business, that gross sexism is acceptable, that crime is normal. These things are so commonplace in our public and private lives that we are not shocked any more. We have become inured to what is wrong, what is unacceptable. Now, when I read the newspapers and watch the news, I think: who are these people?

Worse, though, we have lost our belief in ourselves, our belief that we can change things. The self-belief that propelled thousands of black, white, Coloured and Indian South Africans to take on the apartheid monster seems to have dissipated. We do not believe we can change anything, and so we hunch back into our shells, we hide behind our high walls and our electric fences, we keep quiet when the very freedoms we fought so hard for are trampled upon. We keep quiet when it becomes clear that the many freedoms we enshrined in our Constitution, the freedoms we enjoy with nary a second thought today, are slowly being taken away and will not be enjoyed by our children.

We have walked away from the public square, leaving the thieves in charge.

Writing in *City Press* in 2013, the newspaper's editor, Ferial Haffajee, said: 'For the longest time, I opined we were at a tipping point of being corrupt if we didn't do something about it. Well, now we've tipped. We are well and truly corrupt.'[10]

Why are we corrupt, as Haffajee says? It is because the good men and women of our country have signed out. They are making money, sending their children to private schools and using private cars instead of public transport.

We have said to our beloved country: 'We are out.'

Think of all the countries you know in which the elite has signed out of the system. There is a collective name for them: banana republics. We must avoid being counted among these.

In many ways, this book is not about the politicians who are turning the ANC and Nelson Mandela's legacy into a nightmare. It is about all of us, South Africans, who keep quiet when our voices are needed. It is about those of us who keep quiet when journalists like Mzilikazi wa Afrika are arrested on trumped-up charges.[11] It is about those of us who have forgotten that freedom is never fully achieved, but is defended and renewed every single day, in every square inch of space we occupy in the world.

If the South Africa of our dreams withers and dies, it will be because we have stepped away from the public square. Where is the real ANC? Crucially, where are the men and women who fought so valiantly for this new South Africa?

They are here, all around us, but they have chosen silence, high walls. It is time to reclaim our power.

3

Condemned to the Hewing
of Wood. Again.

'There is no space for him [the "Native"] in the European Community
above certain forms of labour … Until now he has been
subjected to a school system which drew him away from his
community and misled him by showing him the greener pastures
of European Society where he is not allowed to graze.'
– Dr Hendrik F Verwoerd, 'architect' of apartheid

I spent 12 years in school. Ten of those were spent in schools that
were built by my parents and the community where I grew up.

The village of New Eersterus, Hammanskraal, was a creation of the
apartheid state at its worst. The first batch of residents was moved
to Hammanskraal in the 1970s because they were not light-skinned
enough to be part of the Coloured community of Eersterus, near Pretoria. Most of these families had been on the move for more than ten
years. Originally residents of the racially mixed area of Lady Selborne –
razed in 1961 because it was a 'black spot', while a plethora of laws
were enacted in its wake to ensure that blacks never again owned land in
townships – they had been moved from pillar to post by government.[1]

Some had been moved to Indian areas, but were found to be 'not
Indian enough'. Most had been moved to Eersterus, but were declared
'not Coloured enough' by the state. So they were dumped in New
Eersterus, a piece of land near Hammanskraal, 77 kilometres north of
Pretoria, to fend for themselves.

There was nothing in Hammanskraal. No electricity. No running
water. No roads or amenities. Just a piece of land, 20 metres by 20 metres
per family, and one communal tap which soon enough stopped

working. It has not drawn water since I was 12, when the fierce man who oversaw it, known only by his surname, Tshabalala, stopped going to work.

Incredibly, there were no schools. Nothing. Two hundred families dumped in a barren piece of nothing. Rejected for the colour of their skin. Rejected for being black.

It was here that my family came to live in the 1970s. There were no schools, and so the residents banded together and built one. Every family had to contribute a certain amount of money, and a classroom, then two, then several, were built. It was a harsh system. If a family did not pay their share, then their children were not allowed into school, no matter how poor the family. Every January, hundreds of kids would be at home, their parents unable to pay the fees. Then, slowly, in the first three months of the year the children would make it back to class as the parents paid their dues.

That first school was called Kgomba Primary School, and when class sizes swelled, Mmatso Primary was built. The teachers were paid by the government, with regular visits by officious-looking and feared school inspectors, while parents did the rest.

The 'rest' was that parents were engaged with the school. I cannot recall the number of times I heard mothers without a day of learning stomping to the school gates to complain about something, saying in that curious Pretoria patois of Sotho words borrowed from the Afrikaans language: 'Ke patela tshelete e ntshi mo. Ngwana wa ka o tshwanetse akereye thuto ya nnete.' (I pay a lot of money here. My child needs to get a proper education.)

If a teacher was bunking school, the parents were the first to complain. If there was a problem, the parents were the first to complain. If a child was failing, the parents would drag him or her by the ear to the school and ask why they had not been informed that he or she was bunking school. The parents liked teachers who were strict and used the rod – so long as it was not too heavily.

I grew up with parents, not just mine, who believed that education was the only ticket out of poverty. They fought to ensure that their children got as much quality education out of the teachers as they could, though apartheid education for blacks was inferior anyway.

For me, the first seven years of schooling at Kgomba Primary School was probably all the education I really needed. An inspirational English teacher, Joe Modise, forced us all to pick up and read every piece of paper we saw in the street. If he saw you walk past a piece of paper without picking it up and reading it, then you received six or more of his very best lashes. When we were 12, Modise instructed that we address him in English only. For a while silence fell upon the class (there were 123 of us in that classroom), but after a few days we were doing major damage to the Queen's English. But we were speaking, using, the language – very badly, very tentatively, but rolling those words around the tongue. Our pronunciation was so bad I doubt an English person would have understood a word we were saying.

My father forced my siblings and me to read newspapers to him every week and recount to him what we had read when he came home from his job in Joburg at weekends. After a while, we were reading too much, too fast, for him or for teachers like Modise to keep up.

This is not to say that the quality of education then was much to write home about. Very few South Africans who have made it a career to complain about virtually everything in the new South Africa actually understand just how malevolent the idea of apartheid education was, and just what devastation it left behind.

What we were being taught at schools was deliberately, in a deeply Machiavellian fashion, designed to keep the black man out of any kind of skilled work. It was not just inferior to the education provided to a white child of a similar age. It was designed to be four rungs below that of any white man.

Prime Minister Hendrik Verwoerd, the architect of apartheid, was very specific when he set out to implement his segregationist policies in the 1950s. What came to be known as Bantu education was designed to turn people like me – despite the glorious achievements of the likes of academics, lawyers and politicians such as John Langalibalele Dube, Sol T Plaatje, Nelson Mandela and Robert Sobukwe – to be nothing more than 'hewers of wood and drawers of water' for whites. We were not to rise to anything above labourers, as he said: 'There is no space for him [the 'Native'] in the European Community above certain forms of labour.'[2]

To this end, black schools were starved of resources. Buildings, furniture – everything was the most basic available. Little was spent on the black child, while white schools enjoyed the most fantastic facilities and resources. In my final year at Kgomba, there were 123 of us packed into one classroom. In this regard we were a normal black school in apartheid South Africa.

This was the education system that was still pretty much intact in 1993 when my boss at the first newspaper I worked for, the *Star*, took me over to veteran political reporter Phil Molefe and summarily designated him my mentor. I knew Molefe's work from the *Weekly Mail* newspaper, where he had excelled at exposing the iniquities and hypocrisies of Bantu education and the devastation it wrought on black life. A teachers' strike was on the boil, and to cover it properly Molefe needed a leg man. I became the leg man.

Molefe took me across the road to the Elizabeth Hotel, a dingy but popular drinking hole for journalists and down-at-heel Joburgers. He asked me what I wanted to drink. Wanting to impress him, I ordered a whisky and Coke.

'Never!' he shouted at the top of his voice. 'Not in this country! You will not order a drink like that in this country ever again. Maybe in India!'

I had a beer. Thus began two years of reporting, on and off, on the formal end of apartheid education and the changes that Nelson Mandela and his Cabinet tried to bring about in the education system.

Their task was daunting at every level. First, Mandela's government had to create nine non-racial provincial education departments out of the 15 apartheid white, Indian, Coloured, black and Bantustan education departments. Then the whole curriculum, rightly, had to be overhauled to bring it in step with the times and to make it uniform and equitable.[3]

More than 20 years later, as I look back, I am appalled by the mistakes we made and the mistakes we continue to make, as though we have been blind all along. Don't get me wrong. Change was needed then, and radical change for that matter. Yet we have failed at virtually every level, to the extent that the respected academic Dr Mamphela Ramphele made so bold as to say that education was better under apartheid than it is in South Africa today.[4] That is a serious indictment, but it is not without justification.

I do not agree that education today is worse than it was under apartheid. However, that disagreement is merely about the intent of the system: apartheid wanted to destroy the black child and prevent the rise of blacks. I still fervently believe the current dispensation wants to empower and nurture the black child. Yet in this respect it is failing miserably.

The examples of rot and failure are numerous, ranging from infrastructure to quality. In November 2014 Minister of Basic Education Angie Motshekga announced that thousands of pupils at 1 174 Eastern Cape schools were still using beer crates and paint tins to sit on due to shortages of desks and school furniture. She said more than 350 000 pupils still did not have the desks they needed for proper education.[5]

Michael Komape, a five-year-old, died at school in Chebeng village, Limpopo, in 2014 after he fell into the school's unsafe pit latrine. The boy was missing for hours before his mother and teachers found his body. On the Saturday after his death, a news 'brief' appeared on page 2 of a newspaper. It read: 'Eighteen flushing toilets will be installed at a primary school in Chebeng village, Polokwane, where a pupil died in a pit toilet this week.'[6] Another report declared that 'Deputy Human Settlements Minister Zou Kota-Fredericks said on

Friday four toilets had already been built and 16 temporary toilets were brought in for the 190 pupils at the school. The rest of the toilets were expected to be completed in two weeks.'[7]

Why did Michael Komape, the son of a poor man, have to die first before the deputy minister pitched up and set up toilets for his school?

This has become the norm, though. Possibly the worst of the infrastructure failures of the ANC administration happened in 2012, when the Department of Basic Education failed to deliver textbooks to hundreds of thousands of Limpopo pupils, for up to nine months in some cases. It was the work of two NGOs, Equal Education and Section27, that first exposed the department's folly and then forced the minister to act after nearly a year of doing nothing.

You would have thought that the ANC would have done something about an issue as damaging and as terrible as this. But its ministers just talked and talked for a whole year, doing nothing.

The whole thing was extraordinary. You would not have been far wrong to think that the ANC was not in power. The Minister in the Presidency at the time, Trevor Manuel, said: 'Let me be clear that one of the biggest blots on the copybook of this democracy has been the debacle around the provisioning of textbooks in Limpopo province that came to a head with court action by an NGO on May 4 (2012).'

Manuel reportedly went on to say that government, especially the provincial government of Limpopo, could not 'absolve itself of responsibility'.

The arts and culture minister, Paul Mashatile, said at the time that late delivery of learning materials to schools stifled the education of the 'African child'. He said: 'We must condemn any programme that seeks to undermine the process of ensuring that an African child is educated … The 21st century requires that we must be educated and equipped with skills to ensure that we produce prosperous communities.'[8]

Nothing was done.

At the end of June 2012 ANC policy head and justice minister Jeff

49

Radebe said the burning (of old books) and non-delivery of textbooks was a 'shame': 'Six months into the year, our children are still without textbooks … So it is a matter of shame that this has happened.'[9]

It is indeed a shame, but why couldn't all these men and women do anything about it?

Speaking on the SABC on 1 July 2012, Zuma was asked if there would be consequences. He answered: 'Definitely, it cannot be left unattended to – [it] is one of the serious matters. There will be consequences. We can't sit back as government when textbooks were not delivered on time.'[10]

As I write, almost three years later, nothing has been done, no one has been held accountable for what happened in Limpopo. A year of schooling was wiped off some children's lives, and South Africans are not appalled.

What's going on here? Why aren't South Africans up in arms about what is happening in our schools?

Every third week or so we hear reports of schoolchildren – packed up to 20 per taxi – being involved in some horrific accident. One sickening incident happened in Blackheath, in the Western Cape, in August 2010 when a taxi packed with children overtook six cars at a level crossing. The taxi was hit by a train. Ten children died. Four were injured.

The question is this: why are thousands of township or village children leaving home in the dead of night to get to school? What's wrong with the schools in their neighbourhoods?

My abiding memory of Nigeria is this: people boasting about their children in schools in the United States, the United Kingdom and other developed nations. Why were there so many Nigerian kids in foreign schools? The answer was simple: the schooling system in Nigeria had collapsed to such an extent, through the successive wars and coups in that country, that any self-respecting parent would give their right arm – if not their life – to see their child accommodated anywhere so long as it was as far as possible from the Nigerian education system.

This is what many middle-class black parents did under apartheid.

The likes of writer Es'kia Mphahlele organised independent schools so that their children would not drink from the poisoned well that was apartheid education. When these failed due to the apartheid regime's harassment, many parents organised for their children to study elsewhere. That is why you find so many members of the black elite with qualifications from places such as Waterford Kamhlaba in Swaziland. For those who could afford it or could get a scholarship, this was the only alternative to the heinous crime of Bantu education.

So why do so many black parents pack their children into dangerous minibus taxis to get them to 'better schools' in towns and cities across the country? The answer is simple. These parents have lost faith in township and village schools. They know instinctively from looking at the results and the system that they are consigning their children to the dustbin of life if they let them stay in these schools. They are voting with their feet and what little cash they have. They are moving their kids to town.

Respected academic Jonathan Jansen, the inspirational rector and vice chancellor of the University of the Free State, once said that not a single minister in our Cabinet takes their child to a public school.[11] He is correct. Why? All those politicians know that most government schools in South Africa – except for a handful – are nothing short of dire.

In 2012 the national government had to take over the running of the Eastern Cape education department because it had collapsed.[12] The province registered the worst matric results in the country.[13] In 2013 teachers went on a strike for more than six weeks, with no learning taking place at most schools.[14]

What would you do if you were a parent with a child in one of the province's schools? I know what I would do. I would take my child out and put them in a school elsewhere. I would uproot myself from my friends, relatives and home. I would become an 'education refugee', as the opposition Democratic Alliance's former leader Helen Zille put it before she was roundly condemned by the ANC for allegedly being racist.[15] But there is no other way to put it.

It is in the area of mathematics and science education, though, that South Africa has most failed its people and its children. Over the first five years of the Zuma presidency politicians rushed to declare that, as Zuma put it in 2013, '[t]his is the best matric class since 1994'.

He went on to claim that there is a consistently upward trend in matric results, 'with the pass rate going from 62.6 per cent in 2008, dipping to 60.6 per cent in 2009, only to rise to 67.8 per cent in 2010, 70.2 per cent in 2011 and 73.9 per cent in 2012'.

But the man speaketh with a forked tongue. In a comprehensive analysis of the 2013 matric results, the NGO Africa Check points out that there is a flaw in using the matric pass rate as a barometer of national performance because 'thousands of school pupils drop out long before they reach their final year. The dropout rate is not taken into account in the final pass rate'.

'For example, when the 2013 matric class started grade one in 2002, there were 1 261 827 pupils. But by the time they came to sit for their final exams, their numbers had fallen to 562 112,' says the NGO. More than half a million children had already been failed before they even reached matric.

Even worse, though, is that there is a dumbing-down of major proportions going on in formerly black schools in South Africa. Children are being taken off pure mathematics and instead registered to write a soft, easy version of mathematics called maths literacy. If one takes maths literacy at matric, then a career in engineering or a degree that demands proficiency and rigour in pure mathematics is out.

Says Africa Check: 'In 2010, 263 034 full-time pupils wrote mathematics. This decreased to 241 509 pupils in 2013. Conversely, numbers of full-time pupils writing mathematical literacy, the easier subject, increased from 280 836 in 2010 to 324 097 in 2013.'[16]

Think about that. Play with it in your head. Take the model and place it in Singapore, or China, or elsewhere in the world. Instead of stretching every sinew in our bodies to make our children into students as good as, or better than, students at Harvard, Oxford, the Sorbonne,

Makerere, Columbia, UCLA, Cambridge or any other of the great universities of the world, we are instead on a mission to turn our children into mediocre, possibly unemployable people.

This is a sausage machine. We are squeezing children out of a bad system as quickly as we can, cynically inflating the numbers to pretend that these kids are ready for the world out there, while we all know that they are in no way prepared for the workplace or for the complex world they will have to face. We kill them before they even know what kind of complicated and complex reality they have to deal with.

I don't know what your definition of a disaster is. For me, though, this is it.

It is worth noting that the WEF Global Competitiveness Report has for the past five years consistently identified the biggest problem companies face in doing business in South Africa as being an inadequately educated workforce. The report shows the quality of South Africa's higher education and training is ranked fifth worst in the world and the quality of South Africa's maths and science education second worst, after Yemen.[17]

Every year, when this report is released, the government responds by attacking the report. There has been no engagement with the argument that we are dumbing down and killing our children's prospects when it comes to education. When you analyse our education situation, it is hard to argue against Ramphele's assertion that we have done wrong by our children.

Ironically, our government agrees with her. In a voluminous report assessing its achievements over the first 20 years of democracy, the government says: 'International comparisons through the Southern and Eastern Africa Consortium for Monitoring Educational Quality (SACMEQ) confirm that South Africa fares poorly in terms of learner performance in Grade 6 and teacher content knowledge when compared with countries that spend the same or less on education per capita. In terms of the SACMEQ tests, South Africa experienced no statistically significant change in performance between 2000 and 2007.

In contrast, Lesotho, Mauritius, Namibia, Swaziland, Tanzania and Zanzibar experienced improvements in both Mathematics and reading. The 2011 Trends in International Maths and Science Study (TIMSS) points to improvements for Grade 9 learners between 2002 and 2011, especially for learners attending the poorest schools. These improvements are off a low base and South Africa still has a low average in Mathematics and Science performance, below the level expected for Grade 9 learners, as indicated by the recent ANA (annual national assessments) test results.'[18]

I have always been of the view that of all the vicissitudes that apartheid visited upon us, the decision to subject black people to an inferior level of education was absolutely the worst. If one looks at the literature – and an elegant example is contained in Mark Gevisser's biography of former President Thabo Mbeki, a work which also manages to be a history of the nascent black middle class from the late 1800s to the 1950s, when apartheid began to bite[19] – it is clear that the history of modern South Africa is the history of education. The ANC at its formation in 1912 was led by men such as Pixley kaIsaka Seme and John Langalibalele Dube, men who were missionary school-educated and had gained a deep national consciousness in their travels through the world. Nelson Mandela, Walter Sisulu, Oliver Tambo, Nthato Motlana and others were products of missionary and other schools that had at their centre the belief that with education black people could rise up and run a modern South African state on their own.

Apartheid sought to destroy that, and it very nearly succeeded. It destroyed a black middle class, denigrated the intelligence of black people and drummed into the heads of people like me – those who went through school in the 1960s, 1970s and 1980s – that we were nothing, that we were capable of nothing, and that we would be nothing better or greater than 'hewers of wood and drawers of water'.[20]

That is why we were not allowed into 'white' universities, not allowed to study the same subjects as whites, and made to study an inferior mathematics and science as subjects. It brings tears to the eyes, but what is being done to our children through maths literacy is similar.

If there is one thing that we should have fixed in the new South Africa it is education. After my matric I enrolled for an A-level course in Bulawayo, Zimbabwe. Within the first day of studies my South African friends and I knew, without a shadow of doubt, that the South African system had well-nigh destroyed us: the Zimbabweans were far more educated, more assured and more able to grasp the advanced concepts put before us by our teachers. We were left in the dust.

Today, a tour of South Africa's banks, pension funds, asset managers, insurance companies and other financial services firms will show you that it is Zimbabweans and other black Africans who are at the top of the pile. The reason for this is not difficult to find: Zimbabwe and other newly independent nations did not fiddle with their education systems. The system worked in colonial days and under post-liberation administrations. South Africa's education system, however, was allowed to stutter, calcify and rot by our own post-1994 administrations, including that of Nelson Mandela.

What went wrong? Jonathan Jansen has pointed out that we made quite a few mistakes in education; among the first was our attempt at eradicating the apartheid syllabus and replacing it with outcomes-based education. 'Almost 30 000 schools were misled into thinking that, by adopting this complex curriculum plan, teaching and learning would improve. Instead, scholastic achievement is worse than ever, from literacy and numeracy in the foundation years to the disastrous National Senior Certificate results in Grade 12,' he wrote.

Secondly, teachers were offered voluntary severance packages in 1994 in an attempt to 'rightsize' the teaching corps and save money. 'The result? The best teachers left the system. The teachers who remained behind, especially in the most disadvantaged schools, were in general those with weaker teaching qualifications and experience than those who left.'

Of all the mistakes Jansen cites, though, I think the third is the most devastating: 'Mistake number three was closing good teacher education colleges. Let me be clear, some of the colleges had to be closed. Colleges in the homelands produced the worst teachers. But there were good colleges, like the Johannesburg College of Education, the Normaal Kollege Pretoria, the Giyani Teachers' College and the Bellville Teachers' College. But for a government with a reform hammer that sees all problems as nails, all the colleges were shut down or incorporated into universities. That was a mistake, for universities are not the best places for training primary school teachers.'[21]

That is the horror we sit with today. There are few good teachers, and many of those are overwhelmed by the system. Worse, the South African Democratic Teachers' Union (Sadtu) – an ally of the ANC – has essentially taken control of the education system in South Africa. It has wreaked havoc.

In the Eastern Cape, the major scandal is that women teachers have had to sleep with union leaders to get jobs or promotions. Others have had to bribe union officials to become principals.[22] The union has consistently fought against reforms in education, including those aimed at bringing about teacher accountability and improved performance.

At the ANC's elective conference in Mangaung in December 2012, President Zuma said he wanted school inspectors to be reintroduced to the schooling system to catch napping teachers: 'Some might oppose this. Some of our friends in labour, even, don't like this idea. If they don't, then we will just send them to find teachers not doing their work,' he said.[23]

It is now nearly three years since his pledge and nothing, absolutely zero, has happened. Soon after the Mangaung conference, ANC secretary-general Gwede Mantashe emerged from one of the party's numerous post-conference meetings and declared that the ANC would 'leave no stone unturned' in its quest to make education an essential service. This is akin to declaring a state of emergency in education. 'The starting point is, though you are not threatening life and limb, you do threaten the growth and the survival of society. We think that education should be an essential service if we are going to raise this society and the country to the level of being competitive globally,' he argued. He went on to say that to resolve problems in education one had to think beyond the narrow concerns of trade unions: 'We can't just think narrowly, education is essential for society to uplift itself.'[24]

The party has not moved an iota in this regard, either. The people of South Africa are fully aware of the dire state of things, and are voting with their wallets. Writing in *Business Day* in January 2015, Andile Makholwa said: 'The number of learners attending independent schools has risen by 40 per cent over the past five years. At the end of 2014, there were 1 681 registered independent schools with 538 421 pupils, according to the Department of Basic Education's 2014 School Realities report. In 2009, there were 1 174 independent schools with 386 098 learners. The most sought-after boarding schools charge anything from R140 000/year to R209 000/year, while premium day schools demand an average of R90 000/year.'[25] The writer pointed out that many entrepreneurs are setting up chain schools, following in the footsteps of hugely popular listed groups AdvTech and Curro.

Why has the South African state failed so dismally at the one issue that is key to the real transformation of the country and its economy? It is not as if there aren't examples of what clear, decisive leadership can do.

'The international evidence is clear. Schooling reform is possible – in as little as six years and from almost any starting point,' said executive director of the Centre for Development and Enterprise (CDE), Ann Bernstein, after her think-tank released a review of school systems that are improving in over 20 countries. 'For South Africa to make real progress the country needs a new social compact for quality schooling. This will require clear priorities, the mobilisation of the many different interests with a stake in better schooling, and visionary leadership,' continued Bernstein.[26]

In the end, it is a matter of leadership. In education, as in so many other areas, South Africa has no visionary leadership.

The education crisis is now at a stage where a state of emergency should be declared. The grip of the trade unions on necessary reforms needs to be loosened. A new vision and ethos of hard work, application and high standards needs to be inculcated.

South Africa needs to turn its education system around within the next 12 years, or else it faces implosion. Too many of our young people are being pushed out of the education system merely to be left out on the streets, jobless, frustrated, bored and dangerously idle. These are the young people who are recruited into drug-taking and crime; the young people who are falling into the clutches of populist, misguided political elites; the young people who look around them and have feelings that are similar to their parents' in the 1980s. They are the lost generation. More than 20 years after our freedom, this should not be happening. To speak of our young people becoming a 'lost generation', a people with no future and no hope, is an indictment of the new South Africa.

This is what we have wrought. Twenty years of bone idleness, of looting the fiscus, of not paying heed to the fraying of a culture of learning and teaching, have brought us here. Schools in townships and villages are abandoned by middle-class parents. Teachers have sex with schoolchildren. The system is rotten. The matric results are cooked – albeit in a manner that is not outright criminal, yet to all intents and purposes appears so.

We have done many terrible things in the new South Africa. None, however, is equal to the horror we are visiting upon millions of our children by allowing the education system to collapse as it has done. The future will punish us, harshly, when this lost generation of un-educated, hopeless, unemployed young people turns on us. We deserve their anger. We are doing to them what apartheid education sought to do to me and my generation.

4

Race and the Rainbow Nation

'Herein lie buried many things which if read with patience
may show the strange meaning of being black here in the dawning of the
Twentieth Century. This meaning is not without interest to you, Gentle Reader;
for the problem of the Twentieth Century is the problem of the color-line.'
– WEB Du Bois, *The Souls of Black Folk*, 1903

Over the Christmas period at the end of 2014 a black family called the Azure Restaurant at the Twelve Apostles Hotel & Spa in Cape Town and tried to book a table. The caller was told a table was available and was asked for a name. When he gave his name, clearly black, he was told that, well, oops, sorry, there actually was no table available.

Suspecting racism, the family asked a white friend to call and make a reservation: six people, same time. She was immediately told that a table was available. She booked the table.

The black family reluctantly went to the restaurant. On arrival they were told that actually there had been a mistake and there was no booking under the white friend's name. They were offered a table in a private room, away from the main dining area and from other diners.

When the restaurant was called to account, the Twelve Apostles' General Manager, Michael Nel, said in a statement that the incident had occurred due to an unfortunate reservations error.[1]

I think the statement is ridiculous at so many levels: the first call to the restaurant clearly illustrates that there is, or at least was, an explicit policy of barring black people. The course of events at the arrival of the family, to my mind, shows explicitly that such a policy was enforced.

The continued existence of racist policies in South Africa is deeply deplorable, depressing and tragic. What is worse is this, though: visit the Azure Restaurant any time this week and you will find the place packed with ordinary – mostly white, I suspect – South Africans drinking and supping without a care in the world. Many readers will know the story above: it has been carried extensively on radio, on social media and in newspapers. They will still give their money to this establishment.

In October 2014 the Afrikaans singer and racist Steve Hofmeyr tweeted that in his opinion black people were the 'architects of apartheid'.[2] This is the sort of thing that Holocaust denialists say about Jewish people. Yet not much was said about this outrageous statement until comedian-ventriloquist Conrad Koch, in his guise as the puppet political analyst Chester Missing, called Hofmeyr out.[3] Over and above the silence over Hofmeyr's tweet, though, was the fact that corporate South Africa did not mind associating itself with him. Pick n Pay and Land Rover were among the sponsors of an Afrikaans music festival at which Hofmeyr was to perform. Although they later decided not to renew their sponsorship of the event, when first confronted by Koch over their sponsorship of Hofmeyr, a spokesperson for Pick n Pay first said: 'Pick n Pay's reputation for publicly and strongly opposing racism speaks for itself. We are a contracted sponsor of AIG and support Afrikaans music, not individuals.'[4]

Wow. Why couldn't the company have said to the festival organisers: 'This man's utterances are outrageous and unacceptable, and we are withdrawing our sponsorship unless he is removed from the bill'? Why should they have done this? Because Hofmeyr's tweet was against everything we stand for in South Africa. It was racist, a matter that is non-negotiable.

Incidents of racism, and the descent of debates into accusations of racism, have taken centre stage in South Africa recently. In the Western Cape there has been an upsurge in racist incidents, including attacks on black people in so-called white suburbs. Things have become so bad that the mayor of Cape Town, Patricia de Lille, started an anti-racism campaign.[5] However, reports of racist incidents persist.

How do we move beyond these racist eruptions to a conversation that helps us solve our most urgent problems – poverty, unemployment, inequality – as fast as possible? How do we resolve the deep pain, divisions and legacy of the key issue that was at the heart of apartheid?

In May 2012 the Goodman Gallery in Johannesburg found itself at the centre of a firestorm after it came to the attention of the ANC that the gallery had put up a painting of President Jacob Zuma with his penis exposed.[6] The painting was part of artist Brett Murray's 'Hail to the Thief II' exhibition and was inspired by a very famous image of Lenin often used in political literature and pamphlets. The ANC demanded that the painting, titled *The Spear*, be removed from the gallery and that *City Press* remove it from its website.

The party was livid over the painting. The ANC spokesperson at the time, Jackson Mthembu, issued a fiery statement: 'This disgusting and unfortunate display of the president was brought to our attention by one of the media houses and we have physically confirmed this insulting depiction of the president. We have this morning instructed our lawyers to approach our courts to compel Brett Murray and Goodman Gallery to remove the portrait from display as well as from their website and destroy all printed promotional material.

'We have also detected that this distasteful and vulgar portrait of the president has been displayed on a weekend newspaper and its website, we again have instructed our lawyers to request the said newspaper to remove the portrait from their website.'[7]

The party organised a march on the gallery and called for a boycott of *City Press*. Zuma, the ANC and Zuma's children launched an urgent court application against the Goodman Gallery to press their demand that the painting be brought down.

When the matter came to court, something wholly unexpected happened. During the nationally televised hearing Gcina Malindi, senior counsel acting for the ANC and the Zumas, broke down in tears.[8] The case was adjourned for lunch. Malindi later said he had been overcome by memories of the apartheid era.[9]

Now every so often something comes along that affects you so deeply, it shifts the very essence of your viewpoint. When Malindi broke down and cried that Thursday, something happened to me. The very centre of my being moved. I remembered a huge chunk of what I had put away in the deepest recesses of my mind.

I remembered, I was forced to remember, that there is hurt, there is pain, there is anger and there is even hatred in my heart, and in my fellow black people's hearts, about what happened here. I remembered apartheid.

I remembered the disdain with which, whenever I went into the Pretoria city centre, white people treated me. I remembered how, when I was 15 and working as a gardener, a white man made me work all day and at 5 pm told me he was not going to pay me because he did not have money. After an hour of this tawdry squabble, which he thought was hilarious, he finally paid me.

I have had this feeling several times in the past.

When FW de Klerk, the last president of apartheid South Africa, told Christiane Amanpour of CNN that blacks 'were not disenfranchised, they voted. They were not put in homelands, the homelands were historically there,'[10] I recoiled in shock.

As I wrote at the beginning of this book, I grew up in a village called New Eersterus, in the Hammanskraal area just north of Pretoria. The village was, with many others, incorporated into the heinous Bophuthatswana homeland. We all knew this homeland 'democracy' was a sham.

Not once did the people of my village vote for Lucas Mangope, the puppet ruler who acted for the apartheid government through violence, intimidation and torture. When the Bop army attempted a coup in 1988, guess who came to Mangope's rescue? The apartheid government, of course. So much for sovereignty.

Recently, a friend of mine in Cape Town participated in a charity bike ride. After the event, he went to a bicycle shop stall and asked to try out their cycles. He and his two boys hopped on the bikes and rode out. 'Stop that thief!' shouted the shop owner. People ran after my friend. He is black. Virtually everyone there was white. The shop owner, a white man, refused to acknowledge that he had responded in a racist manner.

All these incidents, small and large, bring back the hurt, the pain, the remembrance that once, not so long ago, we were subhuman in this country. They bring back the remembrance that the black man was viewed as a sex-obsessed, lazy ... well, animal, really. We were not human here.

In the sound and fury that accompanied the decision by Zuma and the ANC to take the Goodman Gallery to court, I had been firmly on the side of those who declared the action ill-advised, nonsensical and a poor pandering to one man's whim. I wrote that Zuma had brought this upon himself: his public life has been defined by his flaunting of his sexuality in the guise of nebulous precepts of 'African culture'. This is the man who declared that he had sex with his dead friend's daughter because, he claimed, 'in the Zulu culture, you cannot just leave a woman if she is ready ... To deny her sex, that would have been tantamount to rape.'[11]

Really?

Yet I cannot escape the raw and real pain and hurt that Malindi's breakdown in court underlined. Perhaps, in my defence of the freedom to express oneself, the freedom to exercise artistic creativity, I missed something. Perhaps I – and many of the people who have been batting on this side of the field – forgot that these freedoms cannot be exercised in a vacuum.

There is a hurt that is still not processed. There is a pain so deep and raw that the Truth and Reconciliation Commission did virtually nothing to assuage. To many of the people outside court that day, this pain is raw and immediate. To them, Nelson Mandela and Desmond Tutu, with their talk of reconciliation, are deluded dreamers.

I know this is true because one of my best friends was standing outside court supporting Zuma that day. For him, the Murray painting was an assault on blackness. He feels that 'whiteness' still has the upper hand and that it continues to dictate to and defile black people in South Africa today. His words echoed those of ANC secretary-general Gwede Mantashe outside the court in Johannesburg: 'Even after 18 years of this democracy, they still want us to dance to their tune.'

'They', in this case, are white South Africans. This pain we carry around inside of us, exacerbated and reopened by every new slur, is what Dr Mamphela Ramphele has called our 'woundedness'.[12]

We blacks are not the only wounded. Whites, too, are wounded by 46 years of formal apartheid and centuries of colonialism. You cannot be fine when you are fed a diet of racial superiority, consciously or unconsciously, all your life.

What has hurt most for me, therefore, has been the complete failure by many in the white community to appreciate the true nature of these slurs. De Klerk's casual dismissal of the fact that the homeland system was an assault on every black person's very being reopened all the slights that marked my formative years. Worse still, he reminded me of my brother being asked for a pass, my father being harassed for one, and the incarceration and torture of my friends by the apartheid regime.

More than two decades into our democracy, reminders like De Klerk's, like the racist bike-shop owner's, still occur. It does not help that when these happen, and there is black outrage, the likes of Western Cape premier Helen Zille brand those blacks who make noise as 'professional blacks'.[13] It is as though it is fine to complain if you are white, and not so if you are black.

Did the failure to recognise the deep wounds of our past make us miss a moment in which we could have defused the issue raised by *The Spear*? Could Zuma, in his anger and his shame, have decided to let the matter go, or was his and his advisors' anger so overwhelming they decided to go ahead? Could Murray have, before he raised his brush, wondered about the hurt that we all still carry inside us? Could *City Press*, though wholly within its rights to report on and display the offending painting, have done things differently?

The wounds reopened by the *The Spear*, and by other racial incidents, make Zuma – a flawed character at best – suddenly resonate to more than just his core support base. His pain reminded many of the racist slurs that flare up in the comment sections of news websites and of the callous, casual, denigration of the black form in the past.

These are painful matters. The most painful and challenging, however, is that we are a constitutional democracy, that we have a president who is deeply flawed at various levels, and that rights and responsibilities are entrenched in our Constitution. These rights and responsibilities will not be tested by normalcy. It is when a Murray comes along, uninvited and unwanted, that we have to stand up and contest this space.

With this hurt in mind, with these bags of pain carried by me, the Zuma family and the ANC, I return to our Constitution and its Bill of Rights. We wrote this Constitution. We adopted it, with Thabo Mbeki's majestic 'I am an African' speech[14] ringing in our ears and hearts. We lauded it and we brag about it every day.

It is in the Constitution that our weakest and our poorest and our most ailing, in the Grootboom housing case and the Aids drugs case and the school textbooks case, for example, continue to find protection. It is in the Constitution that we must find a path to resolve the divisions and the hurt.

To read the Constitution, therefore, is to recognise that even when we feel pain, as Malindi so rawly and movingly did, as so many still do every day, the freedoms that we enjoy today, the dignity that we enjoy today, are enjoined in that Constitution.

For us to enjoy all these and to continue to enjoy them, we have to acknowledge that this same Constitution will allow things that pain us, things that kick us in the very heart of our being, to continue.

The depiction of Zuma in *The Spear*, in such a manner, did so to many of our compatriots. Yet that is the bargain we struck.

I have quoted from Mandela's 1994 inaugural speech before. I will do so again: 'Our endeavours must be about the liberation of the woman, the emancipation of the man and the liberty of the child.'

These goals are entrenched in our Constitution. In the case of *The Spear*, perhaps Zuma should be judged within these parameters and not just in the context of our pain. I too feel pain, but the painting should have stayed up, and newspapers must be able to report about it without being boycotted and burnt.

That said, the racist eruptions continue. The conversation around race has intensified. The anger that accompanied the removal of Cecil John Rhodes' statue from the University of Cape Town campus in April 2015 was laced with racial attacks from various forces involved.

Increasingly now, we seem to think that our reality is a straight line, that we lack the complicatedness that makes South Africa a unique place. Many commentators seem to think that we are a nation of black angels, oppressed yet noble, pitted against a nation of white devils, callow and hateful. It is a binary view of the problem, a shorthand. Black is good, white is bad. We are descending into stereotypes, and dangerous ones at that. Even inside the ANC, where for long non-racialism held sway, I am beginning to hear of many fissures that can be ascribed to race alone – even when those accused of racism may be some of the great stalwarts of the non-racial struggle.

In 1999 Britain's *Observer* newspaper reported that 'Helena Dolny, widow of the late South African Communist Party chief, Joe Slovo, has been denounced as a corrupt, nepotistic "racist". No one who knows her would credit the charge.'[15] The accusation was made by one Bonile Jack, a former Ciskei Bantustan official – essentially a collaborator with apartheid. It was enough to ensure that Dolny was pushed out of the Land Bank, of which she was managing director. Such accusations are now commonplace.

You see, things are not always like that. When my friend was accused of stealing that bike in Cape Town, for example, the man who did so was a well-known member of a family of serious anti-apartheid activists. He would never have thought of himself as racist, and indeed one of the first things he said when confronted on the matter was to say: 'But I campaigned against apartheid ...' He invited my friend to come and see the outreach programmes for poor children that he runs in townships across Cape Town. He would never think of himself as racist.

The story of racism in South Africa is more complicated than the surface incidents show. It is layer upon layer, woundedness upon woundedness. We have a long way to go. The past will stay with us for a very, very long time to come. The depth of what apartheid has done to us is unimaginable.

The 'new' South Africa is just over 21 years old. It is an incredibly short time since that glorious day in 1994 when we voted in the first non-racial elections and said goodbye to 46 years of apartheid rule and more than 300 years of colonialism.

No one said our journey would be easy. No one said it would be perfect. No one said there would not be setbacks.

It seems to me that, firstly, we need to acknowledge the deep effect of apartheid racism. No one should ever tell a fellow South African that it is all in the past. It is with us every day and everywhere. No one should ever make light of what apartheid did to black South Africans, and no one should underestimate what it did to the white South African psyche. We are a wounded nation, and 21 years of non-racial democracy has come nowhere close to healing us.

That means we should not be scared by the racist attacks, the racial debates, the racist Twitter wars that erupt around us. That is part of growing up – if we use them constructively to extract good out of the bad.

Here is what I believe is still the truth of our country, one that we do not acknowledge enough: do not underestimate the strides we have made. South Africa today is a very different country to the one we entered in 1994. It will be even better in 21 years' time if we use these racist outpourings to build a better South Africa.

But we need to take care, for we remain a tinderbox. If we do not quickly resolve the structural challenges facing South Africa – unemployment, inequality and poor educational outcomes – then these eruptions of race will take on a whole new hue. We will become a Zimbabwe, where the black poor will point at the prosperous whites, and act in a manner that will set light to the tinder.

This is an urgent problem. Despite the progress made over the past two decades, South Africa remains a country of white haves and black have-nots. This is a problem we need to stare in the face if we are to begin to build this country. This is not a conversation to have in order to apportion blame. We are past that. It is a conversation to have in order for us to move faster to lift up the poorest of the poor, to bring hope into every home.

Those homes are black homes. There is anger in South Africa. Things are not going well. When things don't go well, populists, opportunists and exploiters move in. Race is an easy scapegoat in South Africa. It is convenient for those who seek to hide their lies. It is also real. The only reason why black and white South Africans bought into the détente of the 1990s was because credible leaders told them that we have more to gain from working together than from walking separately.

Today we need to tell – and show – our people that populist policies, such as the expropriation of white-owned land without compensation, leads to the cul-de-sac where Zimbabwe finds itself today. But there needs to be a plan that speaks persuasively and realistically about blacks becoming meaningful players in the economy and in society.

Without such credible leadership and credible – and achievable – policies, we will continue to sit where we now sit, with an angry black population believing that the new South Africa has nothing to offer, and a prosperous white population that feels beleaguered.

The solution is in growing this economy faster, making opportunity available to increasing numbers of black people and ensuring that the ability to be a success no longer depends on being white or a member of a narrow black elite. We need to open up the space for a deluge of young people, from Nkandla to Qunu, to be absorbed into the economy.

That is the silver bullet for our racial problems.

5

The Media and its Discontents

'In this craze of personal aggrandizement, of the creation of these
bogus and corrupt empires and dictatorships, the same thing happened
that happens in real dictatorships, real banana republics. Your society collapses.
Your institutions become corrupt. The daily fabric of your life
comes to be built on lies. Not to mention your economy stops
functioning. Everything is ruined. All is shit …

'Movies are shit.

'Music is shit.

'Magazines are shit.

'Books are shit.

'Radio is shit.'

– Michael Wolff, *Autumn of the Moguls*, 2003

I was sitting in my office in Brooklyn, New York, in October 2002 when my phone rang. I was not particularly busy. I think I was working on yet another beginning to the 'Great South African Novel'.

I picked it up, expecting it to be my line manager in Johannesburg asking me to lift from the *New York Post* and write yet another titillating piece of celebrity gossip to fill the *Sunday Times'* notorious and hugely popular back page. It wasn't. It was a mid-Atlantic accent, which as the conversation got animated took on a more West African tone.

It was a man called Nduka Obaigbena, proprietor of a Nigerian newspaper called *ThisDay* and a serial media entrepreneur.[1] He was setting up a newspaper in South Africa, and he was looking for an editor. I had received two email messages from famed South African journalist John Matisonn, who was acting as one of Obaigbena's consultants in Johannesburg, but I was sceptical. The man was insistent that I should join him. He invited me to fly to London and meet him.

I flew to London on a Friday and met Obaigbena for breakfast at the Lanesborough Hotel the next day. He started off by berating me. He had flown in that morning from Johannesburg and had copies of South African newspapers with him. He was holding up the *Mail & Guardian*.

'What's wrong with your guys? Why do your guys think so small?' he asked.

It was a lead story that was to become pivotal in the history of South Africa over the next 15 years. It declared that Jacob Zuma, deputy president of the country and of the ANC, had allegedly taken a R50 000 bribe from French arms company Thales to influence South Africa's wasteful, unnecessary, misguided and corrupt arms procurement deal. Years after the deal was concluded, most of the arms bought are sitting unused in warehouses, shipyards and hangars. The 1998 deal cost anything from R30 billion to a staggering R91 billion (no one really knows),[2] the biggest arms procurement package in the democratic era.

A minor politician's mistress would not accept that amount to go shopping, he laughed.

I liked Obaigbena, despite the fact that there were a lot of disquieting reports about him in Nigeria. For one, he was notorious for not paying the staff of his very successful newspaper, *ThisDay*, on time.

I was, however, attracted by the ethos he set out for his proposed South African title: world-standard quality of editorial content, editorial independence, robust debate, non-partisanship. Sitting with him and others, we conceptualised a newspaper we believed could beat the world.

I am in, I told him. In February 2003 I started as editor of *ThisDay* newspaper. Just under two years later, in October 2004, it folded. Obaigbena had squandered the money he had set aside for the newspaper by buying a chain of 66 stationery stores that turned out to be complete duds. After spending about R70 million on buying the stores and refitting them, it became clear that he could not keep them going. He had to spend millions more in retrenchment packages.

This meant we could not launch our newspaper on time, and only actually launched in August 2003 without any proper marketing or finances. We were doomed to fail, and fail we did.

You would think there would be bitter memories of this experience, but for me there were never really any. It was the greatest learning experience of my life, and that's because I went to Nigeria with Nduka when I worked for him. I have not stopped visiting.

When I first arrived in Nigeria, in 2003, I saw what happens when journalists, editors, newspapers and media houses are controlled by politicians. I saw newspapers spring up before elections, started by politicians merely to support their run for office, funded on the abuse of taxpayers' money, and then collapse after the politician ascended to office or lost power.

I saw journalists on the take from politicians, and from media barons whose only source of income was largesse from politicians – far beyond the advertising revenues that came from these politicians. In one instance I met a governor of a state who owned a newspaper and paid the proprietor of another newspaper a hefty monthly fee to keep him on the front page and in the good books of editorial writers.

'The one thing you guys must never, ever do,' Nduka, who also swam in these waters, told me once, 'is to become like Nigeria. You have to guard against the corrupting influence of politicians and money.'

In 2010 I saw my friend Dele Olojede, former foreign correspondent of New York's *NewsDay*, travel back to his native Nigeria to start a newspaper that aimed to turn back the tide of this type of corruption. His publication, *Next*, paid journalists well. He recruited people who were not on the take. He encouraged investigations of the high and mighty. He took no side except that of truth, integrity and fidelity to the ordinary man and woman.

Next shut down after three years, starved of government advertising.[3] Sitting across from me at the Wheatbaker Hotel in Lagos, he told me an extraordinary story of how, in the final few days of the newspaper, he had been offered a US$20 million bribe by an oil baron in cahoots with powerful politicians.

He refused to kill the story his reporters were working on. The newspaper folded.

'Never buy into this South African exceptionalism, this belief that it will never happen to you in South Africa. It creeps up on you, and one day it is you,' he said.

As I write this, watching surfers on Muizenberg beach in Cape Town, I have to say that both Dele and Nduka were right. It is here. In November 2014 the *Mail & Guardian* newspaper reported that the ANC's national executive committee had issued an edict that government advertising should be directed towards newspapers and media that supported the party. It was not a new idea.

This idea was first floated in the mid-2000s by Essop Pahad, the Minister in the Presidency during Thabo Mbeki's tenure.[4] Pahad was full of rather idiotic but dangerous ideas at the time as Mbeki was coming under increasing pressure due to his Aids denialism and refusal to roll out lifesaving anti-retroviral drugs to those infected with HIV.

When newspapers derided health minister Manto Tshabalala-Msimang after she went on a roadshow displaying beetroot and garlic at international conferences, declaring that these were cures for Aids, Pahad swiftly got on his high horse and declared that government should pull all its advertising from the *Sunday Times*, which had exposed the minister as a drunk.

President Mbeki's spokesman, Mukoni Ratshitanga, told Independent Newspapers: 'The minister in the presidency holds a strong view that in the light of *Sunday Times* reports on Tshabalala-Msimang and other reporting which, in his view, is sensationalist and deliberate miscommunication of the views and position of government, then the government must not advertise in the *Sunday Times*.

'This is the minister's personal view, it is not a government decision or consideration.'[5]

Of course it was not his personal view. Very few people would have the bravery to utter something so daft in public. The Government

Communication and Information System (GCIS), which is responsible for state advertising, reported to Pahad at the time.

After a massive storm, the idea petered out. It is now back with a vengeance, with the *Mail & Guardian* reporting in December 2014 that three of the country's top independent newspapers – the *Sunday Times, Mail & Guardian* and *City Press* – are going to be punished for 'insulting' Zuma. It said a threat to starve the three newspapers of millions of rands in advertising will soon be implemented by the government. One of the most powerful ministers in the Zuma administration – Lindiwe Zulu – declared: 'How do you continue to pay people who insult you? What's that? Something needs to give.' She continued: 'We know there is freedom of the press. We are not saying people should only write positive things about the government, but you should be balanced.'[6]

The Mbeki administration's interactions with the press were often clumsy but never really came close to the ominousness of the present ANC administration. At best, the Mbeki crowd was gauche.

For example, there was a moment of shame when e.tv reporter Iman Rappetti confronted Mbeki about his inexplicable suspension of NPA chief Vusi Pikoli in September 2007. Pikoli was about to arrest National Police Commissioner Jackie Selebi for corruption. After Rappetti had asked Mbeki if he had seen the warrant of arrest for Selebi, Mbeki hid behind a question – instead of giving a straight answer. Asked the question again, Mbeki still wouldn't give a straight answer. Pahad, who had been friends with Mbeki for over 40 years, hustled Rappetti out of the room, shouting that she was out of order.[7]

The Zuma administration has been far cleverer. It realised right at the beginning that South African journalism has too deep a tradition of independence and insouciance. After all, the ANC had benefited from these traditions as the independent press of the 1980s harried the apartheid government to release Mandela and unban the ANC and its allied organisations.

Mbeki, for all his faults, attacked individual journalists and publications (his weekly online column often referred to some of us as 'some among us', implying that we were traitors of some sort) but he debated, even engaged, some editors.

The Zuma train arrived with a very different strategy in mind, and it has implemented it with single-mindedness and success since it came to power in 2009. That strategy was simple: own and control the media, then squeeze out all independent journalism while starving independent newspapers of advertising. The endgame is simple: ensure that the South African media landscape is exactly like Zimbabwe. The public broadcaster, the press and any other journalistic outlet take their orders from the top. Those who make even a squeak of criticism are soon pushed out. The result is a deadening of debate, a chill, which leads to a homogeneous, 'yes sir' type of media.

The assault began with the launch of the *New Age* newspaper by the Gupta family, notorious for their very close links to the Zuma family. Ironically, the initiative was led by Pahad, who at the time was trying to ingratiate himself with the Zuma faction of the ANC after a lifetime spent as an Mbeki fan. Right from the outset, government departments rewarded the Guptas' newspaper with advertising, despite the lack of audited circulation figures.[8] This was one newspaper that was not going to go the way of my beloved *ThisDay*.

It is important to understand the power of the Gupta family. If just half of the stories that have been published about the family are true, then we have a cancer in our society. As an example of these stories, the *Sunday Times* reported that one member of the family invited the former South African Airways chief executive officer Vuyisile Kona – soon after his appointment – to their home in Saxonwold, Johannesburg, and allegedly offered him a sum of R500 000. Present when this offer was reportedly made were President Jacob Zuma's son, Duduzane, and Free State premier Ace Magashule's son, Tshepiso.[9]

It is all go at the Gupta house. Numerous stories have emerged over the past few years of high-ranking government individuals being invited to the Saxonwold pad and offered goodies or paraded before others to demonstrate the Guptas' influence. The family, owners of

Sahara Computers and the *New Age* newspaper and with interests in mining and aviation, is extremely close to Zuma. Some of Zuma's children and one wife are intimately linked to the family. His son Duduzane is involved in various businesses with the family.[10]

Their closeness to the ANC has not stopped the Gupta family from spreading its largesse even to opposition parties. Everyone seems to have a price. Former Democratic Alliance leader Helen Zille visited their compound and left with a cheque too.[11] She wouldn't return the R400 000 to the Guptas, despite the mounting pile of information about their influence peddling and the general stench of dodginess that hangs over them like a persistent fart.

One of the most astounding things to emerge about their power came when the then Deputy Minister of Police, Fikile Mbalula, apparently broke down in an ANC national executive committee meeting and recounted how he had first heard of his promotion to sports minister from the Gupta family.[12]

Their influence on Zuma has been so great that former ANC Youth League president and now EFF leader Julius Malema warned that South Africa is 'not a democracy of families; this is a democracy of the people of the country'.[13]

'When families are exploiting the resources of this country and are enriching themselves in the name of freedom, when those in political office abuse their power to benefit friends, the youth must rise in defence of the ANC,' he said.

Malema would know: he used to be one of Zuma's closest allies.

One of the main sponsors of the Guptas' media business is the Free State government. We should not be surprised by this. The Guptas have the premier's young son, Tshepiso Magashule, living in their compound.[14] If it is a national or parastatal matter, you can expect the family has young Zuma – or one of Zuma's wives, Bongi Ngema-Zuma, who works for the family[15] – on the phone to the man known as number one.

And so the *New Age* was born. Meanwhile, the ANC was in the process of turning the public broadcaster, the South African Broadcasting Corporation (SABC), into a state broadcaster.

Many of our leaders may not realise it, but it is a very short distance from hope and achievement to despair and mediocrity.

Think back to the SABC of the 1970s and 1980s. This was an institution so deep in the pockets of the National Party that it did not twitch without an express instruction from the Union Buildings. The SABC was useful, for many of us at least, as an alert service: it told us that something had not happened, only for us to deduce that indeed something of significance had taken place.

For lessons on how not to run a public broadcaster, the SABC of the 1980s stands today as a powerful example.

Cast your mind back to the late 1990s and you will remember an SABC that was beginning to reclaim the values, ethos and practices of a real public broadcaster. Journalists of stature from across the globe were recruited, news managers who believed in South Africa and its Constitution – rather than one or other party – were elevated while producers keen for truth ran the programmes from behind the scenes. Great journalistic names, such as Zwelakhe Sisulu, Ofeibia Quist-Arcton, John Perlman, Barney Mthombothi and many others, walked the corridors of the SABC's Auckland Park studios. Hope was in the air. A new country and a new public broadcasting code was being born.

Politicians were grilled – as they should be. Objectivity was prized. In just a few years, we knew that it was possible to take a lethargic, compromised institution and begin to create a broadcaster of quality and pride. In the SABC, despite its size and history, we were a South Africa that was beginning to put its best foot forward. At the SABC we began to build a public broadcaster that many across the world could come and learn from.

That was then. The hope and achievement of that SABC has been terribly destroyed. In its place is an ugly monster, a state broadcaster in thrall to a few callow, incompetent men who see their role merely as delivering a mandate to the ruling party.

Over the past two years South Africa has witnessed the crowing, vanity and self-obsession of the man in charge of the SABC – one Hlaudi Motsoeneng – parading himself through the press and forums, holding forth about his 'achievements' at the public broadcaster. He has cast himself as the hero of the hour, the man giving us a glorious service.[16]

What a fraud. The reality is entirely different. The SABC is today a demoralised, divided, mediocre product where senior staffers cannot work and junior staffers live in fear of persecution. Motsoeneng himself is a fraud who, according to the Public Protector, falsified his qualifications (he claimed to have a matric, when he did not have one) to land his job.

Worst of all, what kind of leader, without any shame, tells the world that someone else suggested that he make up fake matric symbols? Have we no shame? What do the thrusting young staffers joining the SABC today say when they see this sort of practice? I am sure they know now that lying, scheming and jumping into bed with politicians will get you far in this country.

It would be an insult to spaza shops to say that the place is run like a spaza shop. It is worse: it is run like the piggy bank of a tin-pot dictator like the late Nigerian Sani Abacha. Motsoeneng famously said he does not have to understand corporate governance; others are there to do so.

That explains it all. Any senior manager who does not understand corporate governance should not be in the job at all. But the SABC is neither a meritocracy nor a place where the general corporate rules apply.

How depressing, how miserable, how sad it must be for the hundreds of talented and dedicated people who continue to toil at the SABC. It must be dispiriting to be told constantly not to run footage of President Jacob Zuma being booed, or to interview government ministers 'respectfully'.[17]

The obliteration and total capture of the SABC was the second triumph of the Zuma administration. The third triumph was the capture of Independent Newspapers, the group where I started my journalism as a cadet at the *Star* newspaper in Johannesburg.

For those of us who appreciate a robust, independent and free press, though, Independent Newspapers represented one of the remaining pockets of excellence. Under the ownership of Irish millionaire Tony O'Reilly, Independent had been stripped of assets and profits for two decades, but it still maintained a modicum of what newspapers should do in a free and open democracy.[18] Editors still had power to make principled decisions, columnists were wide-ranging and independent and varied, while reporting could still be investigative and fearless. Independent was also powerful because of its national footprint: it owned the *Cape Times* and the *Cape Argus* in the Western Cape, *The Mercury* and *Daily News* in KwaZulu-Natal, and the *Diamond Fields Advertiser* in the Northern Cape. The crowning titles were the *Star* in Johannesburg, the national business insert *Business Report* and the *Pretoria News*.

O'Reilly had bought the newspaper group in a corporate coup following the 1994 elections – in a deal apparently blessed by Mandela – to twin them with his purchase of the *Independent* in London and several Irish newspapers. He fell on hard times after the global economic crisis of 2008. He was under pressure from shareholders in Ireland, and his other businesses were under huge stress. By 2013 things had become so bad he was in talks with various South African entities to sell.

He finally sold to the 'Sekunjalo Independent Media Consortium' for US$227 million. Sekunjalo is led by Dr Iqbal Survé, a former doctor who prides himself on having been close to Nelson Mandela and on having been part of a grouping that saw to the health problems of Robben Island prisoners and political detainees in the 1970s and 1980s.

Writing in the Daily Maverick, journalist Mandy de Waal described Survé thus: 'The founder of empowerment investment vehicle the Sekunjalo Group, he leads Sekunjalo Investments Limited, which is listed on the JSE, and which has investments in the telecommunications, marine, technology, healthcare and biomedical sectors. The listed entity has investments in, or local partnerships with, the likes of Siemens, Microsoft, GlaxoSmithKline, Pioneer Foods, Premier Fishing, British Telecom SA and Saab SA.'

De Waal asked Survé if his purchase of the newspaper group could be read as a political move, and he said: 'That is absolute nonsense. Anybody that knows me knows I am very independent ...

'The decision about what goes into the newspaper won't be mine. It is that of the editorial team. I have gone on record as saying there will be an editorial advisory board which is independent, will have a policy and a charter and will provide independent guidelines for journalists and editors. Anyone that suggests otherwise clearly doesn't know who I am. It is ironic that this is being said while the people I was competing against have very strong political affiliations.'[19]

He has done completely the opposite.

At the *Cape Times*, Survé began by firing the editor the day after Nelson Mandela's death because she led the newspaper with a breaking story – one which reported the Public Protector's findings that Survé's company had been involved in corruption in a government tender. The newspaper group claimed that the editor, Alide Dasnois, should have led the newspaper with Mandela's death.

Indeed she had. The newspaper was wrapped around with a Mandela tribute prepared especially for Mandela's passing.[20]

Since then, major changes have occurred at Independent Newspapers. Editors have been forced out. Some of my favourite journalists, many of them the best in the industry, found themselves unwelcome at the group. Moshoeshoe Monare, one of the finest journalists of this generation, left the editorship of the *Sunday Independent*. Soon after, Makhudu Sefara left the *Star*. Many others left the *Cape Times* and the *Cape Argus*, including Chris Whitfield and Janet Heard (whose father Tony, as editor of the *Cape Times* in the 1970s, defied the apartheid government and published an interview with banned ANC president Oliver Tambo from exile). Many others were hounded out. Lackeys, lapdogs and those who won't or cannot afford to rock the boat – mainly to preserve themselves for personal, professional and financial reasons – have now been put in their place.

At the ANC's 103rd birthday celebrations on 10 January 2014, Survé's group editor-in-chief Karima Brown and the group's head of Opinion and Analysis, Vukani Mde, posted pictures of themselves clad in ANC regalia.[21] The newspaper group's editorial chiefs essentially came out as ANC supporters, if not as card-carrying members.

The group is now a shadow of its former self: quiescent, often running hagiographic profiles of Survé and government leaders, and shorn of any investigative ability. It is a mediocre place, lacking in the spirit that many of us felt we were upholding when we heard Mandela say, way back in February 1994: 'A critical, independent and investigative press is the lifeblood of any democracy. The press must be free from state interference. It must have the economic strength to stand up to the blandishments of government officials. It must have sufficient independence from vested interests to be bold and inquiring without fear or favour. It must enjoy the protection of the Constitution, so that it can protect our rights as citizens.

'It is only such a free press that can temper the appetite of any government to amass power at the expense of the citizen. It is only such a free press that can be the vigilant watchdog of the public interest against the temptation on the part of those who wield it to abuse that power. It is only such a free press that can have the capacity to relentlessly expose excesses and corruption on the part of government, state officials and other institutions that hold power in society.'[22]

I am ashamed to say that all these assaults on the freedom of the press, and the single-minded drive to control all media in South Africa, take place while many journalists keep quiet. I have commented a lot on the SABC saga, on government attempts to cow the media and on the Gupta scandals in my columns and through my television programme, *The Justice Factor,* on the news channel eNCA. To my shame I have kept quiet about what is happening at places like Independent Newspapers, where I began my career.

I also kept quiet when the chief executive officer of e.tv, the media company that owns the channel that airs my show, came out in 2014 and alleged that there were numerous and serious attempts to control news content on the channel. His testimony was chilling.

Marcel Golding was the executive chairman of the Hosken Consolidated Investments (HCI) group of companies, a company built up with the pension funds of the South African Clothing and Textile Workers' Union (Sactwu). Over some 20 years the former political activist, trade unionist and ANC MP had built up the group with his partner Johnny Copelyn to a R20-billion behemoth.

HCI controls Sabido, owners of e.tv, and Golding was also Chief Executive Officer (CEO) of Sabido. In 2007 Sabido launched the eNews Channel Africa (eNCA), where I pitched and was given a politics show called *The Justice Factor*. It has been running since 2008.

In 2014 Golding was suspended as CEO of Sabido, with HCI alleging that he had bought shares in a company called Ellies without first seeking permission from the board. Golding made a submission to the Labour Court that this was a trumped-up charge to get rid of him, as he had for a year been fighting attempts by the Zuma administration to interfere in news content at e.tv and eNCA.

In his submission, he said: 'I have recently been summoned to a disciplinary hearing to answer charges relating to the purchase by Sabido, of which I am the CEO, of shares in Ellies, a JSE-listed company. It is alleged that I did so without the necessary Board's authority. I acted in good faith and at the time believed [it] to be in Sabido's best interests in purchasing the shares.

'The disciplinary hearing has been launched after months of attempts to get me to relinquish the chair of the board of HCI and resign as CEO of e.tv and Sabido as a result of my refusal to permit e.tv to be used for political purposes by a trade union that is invested in the group.

'I believe that two directors of HCI, John Copelyn and Yunis Shaik, are the driving forces behind the attempts to push me out. HCI was originally founded by Copelyn and myself. Copelyn is currently HCI's

CEO and Sabido's non-executive chairman. Over the last year our relationship has deteriorated. The cause of this deterioration included amongst others our differing views with respect to how to manage the concerted pressure Sactwu has been exerting on HCI and Sabido. Sactwu has persistently attempted to influence the editorial direction of e.tv news in order to further its agenda.'

Now, many may believe that these are the ramblings of a man who is caught up in a nasty corporate battle. But the key thing about Golding's testimony is that he points out specific instances which support his argument that e.tv and eNCA were being pummelled to become what the SABC has already become: lapdogs of the Zuma administration.

Golding continued: 'On 24 March 2014 Shaik addressed an email to Bronwyn Keene-Young [COO of Sabido] stating that the Minister of Economic Development Ebrahim Patel had called him and asked that a supplied newsfeed of President Zuma opening a dam be aired on the e.tv evening news. The suggestion in the email was that it "might be a good lead story". It should be noted that this request was made four days after the Public Protector report into Nkandla was made public.

'Keene-Young and I were at a conference and unavailable to respond. Shaik therefore, after receiving another call from Minister Patel, "assumed the responsibility to liaise with" Patrick Conroy, managing director of the news channel, "alerting him of the news and suggested it gets some coverage". On 24 March Keene-Young replied to Shaik's email and explained the inappropriateness of Shaik's conduct to him in the context of news integrity and appealed to him "never to make this kind of request directly to our managers". Shaik replied and contended that he was "not acting as a shareholder representative" when he contacted Conroy and dismissed her stated concern about integrity and independence of the media on the basis that she was having a "temper tantrum" and "protecting turf not values".

'On 28 March 2014 I received an email from Copelyn to alert me to a conversation he was planning to have with me about Keene-Young who had raised the ire of "several important corners of HCI". Keene-Young is my spouse so this situation was understandably awkward for all of us. Copelyn and I met and an altercation ensued in which an ultimatum was posed that either I or my spouse should leave the business. A solution was found in that Keene-Young was designated as Sabido's chief corporate officer and removed from any interface with external stakeholders.'

Golding then went on to list a litany of incidents in which Shaik and Patel have tried to influence the work of journalists on the station. In one instance, Patel tried to co-opt the station to ambush the opposition party, the Democratic Alliance, during a pre-election debate. The interactions became more ominous. He wrote: 'On 14 August 2014 I was sent the following SMS "instruction" by Andre Kriel of Sactwu: "Will call you tomorrow. Violet Seboni Memorial lecture will be on 25 August in Johannesburg, Minister Patel will deliver the lecture. We require e.tv to cover it live. Please arrange".'[23]

It is now a matter of history that Golding and his wife, Keene-Young, were removed. Towards the end of his submission Golding made a statement that would come to haunt me: 'My understanding of the situation is that Sactwu's stance is directly related to a desire by Sactwu to exert greater control over news content at e.tv (and eNCA) by ensuring that a CEO less independent than me assumes control over Sabido.'

This submission haunts me because when he finally left I said nothing, did nothing, and kept quiet. It is an act that unsettled me, but I acted against my better judgement by not speaking out. I acted in a cowardly manner. When they came for Golding and Keene-Young, I should have said something. I should have made it clear that I disagreed, that requests of the nature that had been made to Golding, Keene-Young and Conroy were really what happens at the start of dictatorships.

I had had one meeting, once, with Keene-Young. I had met Golding once or twice in the corridors. I had seen them with their children in the car park, but that was about it. They were not and are not my friends. Yet a matter of principle was at play here, and I was among the many who kept quiet and thought it would never happen to me. I knew when I kept quiet as they were kicked out that I was lying to myself.

I have become a secret admirer of Zuma's cunning. The man is unparalleled at playing ANC politics. He is even better at playing the chess game of South African politics.

Zuma came to power at the intersection of two phenomena. First, Thabo Mbeki's Aids denialism had ravaged too many of us: we lost friends, comrades, relatives, associates, colleagues. We had had enough of Mbeki, his tricksiness and intellectual loopiness while hundreds of thousands of our people died of HIV/Aids. Zuma offered himself up as an alternative to this Mbeki.

Many people climbed on board the Zuma boat. I was a fierce critic of Mbeki, but I found myself deeply troubled by Zuma. The ANC was not doing itself any favours by choosing Zuma. It should have gone back to its values, its traditions and history. Instead, desperate for an alternative, and seduced by Zuma's manipulative ways, it chose him. It took itself backwards.

Many in the news media knew this narrative, knew this story, and opposed Zuma with a vengeance. That is why, when he finally rose to power, he decided to launch a sustained assault against the media. In 2012, for example, when the ANC forced *City Press* to remove from its website a picture of *The Spear*, editor Ferial Haffajee said she had decided to take the image down out of 'care and fear'. In the preceding week she had received death threats, endured a boycott of the newspaper by the ANC, and her journalist was evicted from a party conference.[24]

'Fear' is a word that journalists – and some of the party's own leaders – have come to associate with Zuma's ANC. In the governing party's increasingly paranoid worldview, the media has become the single greatest enemy of the ANC, an enemy that needs to be subdued.

In the run-up to the local government elections in May 2011, ANC secretary-general Gwede Mantashe declared: 'We must realise that in this elections [sic] the main opposition is the media. Leave the [opposition] DA, leave [the opposition] Cope … we will work very hard against that strong opposition.'[25]

The culmination of that 'strong opposition' was the passing in April 2013 of the draconian Protection of State Information Bill, known as the Secrecy Bill, by Parliament. If signed into law, journalists and their sources face up to 25 years in prison for publishing anything deemed to be state information. The Bill provides no recourse to a so-called public interest defence – that publication is in the broader interest of society. It is a piece of legislation that reeks of the stench of the apartheid regime.

In this way the press, which has fearlessly exposed corruption and spoken truth to power while publishing the voices of civil society leaders who warn of a possible slide into a failed state, is being bullied and targeted for control. Journalists have in the past been harassed for exposing corruption, but now the assault on free speech is written into law.

After Mandela's fairly benign five-year term, Thabo Mbeki's prickly personality soon soured his relationship with the press, which heavily criticised him for his Aids denialist views. Though Mbeki's office sometimes used bullying tactics, there was never any move towards legislated gagging of the media under his administration.

It was when Zuma, a former ANC intelligence chief, won the ANC's internal leadership elections in 1997 that the party began to embrace a securocratic, conspiratorial outlook and began systematically putting up the barricades. Under the Zuma administration, power is obtained and maintained through control of the intelligence services and their ability to control the flow of information.

Zuma's genius, and the source of my admiration of the man, stems from the fact that he has not just grabbed at the idea of changing editors and media managers. Zuma's genius is that he understands power, and that power means having control of the money.

Think about it. At the SABC he has chosen the chairman of the board and the foot soldiers, such as the man who lied about his qualifications and yet has now become chief operating officer of the corporation. At Independent Newspapers, which will be the biggest beneficiary of the decision to support only pliant press with government advertising, he has Survé in his pocket. At the *New Age* and the television channel ANN7, his son lives with the proprietors. At eNCA his biggest allies control the business.

Zuma outsmarted all of us in the press who fingered him for his many failings. He is in charge of our salaries, of the purse strings. Our bosses are jumping to his every bidding.

So are the journalists. He has won.

6

The Age of the Traitor

'But I believe, and the black prophetic tradition believes,
that we proceed because black people are worthy of being free,
just as poor people of all colors are worthy of being free, even if
they never will be free. That is the existential leap of faith.'

– Cornel West, September 2013[1]

In late 2014 a little-known, largely incoherent deputy minister in President Zuma's administration accused Public Protector Thuli Madonsela of being a Central Intelligence Agency (CIA) plant.

Deputy Minister of Defence and Military Veterans Kebby Maphatsoe told a crowd gathered at the unveiling of a memorial to Umkhonto weSizwe (MK) combatant Linda 'Lion of Tshiawelo' Jabane in Soweto that Madonsela was on the payroll of the CIA. 'We can't allow people to hijack the ANC. We'll fight and defend the African National Congress. *uThuli umele asitshele ukuthi ubani ihandler yakhe* [Thuli must tell us who her handler is],' Maphatsoe said. 'They are even using our institutions now … These Chapter 9 institutions were created by the ANC but are now being used against us, and if you ask why, it is the Central Intelligence Agency. Ama [the] Americans want their own chief executive in South Africa and we must not allow that,' he continued.[2]

It was a shameless, nonsensical attack, but it was nothing new for those South Africans who stand up for accountability and good governance under the Zuma administration. Maphatsoe, leader of the MK Military Veterans' Association, a wing of the ANC made up of former MK combatants, is known as a political lightweight who is used by President Zuma to garner populist votes from veterans.

After his extraordinary attack on Madonsela, who has been hailed by *Time* magazine and others for her stance against corruption and her efforts to uphold accountable government, Maphatsoe confessed to never actually having fought against apartheid. It turned out that when he lost his arm, which for years he claimed to have lost in battle against the SADF, he was not in combat. He was in fact deserting from an ANC military camp in Uganda, allegedly to expose the terrible conditions there, when he was shot by local forces. His arm had to be amputated.[3]

Maphatsoe is therefore a wounded man. He has no real constituency in the ANC. He has no relevant abilities. He is among those who rose to their current positions by vociferously defending Zuma during his rape trial and battle to avoid facing corruption charges. Hand-picked by the President and handed a deputy minister's position, he is fully aware that he has to constantly sing for his supper.

Madonsela, who has investigated the Nkandla corruption issue and has consistently pointed out the rot at the heart of the current administration, is a target for the corrupt and their praise-singers. Those who raise their heads against the overwhelmingly fawning and deferential culture that has come to represent the ANC are targets. And those, like Maphatsoe, who go after the likes of Madonsela are rewarded with high office despite their patent lack of ability.

Maphatsoe, for example, is in charge of the Department of Military Veterans. He is clearly useless at his job. In October 2014 defence minister Nosiviwe Mapisa-Nqakula told Parliament that the department is in such a shambles that she was unable to produce an annual report, financial statements or audit reports for the entity, said *Business Day*.

'It is with a deep sense of regret that I have to inform you I am not able to table the annual report, financial statements and the audit report … of the Department of Military Veterans in accordance with the Public Finance Management Act,' Mapisa-Nqakula said.[4]

Predictably, Maphatsoe remains firmly ensconced in his lucrative position. He has not been called to account for his failures. Crucially, he has not been publically censured by his superiors for his execrable statements about Madonsela. He has never provided proof for these statements. None can be produced, simply because there is none available. Madonsela was never a spy, and the likes of Maphatsoe know it.

There isn't a single patriotic South African who has stood up against the current rot in our system without being accused of being a CIA spy, an agent of apartheid-era whites, a racist, a sellout or some other such derogatory epithet.

In August 2013 I was visiting friends in Los Angeles when I received an email from my childhood friend Winston Skosana, a staunch ANC member, asking me whether it was true that I was a CIA spy. I had apparently been named in a report doing the rounds in political circles claiming that the strongly anti-corruption then Cosatu secretary-general, Zwelinzima Vavi, and other high-profile South Africans were being paid to advance an American agenda.

Vavi had received and released copies of the report. It was incredible: I was named among political leaders such as Julius Malema, the former head of prosecutions Vusi Pikoli and former director-general in the Presidency Frank Chikane as being among people paid to set up structures in order to destabilise the current South African order.

This fake report named me as a 'media boss' who advised Agang founder Dr Mamphela Ramphele.[5] I had only ever met Ramphele on two occasions – and on both occasions I was interviewing her for my television show. I had never spoken to her privately or advised her. And me a media boss? Really?

I did not even know some of the people I was alleged to be in cahoots with. Worse, though, was that this report, though clearly bogus, made it into the Cosatu central executive committee and, after being leaked, onto the front page of *City Press*.

I was not alarmed, though. Being called a CIA agent or counter-revolutionary has become a badge of honour in South Africa.

Maphatsoe, for example, did not quite get the irony when, just a week after he claimed Thuli Madonsela was a CIA spy, he claimed that the brilliant constitutional law expert Professor Shadrack Gutto was a 'counter-revolutionary' and that Gutto, who was born in Kenya, must 'leave us in our beautiful South Africa'.[6] This was the same Maphatsoe who, as an exile, was helped by fellow Africans, just as the exiled ANC was given succour by other African states.

Unfortunately he is not the only one. It seems like almost every day now, those who speak up against the rampant corruption, the sloth and the looting of poor people's money get labelled as reactionary, counter-revolutionary, treasonous or racist. South African debate is often reduced to these badges.

Where does the paranoia come from? In late 2010 I had an exchange with the ANC intellectual Pallo Jordan – later to be unmasked as a fraudulent claimant to a doctoral degree when he hadn't even finished his junior degree – after I had asserted that it was dangerous to view South Africans as having been liberated solely by the ANC. In fact, liberation came about through a combination of the struggles of internal activists massed under the United Democratic Front, the role of international pressure on the apartheid regime and of course the efforts of the ANC in exile.

In his response, Jordan asserted that, because of the struggles of his comrades, I write my 'wordy, self-righteous columns in *The Times*, certain that he [Malala] won't spend that night in prison.'[7]

It was an extraordinary, and ill-considered, assertion. It was particularly discombobulating because, as outlined by ANC veteran Oyama Mabandla in an article in *African Affairs* in 1990, paranoia was rampant within the exiled ANC, and many in the movement hated those who spoke truth to power – as Jordan often does. The same ANC that Jordan claims fought for my freedom arrested and detained him for six weeks in 1983. This is what Mabandla said way back in 1990: 'Pallo was detained on the orders of [Communist] Party member and Mbokodo [the ANC's security department] chieftain, Peter Boroko ... Pallo was accused of exposing the Mbokodo informant network within DIP [Department of Information and Publicity] by mockingly referring to

Malaya and another man named Ace ... as Amapolisa [police] – warning other DIP staffers to be careful of them. On that basis, Pallo was detained and was to spend six weeks in detention.

'I participated in an informal meeting at Green House [Mbokodo HQ] which discussed Pallo's arrest ... During the discussion one Mbokodo officer made a chilling remark which seemed to capture the essence of the entire saga. The comment went thus, "leli intellectual lase Merika lisijwayela kabi": "this American-trained intellectual is uppity" – and thus in need of straightening out.'[8]

There we go again: all about the Americans, the CIA, the counter-revolutionaries.

This obsession, this paranoia, goes back to the ANC in exile and persists to this day. To be fair to the Zuma administration, the Mbeki administration was probably the most paranoid of the post-apartheid era. The man saw American imperialists and CIA ghosts virtually everywhere he went.

Mbeki, a formidable intellectual, soured his reputation for statesmanship through his denialism on HIV/Aids. Just a year into his presidency, in October 2000, he told the ANC parliamentary caucus that criticism of his HIV/Aids denialism and refusal to dispense antiretroviral drugs to those affected by the virus was a plot by the CIA and international pharmaceutical companies.[9]

So paranoid was the Mbeki administration that in April 2001 the then Minister of Safety and Security, the late Steve Tshwete, announced that respected ANC internal leaders Cyril Ramaphosa, Mathews Phosa and Tokyo Sexwale – who had all been sidelined and had to move into private business – were involved in a conspiracy to overthrow Mbeki with the backing of shadowy foreign forces.

Mbeki, in a live television interview, gave further credence to the plot rumours. 'It's a conspiratorial thing,' he told e.tv's Debora Patta. 'I know you have businesspeople who say, "We will set up a fund to promote our particular candidate and we will then try to influence particular journalists".'[10]

It is in the Zuma era, though, that the practice of branding anyone who dares raise a voice against his maladministration has become institutionalised. Virtually every political opponent, commentator or civil servant who speaks up is called a racist or CIA spy.

We shouldn't be surprised by this. The Zuma administration started out exactly as it aims to finish. In 2003 the National Director of Public Prosecutions, Bulelani Ngcuka, was closing in on a case that would have major repercussions for the future of South Africa. He believed that the Deputy President, Jacob Zuma, had received bribes from Schabir Shaik, a businessman and prominent member of the Shaik family – virtually every member of the family had fought against the apartheid government as a soldier or spy of the ANC – to influence him to pass lucrative government deals to his company, Nkobi Holdings. The most important of these deals would involve the supply of electronic warfare components as part of the controversial arms deal.

The investigation had reached a point where Ngcuka, the Scorpions investigative unit and prosecutors were ready to move against both Zuma and Shaik.

You must appreciate the arsenal in Ngcuka's hands. By the time he was ready to bring charges against Zuma in June 2005, he would claim that in the ten years between 15 October 1995 and 1 June 2005 Zuma had received 783 payments from Schabir Shaik totalling precisely R4 072 499.85. There were 93 000 documents, including bank statements, testifying to each and every one of these transactions.[11]

That is when, in order to protect both Zuma and Shaik, the spy allegations were unleashed. In one of the most shameful attempts ever to manipulate journalists in the history of the new South Africa, two of Zuma's key henchmen moved to tarnish Ngcuka's credentials. The two were Mac Maharaj, a former transport minister in the Mandela administration and a hardened freedom fighter, and Mo Shaik, brother of the compromised Schabir. Both had been key figures around Zuma when he was the party's head of intelligence in the 1980s and 1990s. Maharaj had smuggled a manuscript of Mandela's book out of Robben Island.

First, Shaik planted a story with *Sunday Times* journalist Ranjeni Munusamy claiming that Ngcuka had been an apartheid spy, code-named RS452, in the 1980s. The story was so flimsy that the *Sunday Times* would not print it. When this became clear, the reporter then gave it to the rival *City Press*.[12]

The revelations caused a minor tsunami in the ANC. The party was split in two: those who stood with Zuma and suspected that he was being unfairly targeted by the NPA, and those who felt that the man had a case to answer. It was also a diversion from the real and urgent case of corruption against Zuma and Schabir Shaik. For Ngcuka the allegations were devastating: what freedom fighter, whose wife was a member of the Cabinet, could stomach being exposed as a spy for the heinous apartheid regime?

President Thabo Mbeki appointed a commission of inquiry, under Judge Joos Hefer, to look into the allegations. The matter turned into a farce. Maharaj and Mo Shaik did not present a single piece of evidence to the commission. Instead, Shaik presented what he called a 'reconstruction' of what he claimed was his original report from 1990, in which he said he had found that Ngcuka was 'most probably' a spy for the apartheid government.[13]

Maharaj, who was discredited after allegations that monies had been mysteriously deposited into his wife's account by parties involved in the arms deal, told Hefer that Shaik had showed the report to him at the time. Incredibly, the two men seemed to have invented a fiction and appeared before a commission of inquiry to back each other's fiction up. The judge did not buy it. Before Hefer moved to exonerate Ngcuka, though, the two men then began to backtrack.

The *Sunday Times* investigative reporter Mzilikazi wa Afrika easily managed to find and identify the real agent RS452. In his book *Nothing Left to Steal* he writes: 'Two days later, my friend called to say agent RS452 was a white woman and a former Port Elizabeth-based lawyer. It was believed that she was living somewhere overseas ... With the help of my friend from the National Intelligence Agency, I tried to trace agent RS452. One day he called to say agent RS452's real name was Vanessa Jacinta Brereton and her home phone number was in England.'[14]

Now, both Maharaj and Shaik had appeared on television following Munusamy's report and had said that Ngcuka was most likely agent RS452. In testimony before the Hefer Commission, Maharaj repeated his allegation, saying that 'in all probability' Ngcuka had been an apartheid spy.

Later, after Brereton's confession that she was the alleged spy, the pair's legal counsel, Yunus Shaik, turned around and said: 'That is not their contention.'

The two were utterly humiliated. In his 62-page report, Judge Hefer dismissed their claim. He said both Maharaj and Shaik were 'most unconvincing', their allegations were 'ill conceived' and 'entirely unsubstantiated'.[15]

It is worth reflecting on the fact that when Zuma became president in 2009 he installed Mo Shaik as his new chief of the then South African Secret Service, despite the horrendous intelligence shocker he had delivered at the Hefer Commission. Maharaj was later brought in as his chief of communications.

So it goes.

The question, then, is this: why is it, in South Africa, that holding up the mirror of truth to the powerful is met with accusations of treason? What lies beneath this particular form of defence? Could it be that we all know that it is probably the most destructive charge – on the basis of our history – that we can throw at anyone?

There is a shameful and horrific history behind the accusations that people are sellouts or, in township lingo, *impimpi* (collaborator or enemy spy). In the apartheid era, many MK members were arrested, tortured and 'turned' to spy for the apartheid regime. They were called 'askaris', and they became the most despised species in our political culture.

We don't talk about this history enough. We don't cleanse ourselves of it enough.

On 29 June 1985, the *New York Times* reported on 'necklacing', the horrific method by which suspected police informers or spies were killed by township activists throughout the 1980s. The image is stark in its familiarity. The piece is harrowing:

'A person is taken by a crowd and a used automobile tire is placed around his neck. The tire is filled with gasoline and ignited. The person dies, and a statistic is added to the nation's pain.

'If South Africa's unrest over the last 21 months has acquired its own harsh emblem, it is the form of fiery execution called "the necklace" – the retribution meted out usually by those who call themselves "comrades" as part of what the Government calls a revolutionary onslaught against white rule ...

'On July 10, 1985, in Duduza township, Bishop Desmond M Tutu wrestled with a crowd to save a purported informer from incineration on a blazing car.

'On July 20, 1985, however, no one saved Maki Skosana from being burned to death in front of a television camera in Duduza. Her incineration, which was shown on South African television that night, offered pictorial justification for a partial state of emergency that lasted from the next day until March 1986. The judgment of Miss Skosana was harsh and summary, and some said later that it was a mistake and that she was not an informer after all.'[16]

Many of those killed were innocents. In 1997 the TRC heard testimony about the Skosana case and concluded that she had been wrongly accused. No information existed to indicate that she had been an informer except for the fact that a group of young activists had died from a booby-trapped hand grenade near her house. The TRC said the necklace was 'a gruesome act of extraordinary violence that cast a blight on the struggle for freedom'.

It is unclear exactly how many people died in the 1980s and early 1990s through the necklace method. What cannot be denied, however, is that many perished this way. In townships all across South Africa, communities watched as their neighbours and their children killed their own in the most barbaric manner. Winnie Madikizela-Mandela, controversial wife of the late former president Nelson Mandela and an ANC leader in her own right, once said our country would win its freedom 'with our boxes of matches and our necklaces'.

'Impimpi mayi tshiswe!' (The informer must be burnt to death) was a cry that I heard chanted at meetings throughout the 1980s and early 1990s.

There is no worse way to die than the necklace, I think. But this is what ordinary South Africans, in townships and villages across the country, did to people they knew. In most of these cases there was little evidence proffered. Justice was swift and brutal.

In ANC camps in Angola, Zambia and other frontline states, the organisation was gripped with fear throughout the 1960s right up to the 1990s when most exiles returned home. The apartheid government sent waves of 'turned' young activists or spies to infiltrate the organisation. Comrades were exposed and killed. Few could be trusted. The best bet was to trust no one.

And so it was that, as the ANC's own Motsuenyane Commission found, hundreds were detained in ANC camps, tortured and even killed on suspicion of being apartheid spies.[17]

That suspicion has remained, and continues to dominate the culture of the party now as we gallop towards three decades after it was unbanned in 1990. It is not merely the likes of Maphatsoe, a former exile, who are infected with this dread disease. Young leaders of the party frequently pull out this defence in order to parry allegations of corruption or wrongdoing.

The danger, and it is present and imminent, is that such behaviour will tip over into action – detentions without trial to try and extract 'confessions', jailing and even extrajudicial killings. Investigative journalists in South Africa now live with the knowledge that they are constantly followed and their communications tapped. People like Thuli Madonsela have had to get extra security because they fear for their lives. Trade unionists such as Irvin Jim, the general secretary of the National Union of Metalworkers of South Africa (Numsa), which has split from the ANC's traditional trade union ally Cosatu, has been followed and now lives with extra security as a feature of his life.

There is another, more compelling, reason for the ANC's name-calling and paranoia. It lies in the fact that in exile the ANC was largely powerless, with events happening to it rather than with the party always leading.

Make no mistake, the ANC was a powerful moral force in the world, but it was caught in the middle of the Cold War, its most effective leaders were jailed on Robben Island with Mandela and others, and it was cash-strapped and scattered to the winds in disparate parts of the globe. Inside the country, waves of new thinking challenged the ANC's moral and intellectual hegemony. In the 1960s a radicalism that un-settled the party took hold via the Pan Africanist movement, which called for a more Africanist stance by liberation movements that em-phasised the return of land to the black masses and the call to drive 'whites into the sea'. The ANC lost a significant rump of its member-ship to this thinking.

The 1970s were dominated by the Black Consciousness Movement, which emphasised black pride and was symbolised by the young intellectual Stephen Bantu Biko, who was murdered by the security police in 1977. During much of the 1960s and 1970s the ANC was largely somnambulant, unable to react to the changing winds effec-tively except to receive the fleeing young radicals into its bosom in the frontline states. Similarly, the 1980s were defined by internal civic, trade union and youth activism, which extolled the virtues of the ANC but was in no way directly linked by diktats from Lusaka, the ANC headquarters.

The ANC is today in similar turmoil. Twenty-one years after ascend-ing to power, the party is still unable to run the economy in such a way that its promise of jobs, equality and eradication of poverty is fulfilled. The political space is increasingly dominated by an embold-ened opposition, which has latched on to the abundant failures of

President Zuma to expose the ANC's moral bankruptcy, its institutional failures and its hypocrisy. The ANC's electoral majority is slowly being chipped away. Things are falling apart.

When a party can no longer lead society by dint of its ideas, it begins to clutch at straws. It begins to seek excuses instead of confronting the elephant in the room. It is a terrible yet familiar syndrome: externalise the problem, find a bogeyman.

And so it is now that, helpless and paranoid, the ANC has no answer to the serious charges put to it and its president by someone like Thuli Madonsela. The only way to defend itself is to besmirch her name. The only way it thinks it can besmirch her name is by calling her a CIA agent.

Unfortunately that horse has bolted. South Africans can see through the ruse. The enemy agent is no longer without. The spy who is bringing the ANC down is, unfortunately for the party, itself.

7

Marikana, Our Collective Nightmare

'In 2012? In a democracy? In a new South Africa?
Have we forgotten so soon?
Marikana felt like a nightmare, but that is what our democracy is in 2012.'
– Archbishop Emeritus Desmond Tutu, *The Guardian*, 4 September 2012

On the afternoon of 16 August 2012 a 500-strong contingent of the South African Police Service (SAPS) surrounded a hillock outside the informal settlement of Nkaneng, in the North West province, to quell a wildcat strike by workers at Lonmin's Marikana platinum mine. The several thousand workers on the hill had been involved in violent disturbances over the preceding days. Ten people – workers who had not heeded the call to strike, policemen, mine security guards – had died brutally in the ten days before that fateful afternoon, allegedly at the hands of strikers or provocateurs. One report indicated that one of the dead policemen had been 'hacked to death'.[1]

The chanting workers, many daubed with traditional medicine believed to make them either invincible or invisible,[2] had over the preceding days pelted police with stones and refused to disperse. Many were carrying knobkieries, pangas, sticks and iron rods as they sang on the hill.

The mineworkers were demanding a monthly salary of R12500. Many were earning between R4000 and R5000 a month.

That day, it now seems clear, the police had murder in their hearts. In the morning, two SAPS colonels, named only as a Klassen and Madoda, arranged for four mortuary vehicles to be sent to Marikana from nearby Phokeng. According to the mineworkers' lawyers, they were adamant that 'they were going to close down the miners in Marikana'. In the event, only one mortuary vehicle arrived that afternoon.[3]

What happened next was to become the subject of a commission of inquiry, books, academic studies, journalistic pieces and documentaries. It was to become the SAPS's first post-apartheid massacre. The strikers were massed on the hillock in Nkaneng, and at some point were surrounded by the police.

Then the police mowed the men down. There was sustained gunfire for a maximum of 30 minutes. When silence descended on the hillock 34 mineworkers were dead. More than 70 were injured. More than 200 were arrested.

President Jacob Zuma appointed a commission of inquiry, headed by retired judge Ian Farlam, immediately after the events that day. In June 2015, almost three years later, Zuma announced the findings of the Marikana Commission of Inquiry. In essence, the commission found no one culpable for the killings, and it exonerated the major political figures involved. It questioned National Police Commissioner Riah Phiyega's fitness to hold office, and recommended that high-level investigations into all the killings, before and during the massacre, be carried out by experts.[4]

Three years after the Marikana Massacre, that was it. Or is it? It is worth revisiting some of the evidence of this most heinous of crimes, and wondering out loud how, in the new South Africa, police could kill so many of their own so brutally.

It seemed that the police shot to kill, if not during the first furious fusillade then certainly afterwards, on that afternoon. According to the mineworkers' lawyers, several of the strikers were shot in the head. 'We want to show that according to the [postmortem] records, fatal wounds that were sustained by all the 16 people who were killed at [one of the] scene[s] were in the upper body,' Advocate Dumisa Ntsebeza later told the commission.[5]

His list was chilling: Patrick Akhona Jijase (26), gunshot wound in the head; Mphangeli Tukuza (41), gunshot wound to head, entrance wound at earlobe, exit wound (of bullet) over left eye; Mgcineni Noki (30) – who had shot to fame as 'the man in the green blanket' as he led workers through the strike – was shot in the face, neck, lower limbs and buttocks.

And so it went on. Ntsebeza presented evidence showing conclusively that 14 of the dead were shot in the back. However, in its final report the commission said: 'The lack of clarity around the death of the 17 deceased persons at scene two, places the commission in the difficult position of not being able to make findings as to the circumstances surrounding the death of each deceased. To accept or reject any version, with any degree of certainty, requires further interrogation of many factors.'[6]

I find this conclusion inadequate in the face of the evidence presented to the commission. How can so many die from bullets fired from behind them? If it is not murder, then it is cowardly. Let us say so.

The award-winning photojournalist Greg Marinovich, writing in the Daily Maverick, had presented even more chilling testimony just days after the massacre. According to his account, some of the dead were cornered and, instead of being arrested, were shot in cold blood. 'It is becoming clear to this reporter that heavily armed police hunted down and killed the miners in cold blood,' he wrote.[7]

The Marikana Massacre, as it has come to be known, was the deadliest single police action since apartheid police killed 69 people and injured 180 at Sharpeville in March 1960. As at Marikana, many of those killed at Sharpeville were shot in the back as they tried to run away from police fire. Eight of the dead were women and 10 were children.

How did we get to such a low point in South Africa, in a free and democratic country in which the party of Nelson Mandela was in power? How did we get to a point where only one government leader, defence minister Nosiviwe Mapisa-Nqakula, has had the guts not only to go to the bereaved communities but also to apologise? What happened to us?

The Marikana Massacre underlined everything that was wrong about the new South Africa. If there is in any way a nadir for our failures over the past 21 years of our democracy, this was it. Marikana exposed the myth of black economic empowerment (BEE) as a tool that does not actually empower workers and communities but creates a small, mollycoddled, arrogant, selfish black elite.

It exposed the continued exploitation of ordinary workers who live in abject poverty despite the massive wealth they help create. It showed up the hypocrisy of many mining conglomerates when they assert that they look after their workers; many of the mineworkers around Marikana lived in the squalid informal settlements, such as Nkaneng, around the mine, instead of in mine accommodation as is required by numerous pacts signed between employers, government and trade unions.[8]

Marikana showed how we took over from the apartheid government in 1994 and did very little to change our society. We merely took up where apartheid-era legislation left off, and did nothing to fundamentally change the structure of our society and its labour relations.

The Marikana story is long and complex and ultimately shameful. It starts with poor labour relations, with poverty and inequality, and stretches through our current government's obsession with a macho, discredited, 'shoot to kill' attitude towards policing. It is the story of a trade union that lost its way and cosied up to big business; of an upstart and populist new union that exploited real frustration with low wages and poor living conditions to establish itself; of police failure to heed signals that a bloodbath was looming. Indeed, it is the story of a police force that believes that a bloodbath solves most problems.

It is a story that exposes South Africa's structural weaknesses, too. We are one of the world's two most unequal societies (with Brazil) and the poor are talking to the cosy elites and saying they can and they will rise up. Poverty, inequality and unemployment are at the heart of the shootings.

The Marikana story starts with the 360 000-member National Union of Mineworkers (NUM), formed in the 1980s to fight apartheid labour laws. Under the leadership of Cyril Ramaphosa, the union became the biggest affiliate to Cosatu, the powerful trade-union ally of the ruling ANC. Ironically, the unionist-turned-businessman Ramaphosa became a key player at Marikana: from his seat on the board of platinum miner Lonmin he urged the authorities to take 'concomitant action' against the striking workers.[9]

For over a decade, up to the time of the shootings, Cosatu had concentrated on socio-economic and political issues. Instead of organising on the shop floor, it became involved in factional ANC politics, while sometimes harrying the ANC government to adopt increasingly left-leaning policies and protect workers at the expense of the unemployed. The NUM, one of the two biggest unions within Cosatu, was at the forefront of these struggles.

Over the past few years, the NUM has been split by the succession battles inside the ANC, with the leadership campaigning hard in 2012 for ANC President Jacob Zuma to win a second term as party leader and therefore a second term at the helm of South Africa. The union paid a heavy price for this.

At the Lonmin mines, the NUM's membership declined from 66 per cent of workers to 49 per cent – it has declined further since then – and the union lost its organisational rights.[10] Disgruntled and expelled union leaders started a new union, the radical Association of Mineworkers and Construction Union (Amcu), and began organising on the NUM's turf.

The NUM's Achilles heel was that its relationship with mineowners and the Chamber of Mines had become cosy. The union's former general secretary, Frans Baleni, was often a more strident critic of the nationalisation of mines than many business leaders.[11] The union has also allegedly accepted wage settlements that tied workers into years of meagre increases.

Amcu dangled a ripe piece of fruit before the workers' eyes: rock drillers (who formed the core of the Lonmin Marikana strike and do the most physically demanding work underground) earning about R4 000 a month were promised R12 500 a month. The union's support in the Lonmin mines shot up to 19 per cent by August 2010 and it embarked on an illegal strike to force its pay demand.

The strike soon turned violent – a harbinger of things to come. On the ground, armed workers were promising to 'take a bullet with my fellow workers'. One of the key features of the strike was the ubiquity of a traditional doctor among the strikers, anointing them with herbs and potions allegedly making them invincible. The Amcu leaders were girding for war.

The NUM had lost all leadership and credibility in the matter and was bleeding members fast. Baleni had been awarded a salary increase of more than 40 per cent in the previous financial year and his total salary package was just more than R105 000 a month in 2012.[12] NUM leaders had, in the days preceding the massacre, refused to get out of police armoured vehicles to address workers. In May 2010 an NUM leader had been struck in the eye with a brick, and later lost the eye.[13] The NUM had no cogent plan to end the strike.

The police, too, had lost credibility in the two years leading up to the massacre. Although indications are that they were shot at, a death toll of 34 in 30 minutes suggests panic, ill-preparedness, fear and a plethora of other issues. Crucially, the killings unmasked a police force with no sense of perspective about how to keep its people safe, how to enforce law and order, and how to be a police service in a country at peace.

Unfortunately, a violent beast beats inside the heart of our SAPS, a beast that is connected to the police's violent apartheid history and has been awakened by the securocrats that the ANC administration has sent in to lead the police since 2009.[14] Nothing illustrates this change more starkly than the case of Mozambique immigrant Mido Macia, a taxi driver. On 13 February 2013 Macia was arrested by police in Daveyton for parking illegally. He allegedly resisted arrest, and was then handcuffed behind a police van and dragged down a street by eight policemen. He later died of his injuries. Onlookers took video footage of the atrocity, and it shocked the nation.[15]

The only surprise about the outrage that followed Macia's killing was that South Africans – and knowledgeable observers of the country – were surprised by this outrage at all. Macia's tragic murder was merely the latest in a long and growing list of innocents violated by our police. Macia's name is preceded by others, reflecting the remilitarisation of the SAPS since President Zuma came to power in 2009, and the consequences of that process.

Take Atlegang Aphane. He was three years old when police shot him dead in November 2009, allegedly because they thought the toddler was carrying a gun. He was just three years old. Think about that. Three years old.[16]

Then there was the activist and teacher Andries Tatane. He ran to stop policemen beating up and abusing an old man during a service delivery protest in Ficksburg in 2011. Police members beat him to death with batons in front of television cameras and fired rubber bullets at point-blank range. The footage was shown on live television. A court later acquitted seven of the policemen.[17]

It tells you something about the posture of the SAPS that, when the Marikana workers were mowed down in under 30 minutes by police, the surviving mineworkers were, bizarrely, charged with the murder of their own colleagues. As if that was not enough, National Police Commissioner Riah Phiyega later told her members that they should not feel sorry for what had happened. Remember that more than 14 of the Marikana dead were shot in the back.[18]

The reason for the increase in cases of police brutality in South Africa is not hard to find. It goes straight to the heart of the administration of President Jacob Zuma, which, since its inauguration in May 2009, has beaten the drum of 'tough action' against the admittedly high and rampant crime in our country.

In 1994 the Mandela administration began demilitarising the apartheid-era South African Police. Military ranks were abandoned, and the word 'service' was added to the name. Civilians were encouraged to become active in police structures through the introduction of community policing fora.

Not so under Zuma. A process of remilitarisation of the police started, coupled with tough talk from politicians and police top brass. Zuma's administration was particularly enamoured of the word 'bastard': 'We cannot say to the police, retreat. We cannot say to South Africans, despair. Our job is to give people hope. Yes. Shoot the bastards. Hard-nut to crack, incorrigible bastards,' said then deputy police minister Fikile Mbalula in 2009.[19]

He was echoing words used by the then justice minister, Susan Shabangu, who had said the year before: 'You must kill the bastards if they threaten you or the community. You must not worry about the regulations. That is my responsibility. Your responsibility is to serve and protect.'[20] Shabangu was mineral resources minister, responsible for the mines, at the time of the Marikana Massacre and was among those who were involved in Marikana in the days up to 16 August. The Marikana Commission of Inquiry cleared her of any wrongdoing.

In the period since 2009 military nomenclature has returned to the SAPS. The police commissioner now carries the rank of general. Crack units have been established, and the notorious paramilitary unit 'Ama-Bherete' is feared for its brutality in enforcing the law in townships. Numerous victims have provided footage of the unit's brutality, in one case beating up restaurant patrons without any provocation, but no action has been taken.[21]

Police brutality is generally not punished in South Africa. *City Press* reports that in the 2011/12 financial year, 720 deaths allegedly at the hands of police were investigated by the Independent Police Investigative Directorate (IPID). Only five officers were dismissed and 13 convicted of crimes during that period. In the 2008/09 financial year, 912 deaths at the hands of police were investigated. Just three officers were dismissed.[22]

It is not just that the police do not want to act. As demonstrated by the incompetence of Hilton Botha – the investigating officer in the Oscar Pistorius case, who was at the time facing seven charges of attempted murder for shooting at a taxi with seven passengers in it – our police service is terrible at investigation. Out of an average of 65 000 sexual offences reported every year in South Africa, the police are fortunate to record more than 4 000 convictions.[23] It is almost just not worth reporting the crime.

The composite that emerges is disturbing: a country that leads the world in murder and rape; an incompetent police force that is quick to pull the trigger; and a populace awash with guns and enamoured of gun culture (Pistorius allegedly slept with one at his bedside and a rifle on the window sill).

All these elements came to the fore at Marikana.

The militarisation of the police is, however, part of the DNA of the current ruling faction of the ANC. Many South Africans, like the former defence minister Mosiuoa Lekota – who left the ANC to form the Congress of the People (Cope) in 2008 – have said that they find Jacob Zuma's singing of his signature tune, 'Awu Lethe uMshini Wami' (Bring Me My Machine Gun), to be inappropriate. Lekota, while still in the ANC, argued that the armed struggle is long over and asked why anyone in their right mind would be asking for a weapon in a peaceful and democratic South Africa.[24] Zuma's favourite ditty is especially revealing when one considers who is propping up his throne and who is on the ANC's current national executive committee.

A large chunk of the team that propelled Zuma to power is comprised of former army and intelligence operatives.[25] They are drawn from MK and ANC intelligence cells, and they organised Zuma's election like a military operation. Zuma, as discussed in a previous chapter, was the ANC-in-exile's head of intelligence between 1985 and 1995. It is no wonder that with Zuma came not peace, but a remilitarisation of the police and a focus on intelligence gathering.

Chief among his advisors, and swiftly appointed to head up the South African Secret Service when Zuma came to power in 2009, was

Mo Shaik, the ANC underground operative who became the democratic South Africa's first chief of National Intelligence. He was disgraced when he tried to besmirch the NPA head, Bulelani Ngcuka, in 2003. In the two and a half years preceding Jacob Zuma's ascent to power at Polokwane, Shaik built a formidable network of volunteers, funders and recruiters to back Zuma's campaign.[26]

Siphiwe Nyanda, the former Chief of the SANDF, worked indefatigably with many present and former army personnel to ensure a Zuma victory at Polokwane. Nyanda left the defence force in 2005. For his efforts, he was placed high on the first Zuma NEC nomination list and made it in at No 22. He also became Zuma's first communications minister in 2009.

Also close to Zuma, at least initially, was Tony Yengeni, another army man who, despite his incarceration in Pollsmoor prison for fraud connected with the arms deal, worked energetically for Zuma in the Western Cape. Che Masilela, the secretary of defence and a staunch Nyanda ally, was crucial in mobilising support for Zuma in Mpumalanga. Then there was Billy Masetlha, the sacked and publicly humiliated former head of National Intelligence. Masetlha, once close to Thabo Mbeki, angered the President by being taken in by the false emails that alleged a plot against Zuma by pro-Mbeki Cabinet members and businessmen.[27] A prominent fixture of the Zuma campaign, Masetlha made it onto the Polokwane NEC list at No 28.[28]

In 2008 I asked in a column whether a Zuma presidency would become a militarised entity. Would he rule by using the secret services to gather information to use against people? In a proper democracy, the police, army and secret services are subservient to the civilian authority. But in the Zuma years the civilian authority has become the police, the secret service and the army.

That is why, in my view, we saw state-sanctioned murder on the afternoon of 16 August 2012 in Marikana. The seeds were laid long before that dusty winter day. Under Zuma, in the period from 2009, the seeds had been watered and had grown.

The other major myth that was exploded by the Marikana Massacre was the myth that the policy of Black Economic Empowerment (BEE) equated to true empowerment of black South Africans. Since the 1990s the ANC has vigorously – and in my view with all the right intentions – pressured big business to sell a portion of their shareholding to black businesspeople in order to comply with BEE legislation. This was done through policy, legislation and regulations modelled on the Malaysian system, originally developed by Prime Minister Mahathir Mohamad, that sought to redress past inequalities.

According to the Department of Trade and Industry, 'broad-based' black economic empowerment 'is essentially a growth strategy, targeting the South African economy's weakest point: inequality …' It concludes: 'As such, this strategy stresses a BEE process that is associated with growth, development and enterprise development, and not merely the redistribution of existing wealth.'[29]

Minister of Trade and Industry Rob Davies loves repeating this mantra, as he did at a breakfast in late 2013 when he declared that BEE was indeed a success: 'Achieving broad-based black empowerment was a political imperative … and a matter of equity.'[30]

Has BEE succeeded? The legacy is mixed, if one follows the numbers. The Johannesburg Stock Exchange (JSE) has only 3.9 per cent of its value owned by black enterprises, more than 15 years after the policy was introduced. Anecdotally, some black South Africans have become extremely wealthy. Patrice Motsepe, a doughty billionaire mining entrepreneur, is often listed among the top three wealthiest South Africans. *The Economist* magazine reported in 2010: 'Among the 295 companies listed on the Johannesburg Stock Exchange (JSE), blacks account for just 4 per cent of chief executive officers, 2 per cent of chief financial officers and 15 per cent of other senior posts. In non-executive ones, they do a bit better, accounting for just over a quarter of board chairmen and 36 per cent of directors, but still nowhere near their share of the workforce.'[31]

South Africa is today considered one of the most unequal societies in the world. The biggest criticism of BEE is that it has made a handful of mainly politically connected individuals extremely rich, while the majority of South Africans remain poor.

It is within this context that the events at Marikana should be viewed.

Lonmin, owners of the Marikana mine where the events of 16 August 2012 unfolded, had a South African black partner as prescribed by the law. That partner was a company called Shanduka,[32] founded by ANC leader, current deputy president of the country and revered anti-apartheid trade unionist Cyril Ramaphosa.

Ramaphosa is no ordinary man. In the 1980s he launched the NUM and in 1987 led the longest and most violent mineworkers' strike in South Africa. He fought against apartheid and was one of the few leaders to stand up to Winnie Madikizela-Mandela, the then wife of Nelson Mandela, when she was accused of grave human rights abuses through her gang of bodyguards, called the Mandela United Football Club. When Mandela walked out of prison in 1990, Ramaphosa walked beside him. In the years up to 1994, he was a key advisor to the leader.

It is Ramaphosa and his counterpart on the National Party negotiating team, Roelf Meyer, who are credited with some of the most important deadlock-breaking mechanisms during the negotiations for democracy in the 1990s. In the new South Africa, Ramaphosa led the Constituent Assembly in negotiating and drafting the final Constitution adopted in 1997 – hailed as one of the most progressive in the world.

Mandela was set to step down as ANC president in 1997, and by all accounts his preferred successor was Ramaphosa. Mandela was, however, out-manoeuvred by his deputy, Thabo Mbeki, and the so-called exile wing of the ANC. By the time Ramaphosa was ready to run, the Mbeki grouping had already amassed enough support within the ANC to take the lead.

Ramaphosa decided to go into business. By 2012 he had amassed a fortune that put his net worth at R2.2 billion, according to the *Sunday Times* Rich List. *Forbes* magazine, however, in 2014 put his wealth at a staggering US$700 million.[33] Through a series of BEE deals he acquired stakes in a variety of major companies – from Bidvest to Mondi, MTN Group, Standard Bank, Coca-Cola and McDonald's. He sat on a number of boards, including that of Lonmin.[34]

Ramaphosa's role in the Marikana Massacre has put a question mark over the role of black shareholders and board members in major corporates. Ramaphosa's own role in events remains controversial. The key question is: did he put so much pressure on government ministers – all of them his juniors in the ANC – and on the police to the extent that they had to act with 'maximum force' against the mineworkers?

In the run-up to the events of 16 August, Ramaphosa, in his capacity as a Lonmin director, seems to have run himself ragged to get government officials to take what he called 'concomitant action' with regards to the strike at Marikana. He was in touch with the then Minister of Police, Nathi Mthethwa, and the Minister of Mineral Resources, Susan Shabangu, by telephone and email to urge them to take action.[35]

As the Daily Maverick puts it: 'Ramaphosa claims his call for "concomitant action" was merely a request to stem the loss of life in Marikana: "The reference to 'concomitant action' in my email communication of 15 August 2012 was to indicate that appropriate steps should be taken to bring the violence and deaths to an end. I was calling for peace and for the necessary steps to be taken to save lives."'

The Daily Maverick notes that 'Ramaphosa, however, had had two discussions with Shabangu in the lead-up to the massacre. After the first, a telephonic discussion, he told colleagues: "I called her and told her that her silence and inaction about what is happening at Lonmin was bad for her and the government."

'After meeting Shabangu in Cape Town, Ramaphosa says:

'1. She agrees that what we are going through is not a labour dispute but a criminal act. She will correct her characterisation of what we are experiencing.

'2. She is going into Cabinet and will brief the President as well and get the Minister of Police Nathi Mthethwa to act in a more pointed way.

'3. She will be in Johannesburg by 5 pm and would be able to speak to Roger [Lonmin executive].

'He concludes his email with: "Let us keep the pressure on them [government] to act correctly."'[36]

So what was Ramaphosa's role on the board of Lonmin? What is the role of politically connected directors on the boards of companies that may be exposed to this sort of occurrence or any other calamity that needs government action? There have been many accusations that the enthusiasm with which corporate South Africa has embraced BEE is for exactly this reason: companies have been buying cover against government policies and any adverse action by workers or communities in areas where they operate. In essence, the presence of black shareholders has nothing to do with their business acumen, but with their connectivity.

Advocate Dali Mpofu, acting for the mineworkers, told the Marikana Commission of Inquiry: 'The Constitution says very clearly the police must not be involved in making political considerations. One of the people who wrote that Constitution (Ramaphosa) caused that to happen. He caused the police minister, police commissioner and everyone to cross the lines that are set by our Constitution.'[37]

The Daily Maverick observed: 'Ramaphosa's email correspondence with other Lonmin officials exposes the extent to which the British company relied on Ramaphosa's relationship with government to rally government agencies like the SAPS to Lonmin's side.

'It remains to be proven that Ramaphosa had a direct influence on how police acted on 16 August – that he was responsible for the police opening fire on the striking mine workers. However, what Ramaphosa's own statement to the Farlam Commission and his email correspondence reveals is a businessman with inordinate access to – and influence over – the South African government.'[38]

The report of the Marikana Commission found that Ramaphosa had done nothing untoward. It said: 'The Commission is of the view that it cannot be said that Mr Ramaphosa was the "cause of the massacre" ... There is no basis for the commission to find even on a prima facie basis that Mr Ramaphosa is guilty of the crimes he is alleged to have committed.'[39]

And that was that. But is it really? What is even sadder about Marikana is that the idea of 'broad-based' empowerment, meaning that as many people as possible should benefit from empowerment schemes, seems to have also fallen by the wayside in the Lonmin deal. The *Mail & Guardian* reported that Lonmin paid millions of rands in dividends to Ramaphosa's company in the three years leading up to the massacre while failing to meet promises to build houses for its workforce and pleading poverty over wage demands. It said evidence before the Marikana Commission showed that the payments, totalling US$46 million, were made despite business conditions being so tough that the platinum mines paid zero dividends to the British parent company, Lonmin plc.

The most appalling admission, however, came when it emerged that in 2006, when Lonmin successfully applied to convert its old-order mining licence, and therefore to secure its right to continue mining on the platinum belt, the company promised to spend R665 million building 5500 houses for mineworkers at Marikana. 'But during questioning, Lonmin's former chief of operations, Mahomed Seedat, conceded that, although the living conditions at Marikana were "truly appalling", Lonmin had built no more than three show houses,' the newspaper wrote.[40]

Ramaphosa is a star of the BEE story, a giant of South African business. All this happened on his watch. What happens at many other entities that proudly speak of their BEE credentials?

The words of Malaysia's Mahathir Mohamad, reflecting on affirmative action and Malay economic empowerment in 2002, just a year before the end of his prime ministership, should give us pause when we reflect on South Africa. He said: 'In business, the vast majority [of Malaysians] regarded the opportunities given them as something to be exploited for the quickest return. Very early on they had sold off their opportunities in order to become sleeping partners in an arrangement cynically known as "Ali Baba", in which Ali merely obtains the licences, permits, shares or contracts and immediately sells these off to non-Malays, mainly Chinese. They learn nothing about business and become even less capable at doing business and earning an income from their activities. They become mere sleeping partners and at times not even that. Having sold they no longer have anything to do with the business. They would go to the Government for more licences, permits, shares, etc.[41]

This, sadly, is the face of BEE in South Africa. This is what the Marikana Massacre has exposed about the roles played by many so-called black industrialists at board level. It is a shame.

But what does it all matter? Well, for me, this is the point: for all its faults, its incompetence and its inability to keep its eye on the ball, we owe the ANC a debt of gratitude. We owe the ANC this for a single but powerful overarching achievement.

In the depths of the despair of the late 1980s and early 1990s, the ANC was the single organisation that managed to keep us all – left and right, white and black, young and old – together. The key to that was the articulation of the party's vision that, as Thabo Mbeki put it, our tomorrow would be better than our today, that our future would hold something better for each one of us.[42]

This vision was particularly important in making sure that the poor of South Africa bought into the 1994 democracy project. Instead of a winner-takes-all political and economic settlement, we had a pragmatic and consensual dispensation.

It was not perfect but that consensus has given us a great country for more than 21 years. We have not achieved to our expectations, but we have not been total failures either.

Somehow, today, the ANC still manages to convince many of us – and particularly the desperately poor, who feel most the effects of massive food-price rises, inflation and other ills – that tomorrow will be better than today.

What happens when the ANC loses this ability to convince the poor and marginalised that there is a better tomorrow, and an even better day after that? What happens when, like the Marikana mineworkers, this constituency starts to believe that, in fact, tomorrow will not be better?

What happened on the platinum mines is that those poor, uneducated men sought a better tomorrow elsewhere. First, they dumped the NUM. Then they believed in Amcu, which has on many occasions promised, but not always delivered, exorbitant salary increases. Then those workers abandoned both unions and went up that hill of death. Though Amcu's representatives received a somewhat warmer response than the NUM president Senzeni Zokwana, who was told in no uncertain terms to pack up and leave,[43] the truth is that those workers were unorganised and unrepresented.

Formal structures of representation had, in their view, let them down. They were open to a flirtation with Amcu, and with the likes of the expelled ANC Youth League leader Julius Malema, but they were alone.

For many among them, the only weapon they had was a desperate one: that good, decent people would not kill them. That belief, too, was abandoned and betrayed when the police mowed them down and finished them off with bullets in the back.

What happens when the 8 million unemployed young people in our country reach these levels of desperation and disillusionment? What happens when they stop believing that tomorrow will be better than today? It might make many of us quiver with fear, but here is the cold, hard truth: they will opt out of the current social, economic and political arrangements and they will choose anarchy.

So what now? Several scenarios offer themselves. The first is that the ANC wakes from its slumber and realises that, after 21 years of promises, it is what it does and not what it says that matters now. It can no longer blame apartheid for anything. It is in charge of the purse strings and it has received the people's votes. It has to govern, and govern decisively and well.

When people see the fruits of such governance – jobs, schools that work, less corruption – then they will reinvest in the dream they bought into 21 years ago.

The second scenario is that the ANC remains in the grip of the rapacious, me-first, it's-our-turn-to-eat brigade that is dragging it down. If the party stays on this trajectory, it opens the way for two types of new player to emerge. One would be a credible, ethical and believable opposition that can convince the electorate that the 1994 project of hope and prosperity can be continued by others and not just by the ANC.

The other new player would be a coalition of populists of the sort of Julius Malema and his EFF. That coalition would promise largesse, milk and honey, without proffering a shred of evidence about how exactly these would be achieved.

This path will lead to disaster. We would be on that well-trodden path most lately walked by Zimbabwe.

The choice is ours.

Crucially, it is the ANC's too. Looking at the events of Marikana, however, I have very little confidence that the ANC has a clue about the magnitude of what it faces and even less of an idea of what is required to get out of the mess we find ourselves in.

How did we get here? We turned a corner in December 2007, in a muddy town called Polokwane.

8

Arrival of the Man of the People

'Look upon my works, ye Mighty, and despair!'
– Percy Bysshe Shelley, 'Ozymandias'

Mmachidi Maria Kgatla shook her head vigorously and wagged her finger at me.

'They cannot get rid of that man,' she said emphatically. 'President Thabo Mbeki has done a good job. They must let him continue. Look around you.'

Kgatla was sitting in the shade between her rondavel and a solid, four-roomed brick house with several of her grandchildren.

The four-roomed brick house in the village of Mawa, near Tzaneen in the far north of Limpopo, had been built as part of the government's housing programme, and she was very proud of it. Although she kept her rondavel to remain rooted in her culture, in her view Mbeki had done a wonderful job and deserved to remain leader of the ANC and the country.

They'd had good rains that year in GaModjadji, the seat of the legendary but unfortunate Rain Queen Modjadji, and it showed. The valley was lush, green and breathtakingly beautiful.

And on the Saturday before the beginning of the ANC's national conference in December 2007 GaModjadji was a sea of calm, far from the police sirens and the singing in Polokwane, the capital of Limpopo province, where more than 7 000 delegates and visitors had arrived for the conference.

Kgatla was my grandmother. I had taken some time off from the conference, where only the deluded did not believe that Mbeki was set to lose the presidential battle to Jacob Zuma, to ask her what she thought of the contest.

She did not even know that the conference was taking place, but became extremely agitated at the prospect of losing Mbeki.

'Mbeki gave us very good laws and brought some important initiatives. Do you know that Aids orphans get paid a grant? In this village nearly everyone gets a grant of some sort. There is no more hunger. It is Mbeki who did all that,' she said.

Over and above the house, Kgatla received a monthly pension of R870. The grandchildren who live with her also receive a child grant, alleviating the financial burden on her.

The road to her village was being tarred. The work had been going on for two years, but she said she had no doubt that in the next three years the road would be tarred up to her village.

'Tell me of any black person in South Africa who has ever seen a child's grant or a generous pension like the one I get? Houses for free? Roads? Peace in our country? It is because of Mbeki,' she said.

And Jacob Zuma? She said he seemed more interested in getting married than he was in running the country. My grandmother was the second of two wives. She hated the institution of multiple marriages. Zuma, married six times (one wife had divorced him and another had committed suicide), was all her nightmares come horribly true.

My aunt Matseleng Kgatla, also a beneficiary of housing and other improvements by government, said it does not matter that Zuma had very little formal education. 'Look, all these good things will continue: the water, the RDP houses and the other things. The fact that the man has only Standard Three does not count. The issue is whether he can lead or not. It is not the certificates you have, it is what is in your head that counts,' she said.

On education, she pointed out that a perfect example is President Robert Mugabe of Zimbabwe. She said that there are so many desperate and destitute Zimbabweans in the GaModjadji area people refer to them as *'matlola trata'* (the border jumpers).

'How many degrees does Mugabe have? Twenty-three or more. Yet this place is full of Zimbabweans running away from him,' she said.

118

To be sure, the transformation of Mawa was breathtaking. There is electricity in most parts of the village and there was a sense of progress and prosperity in the area. Many people I spoke to believed Mbeki was responsible for these changes.

'He is not like Mandela, but he is his real son,' said Maria Kgatla.

Those who shared Kgatla's view were a minority in the Limpopo province that week. After a day's visit I turned my car south to Polokwane, where South Africa's future was about to be decided. The titanic battle between Zuma and Mbeki had started when the President had fired Zuma, his deputy, in June 2005.[1] Two years later, the two men were about to face off in a battle that was to change South African politics forever.

When Shelley wrote his celebrated sonnet 'Ozymandias' in December 1817, little did he know that it would resonate powerfully on the southern tip of Africa exactly 190 years later. It was, after all, penned for a small literary competition.

'Ozymandias' is about a wanderer in the desert who comes across the decaying, yet powerfully arrogant, statue of Ramesses the Great, Pharaoh of the nineteenth dynasty of ancient Egypt.

The traveller tells how the sculptor managed to depict Ramesses' 'wrinkled lip and sneer of cold command'. In just 14 lines, Shelley powerfully summed up the rise and fall of empire and its architect's vaulting arrogance and hubris. The words on the statue's pedestal read: '"My name is Ozymandias, king of kings: / Look on my works, ye Mighty, and despair!"' The poem concludes with the wanderer's observation:

> Nothing beside remains: round the decay
> Of that colossal wreck, boundless and bare,
> The lone and level sands stretch far away.

Mbeki is a student of Shelley. He quotes the poet often and turns to his work in private to draw inspiration and sustenance. On the morning of Sunday 16 December 2007, as Mbeki walked to the podium to deliver what was to be his last address to the ANC as the organisation's president, the parallels between him and his literary hero's subject were striking.

Mbeki had over the previous three days compiled a 42-page political report that recounted every little success he had achieved in his tenure as party and state president. Essentially, he entreated the almost 4 000 voting delegates and assorted hangers-on and guests to 'look upon my works, ye mighty, and despair'.[2]

It did not work. Instead, the first three days of the ANC's 52nd national conference, held at the University of Limpopo, will be remembered for the way the delegates saw, and got rid of, Mbeki's 'wrinkled lip and sneer of cold command'.

Right until the bitter end, at 8.45 pm on Tuesday 18 December 2007, when Mbeki was finally humiliated, it was all about the man who had been groomed for power – by ANC leaders such as OR Tambo – and whose hubris was his undoing. He refused to listen to anyone around him, set on the belief that he was the only person who could defeat a clearly rising Jacob Zuma.

As the crowd in the sodden white marquee erupted into song and dance at the announcement that Zuma had pulled off one of the most extraordinary comebacks in South African political history and trounced Mbeki for the ANC presidency, the place to look was Mbeki's face.

How would he take it? How would he react? In an attempt at showing unity, Mbeki walked with the new ANC president onto the stage and gave him a hug. Then, smiling nervously and throwing short waves at those on stage, intermittently clapping his hands, he walked the few metres to the steps that took him away from the presidency he had been groomed for over decades.

It was the loneliest ten metres the ANC president had ever walked. After years of bitter acrimony, he had lost his bid to cling on to power in his party and the ability to anoint his own successor. Mbeki was a humiliated and broken man, and you could see it in every line on his face.

How did it get to this point? There had not been a contest for the presidency in the ANC since 1949. In 2007, too, party leaders had been saying one was not necessary. Mbeki should have started a succession process a long time before, but had failed to do so.

Mbeki had failed to listen to advice on the leadership race and failed to take advice on other issues in his tenure as ANC president. That was his undoing.

The events at Polokwane that week mirrored almost exactly the groundswell of discontent in the ANC and in South African society in general about Mbeki's rule. The crushing defeat he suffered was not an endorsement of Zuma. It was a plea from his own comrades saying they had had enough of his vaulting arrogance and his refusal to listen to advice, let alone take it, from those who worked with him.[3]

The revolt began as soon as the meeting started, on the Sunday morning, when delegates shouted down and heckled conference chairperson Mosiuoa 'Terror' Lekota. The ANC chairman, a staunch Mbeki supporter who had traversed the country beating the drum on behalf of the President, had said in the past that Zuma was 'not right in the head' because of his singing of 'Awu Lethe uMshini Wami'. (Lekota was later to peel off from the ANC and start the Congress of the People [Cope], a party formed by ANC members disgruntled with Zuma's ascendance to power, and which attracted more than 1.3 million voters, or 7 per cent of the vote, in the 2009 national elections.)

It was just the beginning of a very bad day for Mbeki and those close to him. For the rest of the day they were heckled and harangued by delegates and members of the ANC Youth League who fought them on every point, whether procedural or constitutional.

In a clear sign of the deep suspicion with which Mbeki was held, the ANC Youth League's Sihle Zikalala – now a senior provincial leader in KwaZulu-Natal – led and won a motion to have counting of votes done manually instead of electronically.[4] The subtext? We do not trust Mbeki to behave honourably in these elections and suspect that he will try to steal the result.

It was an extraordinary assertion, but a pointer to the isolation of Mbeki and the hatred felt towards him by his adversaries in the party.

When Mbeki delivered his speech, only a sprinkling of respectful applause was heard. As soon as he finished, the crowd immediately started singing the Zuma machine gun song.

The humiliation was akin to the scenes at the ANC's national general council in 2005, when Mbeki had first fired Zuma from his job as deputy president of the country and then stripped him of his powers as the party's number two. But, in a reversal that humiliated Mbeki, delegates at that council reinstated Zuma with full powers and ordered Mbeki to get the state to pay his legal fees.[5]

A strange thing happened back then. After his public humiliation, Mbeki immediately left the meeting and gave an interview to the SABC in which he said he would accept nomination for the presidency of the party. It was a baffling declaration given that he could see clearly, two full years ahead of the 2007 national conference, that his own people were tiring of him.

The same failure to see the writing on the wall showed itself again in the week he lost power in 2007. On the Sunday evening, after the chaotic events earlier in the day, members of Mbeki's kitchen cabinet advised him to withdraw from the race. 'The writing is on the wall. You can see the mood,' the director-general in Mbeki's office, Frank Chikane, apparently told Mbeki in a frequently quoted and yet unverified conversation. Mbeki, although clearly on the verge of defeat, refused.

Other reports have suggested that, later that same evening, Mbeki received a call from Nelson Mandela also asking him to step down for the 'sake of unity in the ANC'. Mbeki apparently refused and demanded that Zuma and ANC secretary-general Kgalema Motlanthe also step down if he did so.

'How could he do that? He was way behind in support and they were way ahead. They had nothing to lose and were not going to agree to that,' said one ANC leader, exasperated, to me.[6] And yet

Mbeki's arrogance and hubris over the few days of the conference mirrored his obstinacy and refusal to listen to anyone throughout his presidency.

An example was Mbeki's handling of the *Daily Dispatch*'s exposé in 2007 of the appalling conditions at Frere Hospital, in East London. Faced with evidence and a declaration by the then deputy health minister, Nozizwe Madlala-Routledge, that conditions in the maternity ward were a 'national disaster', Mbeki chose to call the exposé a bunch of untruths. He later fired Madlala-Routledge for reasons generally seen as a cover-up.[7]

The list of incidents of Mbeki's belief in himself and his dismissal of advice is long. For eight years up to the Polokwane conference he held on to discredited views on HIV and Aids, which brought the ire of the likes of Archbishop Desmond Tutu, the country and the international community upon him. On Zimbabwe, he steadfastly refused to act with decisiveness and a clear moral voice against the outrages of President Robert Mugabe. Instead, he tried to implement, for nearly ten years, the discredited and ineffectual 'quiet diplomacy' he punted without success. In that time South Africa saw a dramatic influx of desperate Zimbabweans – some braving wild animals and flooded rivers – seeking sanctuary in the country.

The 3 900 voting delegates who effectively kicked Mbeki out at Polokwane were responding to what ordinary South Africans had felt for a long time. Mbeki's numerous successes – mainly on the economy and foreign affairs – were overshadowed by his increasing belief that he held a monopoly on truth, insight and wisdom.

Inside the ANC itself, he had centralised power around himself to the extent that almost every decision had to be sanctioned by him. His appointment of premiers, for example, had raised massive unhappiness in the provinces.[8] Mbeki confidant and businessman Saki Macozoma, in the run-up to the 2007 conference, alluded to this problem: 'In the provinces, a lot of people have a sense of grievance that they haven't been given recognition. Take Ace Magashule in the

Free State; he's been leading the province all this time, but he hasn't been given the responsibility for running things. People like this throw in their lot with Zuma or vote for themselves and for their issues.'[9]

Mbeki never acknowledged that the decision to centralise power was a problem, saying instead that he consulted with the provinces on appointments. At the end of the day, however, it did not matter what Mbeki thought. The delegates to the Polokwane conference increasingly and noisily made it clear that they had found their voice, and that voice clearly and loudly said they did not want Mbeki's style of leadership.

Their vengeance was harsh.

Zuma received an overwhelming 2 329 votes to Mbeki's 1 505. Mbeki's entire team of nominations was walloped by the Zuma faction. Their rejection was not about the individuals, but because they were seen as being Mbeki favourites.[10]

As the conference tapered off after four days, there was a lot of singing about Jacob Zuma. But all the songs started with a complaint about Mbeki. The most popular went: 'Mbeki you control the Scorpions, tell us what Zuma has done wrong.' The delegates prepared to give interviews spoke about how bad Mbeki was, not about how good Zuma was.

The words sung by those delegates, however, were to return to many of us again and again as Zuma consolidated his power, and as his scandals continued. Why did so many vote for him? In many ways, the story of Zuma and Mbeki is the story of people hoping that Zuma would reform, mend his ways and adopt a new path.

When former President Nelson Mandela transferred R1 million into the bank account of the then recently fired Zuma in June 2005, he was acknowledging a truth many other ANC leaders knew full well. Zuma, since his return from exile in 1990, had battled with the financial demands on him and had slowly but surely drifted into a position where he was no longer his own man. He was beholden to benefactors in business to look after his many children and his burgeoning number of girlfriends and wives.

The hope for Mandela was that Zuma would cut his benefactors loose and start on a new path. Zuma, despite the scandal of the Schabir Shaik case, did not. In his battle against rape and corruption charges, he accumulated even more benefactors.[11]

Luckily for him, his political star was on the rise. Mbeki's increasingly brittle and paranoid manner had alienated many (and not many of them were so saintly, by the way) and they began to coalesce around Zuma. That 'coalition of the wounded' – taking in the South African Communist Party (SACP), Cosatu and many others left bleeding from Mbeki's lashings – noisily took power in Polokwane that week in 2007.[12]

They were ruthless in their exercise of it. They fired Mbeki from the presidency of the country within nine months of taking over the ANC, making sure that he did not finish his second term.[13] They hounded out civil servants perceived to be on Mbeki's side. They splintered the ANC.[14] Yet the rump of the party stayed, and managed to win elections in 2009 with 65.9 per cent of voter support.

The Zuma problem would not, however, go away. Zuma's ascent to the top seat did not see him change his wayward ways. His dependence on the largesse of benefactors seemed to increase substantially as he prepared to enter office in 2008 and 2009. Newspaper reports detailed his closeness to one family in particular: the Guptas of Saxonwold.

We all now know the crassness of the relationship: the son who is kept by the Guptas; the shag pad paid for by the Guptas; their boasting of their closeness to him; their telling prospective Cabinet ministers, even before announcements are made, what positions they are likely to get. Then there was the wedding scandal, when the Guptas landed a plane full of guests at a national key point, the millions pumped by government into the *New Age* newspaper (government spent more than R10 million on advertising in the *New Age*, which has a readership of only 15 300, while spending R10.4 million on the *Sowetan*, which has a readership of 1.6 million), and many others.[15]

This must have been what Mandela was hoping to avert when he ponied up that million rands for Zuma. He must have known that the

ANC was headed for a problem here. He did not tell us, nor many other ANC leaders.

With days to go before the Polokwane conference, Mbeki and his advisors still clung to the hope that they would see Zuma off. We all knew that this was impossible. Zuma had secured the support of key voting constituencies in the party, and was going to win easily.

I believe it is now clear that Mbeki stood against what was called the 'Zunami' because he knew that the ANC was headed for a reckoning with its Zuma problem. Like others, he knew that the ANC was electing to power a man who walks, runs, moves, dances to the tune of those who keep him financially afloat and take care of his children. Mbeki and his faction knew then that, at the very least, the ANC needed to be saved from him.

The man who stood by Zuma's side in Polokwane was Kgalema Motlanthe. Sober, studied, respected and viewed as being non-factionalist, he threw his weight behind Zuma and essentially made the man from Nkandla look respectable. Zuma was still facing serious corruption charges and had just survived an embarrassing rape trial, so Motlanthe was the sober face of this coalition. It was he who was sent to the Union Buildings to be caretaker president when Mbeki was fired in September 2008.

Within five years, Motlanthe was running against Zuma for the presidency of the ANC in Mangaung. Why did Motlanthe do this? What did he learn about Zuma in five years that made him feel that the man was patently unsuitable for the presidency?

He did not tell us. He expected the ANC's delegates to Mangaung – and the people of South Africa – to decipher for themselves what was wrong here.[16]

The truth of it is that the ANC has a Zuma problem. No matter how powerful he may be inside the party, with his ability to pull off a 75 per cent majority in internal elections in Mangaung in December 2012, the man is bringing the ANC into serious disrepute. No matter how many commissions of inquiry clear him, the truth is that the Guptas were able to land a plane at Waterkloof Air Force Base – a national key point – because they are his friends.

You don't have to look far for why we are where we are today. In trying to get rid of Mbeki in 2007, the party clutched at straws and chose anyone, absolutely anyone, who was prepared to stand against the man.[17] Zuma, warts and all, was the only man brave enough then to do it. The ANC rump, knowing what a compromised individual he was, did not care. Zuma could do the job.

And so here we are, stuck with a compromised leader who has absolutely no idea how to run a country for people rather than for himself.[18] We chose him, and now we are paying for it as Zuma destroys every single institution of accountability in the country. By 2019, when he has to step down, Zuma will have destroyed these institutions to ensure that he never goes on trial again, let alone sees the inside of a jail cell.

9

This is How the End Begins

'Our government is worse than the apartheid government,
because at least you were expecting it from the apartheid
government … We were expecting we would have a government
that was sensitive to sentiments of our Constitution.'
– Archbishop Emeritus Desmond Tutu, *Mail & Guardian*, 4 October 2011

We will be talking about the fugitive from justice, President Omar al-Bashir of Sudan, for decades to come. We will talk about him when we remember that, in the 2000s, when leaders such as Thabo Mbeki and Olusegun Obasanjo were preaching about a new Africa of responsible leadership,[1] al-Bashir allegedly sent his army and the notorious Janjaweed militia into the Darfur region to rape, maim and kill 300 000 of his own people.[2]

We will talk about him when we remember the energy and vigour with which South African government leaders bent over backwards to explain away their decision to allow him to leave South Africa following the African Union (AU) summit in Johannesburg in June 2015.[3]

Al-Bashir's legacy for us, though, is that it was in his dramatic escape that our political leaders showed their disregard for our own laws and the courts in South Africa. We have spent months debating various aspects of the al-Bashir case, but the most crucial one is that something horrible happened in Court 4F of the Pretoria High Court on Monday 15 June 2015.

The horrible thing is that the President of South Africa and his government ignored a court order to arrest the fugitive and keep him here.[4] The implications are immense. If the executive is allowed to ignore the judiciary and act as it wishes, then we have descended into anarchy. The executive has essentially stolen our democracy; it abides by the laws it likes and ignores the ones it doesn't. This cannot be allowed.

What happened here? We know that on Sunday 14 June 2015 the court handed down an order that al-Bashir not be allowed to leave the country until the court had dealt with the application to have him arrested. On Monday the court then handed down its order that al-Bashir indeed be arrested.

Between Sunday and Monday the South African authorities were supposed to comply with the court order that the man had to remain here. Our authorities clearly did not think this was necessary.

On Monday state counsel William Mokhari stood up in the High Court in Pretoria and stated: 'I have been informed by the government that they have reliable information that President al-Bashir has departed from the republic.'

Journalists and government representatives in the public gallery laughed. They laughed because they knew that our government had ensured that, at 11.46 am that day, al-Bashir had jetted out of Waterkloof Air Force Base. They laughed because they knew that our leaders had laughed at the courts.

Judge President Dunstan Mlambo said: 'It is of concern to this court that it issues orders and that things just happen in violation of these orders.'[5]

There is now no doubt that al-Bashir's escape was deliberate and was orchestrated by the President of our republic himself. Robert Mugabe, President of Zimbabwe and current African Union chairman, told reporters: 'He [President Jacob Zuma] said President Bashir would not be arrested, as he would not allow police here to arrest him.'[6]

The *Sunday Times* and the *Mail & Guardian* wrote days later of a high-level plot to ensure that al-Bashir escaped arrest. At a meeting at the Taj Hotel in Cape Town, security cluster ministers allegedly promised maximum protection to al-Bashir during his visit here.[7]

And so it was that every wing of our government was set in motion to protect this fugitive, all in the name of 'African solidarity' and realpolitik.

What is amazing is that government leaders did not foresee any of the events that later unfolded. They could have just told al-Bashir to stay home while South Africa withdrew from the Rome Statute and the International Criminal Court (ICC) – if that's what we want to do. Alas, we chose a dangerous and unpredictable new route. We violated an order of our own court.

What now? A mighty precedent has been set by government's deliberate violation of a court order. There will be many instances in future when ordinary people will seek remedies via the courts. Remember when the Mbeki administration would not provide anti-retroviral drugs, it was orders of court that forced them to do so.

If this administration can ignore this one court order, what stops it from ignoring another one? And then another? Before you know it, the judiciary will be rendered meaningless. We will be lawless, a place where the executive acts with impunity and only complies with the laws it likes. This is how dictatorships are formed.

There will be a lot of heat over the next few years about the justness or not of arresting al-Bashir or not. Two things will be certain, though. First, the man has been indicted for the killing of 300 000 of his fellow black Africans. Who speaks for them? Second, the man forced the Zuma administration to show its disregard for its own courts and the law.[8]

Don't say you did not know, for it happened right in front of our eyes.

Another element is in play.

When al-Bashir was allowed to escape the country, Nelson Mandela's democracy stood in solidarity with the Big Men of the African Union (AU) who have declared the ICC a racist organisation that targets Africans for trial.

In December 2014, Ugandan President Yoweri Museveni, who has been in power since 1986, said the ICC was a 'tool to target' Africa.[9] Rwanda's President Paul Kagame, who has been in power since 1994 and wants to extend his term by seven years, has accused the ICC of 'selective' justice.[10] This is in some sense true: since its establishment in 2002, the ICC has heard 22 cases and indicted 36 individuals. All of them are African.[11]

South Africa, though a signatory to the Rome Statute, through which the ICC was established, has lately joined this chorus, with the governing ANC saying that 'the ICC is no longer useful for the purposes for which it was intended – being a court of last resort for the prosecution of crimes against humanity'.[12]

This stance has endeared it to the rest of the AU, by which the country seeks to be seen as a significant player. However, the government's contradictory stance – signatory to the Rome Statute on the one hand while flirting with those who seek to defy its precepts on the other – has never been challenged.

Since 2008 South Africa has fully sided with the dodgiest leaders in the world in the name of 'national interest'. Three times we have refused the Dalai Lama a visa to enter South Africa, most recently to attend a peace summit at the invitation of Archbishop Desmond Tutu and other Nobel laureates.[13] This is seemingly at the behest of China, with whom we have signed a ten-year agreement pledging 'political mutual trust and strategic co-ordination'.[14] Our president is having a full-on bromance with Russian strongman Vladimir Putin[15] while our silence at the killing of journalists and opposition politicians in that country is deafening.

Robert Mugabe, accused of the murder of thousands of his own citizens in the 1980s and the torture of thousands of others in the 2000s, was wined and dined on a state visit here in early 2015. And al-Bashir? We have defended him since the ICC issued the first warrant for his arrest, in 2009, under the guise of building alliances with fellow BRICS members – the five major emerging economies – and with the AU.[16]

But it is the fact that South Africa has broken its own laws and acted in defiance of a court order that is most chilling. William Mokhari told the Pretoria High Court that al-Bashir's departure would be fully investigated.[17] But that is academic. The government did nothing to arrest him. What orders of our courts will our government now ignore, many of us ask?

The future is now uncertain. This is how democracies are stolen. This is how the end begins.

PART TWO
The Road Ahead

10

The Prince and the Redemption Narrative

'At every moment of our lives, we all have one foot
in a fairy tale and the other in the abyss.'
– Maria, a sex worker in Paulo Coelho's *Eleven Minutes*

As the first 21 years of a democratic South Africa have turned bitter and sad as the ANC turns on itself and its foundations, one hopeful narrative has remained in the country as a whole and among many ANC intellectuals. It is an idea that says the ANC can self-correct, that it can realise it is facing the abyss and pull back from violently destroying itself and the country it has gifted with freedom and democracy.[1]

From this glimpse of the apocalypse the ANC would then, according to this narrative, change course and attempt to return to its true north.

Well, the ANC is facing that abyss now.

In the May 2014 national elections the party suffered huge losses in the urban centres of Johannesburg, Tshwane, Ekurhuleni and Nelson Mandela Bay (Port Elizabeth), and slipped further in Cape Town, where it continues to retreat in the face of the rampant opposition Democratic Alliance (DA), which also governs in the Western Cape.

For example, in Johannesburg the ANC enjoyed 59.3 per cent support in 2011. By 2014 it was down to 52.3 per cent. In the City of Tshwane (including the administrative capital of the country, Pretoria) the ANC went from 56 per cent to just 49.3 per cent. The ANC won 67 per cent of Nelson Mandela Bay in 2006. In 2011 it got 52 per cent, and in 2014 just 48 per cent.

These results indicate that the ANC is losing a constituency that was at the heart of its formation: the black elite and middle classes. The key player in the party's formation, Pixley kaIsaka Seme, was a lawyer. The party's first executive committee in 1912 was made up of journalists, priests, lawyers, teachers and other members of the black professional class.

Throughout its history, that educated black middle class has been the strand running through the party's leadership: Nelson Mandela and Oliver Reginald Tambo, the men who held the party together through three decades of exile, were lawyers. Walter Sisulu was a businessman. Many others were in the professions.

One of the ANC's extraordinary achievements over the past 21 years has been the explosive rise of the black middle class. In late 2013 global investment bank Goldman Sachs issued a report claiming that 'in absolute terms, Africans now dominate the middle-class consumer segment'. It said some 10 million people had 'graduated into the middle to upper band' in the ten years between 2001 and 2010.[2] That figure may be a little bit too generous, but even conservative figures do show quite revolutionary growth: a 2013 report by the Research on Socio-Economic Policy unit at Stellenbosch University showed that the black middle class had grown from 300 000 in 1993 to 3 million in 2012. Moreover, the black share of the middle class *rose* from 11 per cent to 41 per cent.[3]

So why, then, are all these people either not voting for the party that made them so prosperous or defecting to other parties? Former DA leader Helen Zille claims that of the party's 1 million new votes in May 2014 at least 700 000 were from black South Africans who had never voted for the DA before. She said 40 per cent of the party's new black voters were from Gauteng, the economic powerhouse of the country.[4] Julius Malema's EFF also attracted a total of 1.1 million voters, most from urban centres in Gauteng.

The loss continues elsewhere among the black intelligentsia. In May 2015 the DA's student wing, the DA Students' Organisation (Daso), thrashed the ANC-aligned South African Students' Congress (Sasco) at the University of Fort Hare to take control of the Students' Representative Council. Daso won 52.5 per cent of the vote, up from 20.5 per cent in 2014. Sasco scraped together a measly 37 per cent of the vote.

This stunning outcome was even more extraordinary given that Fort Hare is a key site in the ANC's historical iconography. Virtually all the party's struggle icons studied there: Mandela, Tambo and other great leaders from Govan Mbeki to Nthato Motlana and ZK Matthews walked through its halls.

'You cannot complete a conversation about the struggle for liberation without mentioning Fort Hare,' ANC Eastern Cape provincial secretary Oscar Mabuyane told the *Times* after the comprehensive drubbing. 'It is not an easy thing to accept [that we lost] Fort Hare. The institution is a cradle for continental leadership in progressive politics. It's a very sad moment.'[5]

Clearly, the ANC is losing its oldest constituency: the educated elite, the students and the black middle classes. What is to be done? Crucially, what will the ANC do? And why is the ANC losing its core constituency, a constituency that has benefited more than any other section of South Africa from the party's policies since 1994?

The inevitable answer is leadership, and the raised finger inexorably points to one man, and one man only: Jacob Gedleyihlekisa Zuma. And so the eyes begin to move away from Zuma to seek a new leader, a man or woman around whom the ANC can coalesce and find its centre again.

Who, however, will ask the key questions that will lead to the start of this process? One of the ANC's top intellectuals, a key member of the party's NEC, has said in private conversations that a drubbing at the polls and the continuation of the current intellectual and policy drift will inevitably lead to a middle tier of party activists revolting against the status quo.

They will not do so in a loud voice, but in quietness and stealth. Why will they do it? Well, if the ANC suffers yet another electoral whipping then it will lose yet another big chunk of its middle-tier activists. They will be out of the lucrative political positions that they currently enjoy. They will be out in the cold, and wondering why. They will ask these questions, and will look around for a figure who might step forward to lead them and their party out of the morass in which it finds itself.

There are many such individuals. They are in the local councils, in the provincial government structures, in the National Assembly and in government. They are everywhere, and with every voter the ANC loses one or more of them is in danger of losing his or her position. In the national elections of May 2014 the ANC won 249 seats out of a total of 400 seats in the National Assembly. In the 2009 elections, the ANC obtained 264 seats. This was down from 279 seats won in 2004. This downward trend is expected to continue at a faster pace, particularly at local government level, where the ANC has already experienced considerable losses, as seen in Tshwane and other centres. In the May 2014 elections the ANC lost support in key areas and skirted close to the 50 per cent mark in Johannesburg, Tshwane and Ekurhuleni. The real danger for many of the ANC activists at this level of leadership is that they will not return to power.

The selfish and myopic among them will dig in and accelerate the corruption that has flourished so much under Zuma and his cronies. These leaders are the kind that Zwelinzima Vavi, the deposed former secretary-general of Cosatu, warned in 2010 were turning South Africa into a predator state: 'We're headed for a predator state where a powerful, corrupt and demagogic elite of political hyenas are increasingly using the state to get rich,' Vavi told a press conference then, adding that just as the 'hyena and her daughters' eat first in nature, the 'chief of state's family eats first' in this predator state.[6]

'We have to intervene now to prevent South Africa from becoming a state where corruption is the norm and no business can be done with government without first paying a corrupt gatekeeper,' Vavi said.[7]

In South Africa today, there are many young leaders who have made themselves the gatekeepers of any kind of business with the state.

There are already many of them, and many more are emerging. If there is any opposition to their plans then those who speak up are ruthlessly removed. Today, every institution of accountability has spat out a leader – Anwa Dramat at the Hawks, Vusi Pikoli and Mxolisi Nxasana at the National Prosecuting Authority, for example – who developed enough of a backbone to ask difficult questions about corruption related to ANC and government bigwigs.[8]

This is the path down which the ANC is headed now.

The alternative is that an enlightened majority chooses to seek a new, conscientious leadership that will once again reconnect with the people and the party's ethos. This new leadership carries within it the inclusive leadership culture of Nelson Mandela, Ahmed Kathrada, Walter Sisulu and many other ANC leaders of the past.

Of course, it will not be leadership alone. It will be the ability not only to articulate a new vision for South Africa but also to take all of us along with him or her on the long and bumpy road that lies ahead. That leader will have to inspire confidence in South Africans that we are embarked on a new path.

We have been here before, and we can do it again.

This is because the main ingredient of the political settlement that led to the 1994 elections and the post-apartheid democracy we enjoy today is confidence.

As in South Africa today, in 1990 FW de Klerk had a crumbling economy on his hands. Even worse for him and his fearful lieutenants and constituency, the jails were full of political activists. White youth were refusing to buy into the apartheid system and serve in its army. The world was laughing at him and his discredited government. The townships were wracked by violence.

Nelson Mandela and his comrades walked out of jail after 27 years into a changed world. Oliver Tambo and the ANC returned from exile to a country many hardly remembered or recognised. The United Democratic Front had fought against the apartheid government internally and could hardly recognise a future partner among apartheid's leaders.

These were the two main protagonists in the talks that began, publically anyway, in 1990. Certain key steps were necessary for these two sworn enemies to sit at the table and begin a meaningful dialogue. These are what we would call confidence-building measures.

The ANC needed to convince a hostile world – remember that the likes of British Prime Minister Margaret Thatcher and US President Ronald Reagan regarded the liberation movements as 'terrorists' – that it was ready to govern and that it could. At home, the right wing stridently told its constituency that a combination of *'swart gevaar'* (black peril) and *'rooi gevaar'* (red, communist peril) was at hand. The likes of the Pan Africanist Congress and many in the ANC, such as the late Harry Gwala, plainly said the apartheid government could not be trusted and would not hand over power.

The key leadership lesson of Mandela and De Klerk (together with a core group of younger leaders such as Thabo Mbeki, Cyril Ramaphosa, Roelf Meyer and others) was that from this morass of mistrust they managed to spread a seed that proclaimed: we can do this, we can see our way through this deep and dark tunnel, we can emerge on the other side better able to face the future.

That seed is called confidence. These leaders managed to indicate to world leaders, to constituents at home, to the international markets, that South Africa could face and resolve its problems. South African leaders built up our confidence in ourselves and the democracy pact – flawed as it surely was in some respects – to the extent that all of us could sell it to the world and proclaim that we believe, as Mbeki was to put it years later, 'that tomorrow will be better than today, and today was better than yesterday'.[9]

That is why South Africans were able to walk the world with a new confidence. That is why we began to roll back the tide of low growth, joblessness and poverty.

Today confidence in our country – internally and externally – is waning. Since 2009 we have been losing the war against corruption, poverty and unemployment. Our economy is growing at appalling

140

levels compared to the rest of the continent. We are no longer the darlings of the world. If the increase in what are called 'service delivery protests' is anything to go by, we are no longer the darlings of our own people either.[10]

All this is happening because we have not taken the right confidence-building steps. Instead, we are becoming a country in which a few are intent on enriching themselves at the expense of the many, a country in which our elites are burrowing away to fill their pockets before everything explodes. Even they have lost confidence. They are looting so they can escape.

The key challenge for the leader that these young ANC leaders will be looking for is confidence and confidence-raising measures. They want that leader to start the hard work of making small, meaningful changes that can restore our people's confidence in our political structures and in our leadership.

For all these, many are increasingly looking towards business tycoon and current Deputy President Cyril Ramaphosa. But Ramaphosa may lose out yet again.

The case for a Ramaphosa presidency is compelling. Schooled in the trade union movement, rising through the United Democratic Front and at Mandela's side during the pre-democracy talks of the early 1990s, he chaired the Constituent Assembly that gifted South Africa with the most widely praised Constitution of modern times.

The problem is not the case for the man. It is the man. What, many are asking, is Ramaphosa's game? As in 1997, when he waited too long and was outflanked and outgunned by the wily Thabo Mbeki, the man who is lauded by many as a master strategist and tactician seems to be keeping his powder dry.

In early 2015 a unique set of events presented themselves to a possible challenger to Zuma's throne. First, Zuma was under fire from the opposition, civil society and ordinary South Africans. In Parliament, in public meetings and in other fora, some elements of power were clearly ebbing from the man from Nkandla.

The denigration of the President of the republic cast possible new outcomes within and outside the governing ANC: a power and governance vacuum as the President concentrates on his many scandals; the rise of new contenders to replace him; the hammering of the ANC at the polls in 2016; and the strengthening of the opposition – particularly the EFF – as they continue their relentless (and justified) stalking of the man.

Here is the problem, though. Ramaphosa has flip-flopped, been reticent, failed to raise his voice at crucial periods, and just not made it clear where he personally stands on the key issues facing his organisation and the country. He has failed to be clear, to take those who have supported him into his confidence, and has largely added to the confusion that surrounds the ANC and its succession strategy. It is time for him to step up, otherwise he could find himself being remembered as the man who stood at the door of history and failed to cross his own personal Rubicon.[11]

Ramaphosa has been here, there and everywhere over the first year or so of the second Zuma presidency. He has brokered peace deals in Lesotho and elsewhere. He has popped into Parliament to deflect anger against Zuma's no-shows. He has tried to save Eskom, the embattled electricity utility.

What is his game? Will Ramaphosa run for the ANC presidency in December 2017? He does not seem at all bothered about building a constituency inside the party. These are, after all, the people who really matter; they are the ones who will vote at the ANC national conference. None except elements of the weak Gauteng ANC have come out in support of Ramaphosa.

His failure to organise within the party, and his reticence on his future plans, could lead to him being bypassed as other contenders emerge and race to the top. After all, Dr Nkosazana Dlamini-Zuma is already being pushed quite hard by elements in the powerful KwaZulu-Natal ANC, and by Zuma himself. Zweli Mkhize, once a contender but whose star has waned somewhat, is once again being mentioned as a key man. Jeff Radebe, the ANC stalwart who is Rama-phosa's brother-in-law, is now also suddenly back in play.

Ramaphosa, meanwhile, is the man at the crossroads. Many want him to run, to bring the ethos of the Mandela presidency back to the Union Buildings, but he remains the quiet man. He is not showing his hand.

What happens now? Zuma ascended to power by persistently tell-ing the world that his predecessor and comrade, Thabo Mbeki, was trying to subvert ANC culture and traditions. According to these tra-ditions, said Zuma, there has always been an understanding in the party that the deputy president succeeds the sitting leader.[12] Why, he would ask in the mid-2000s when there was a massive movement to stop his ascendancy, was his possible rise to the top suddenly being questioned?

Well, Zuma seems to have somersaulted somewhat on this 'culture and tradition' business. On 5 May 2014, he told a press briefing: 'The ANC has come in to say women must be in power. I think the coun-try is ready for a woman president. The ANC has capable women [who can serve as president]. The ANC would enthusiastically [support] the election of a woman president. That might happen sooner than we think.'

He continued: 'This [contestation] is what the ANC needs. But what needs to happen is for people to allow democratic processes. We must afford members of the ANC space to choose their own leaders. Con-testation will happen in the next [coming] years. I will be at my Nkandla [at that time]. But I will continue to contribute as an ordi-nary member of the ANC.'[13]

After he won the deputy presidency of the party in Mangaung in December 2012, many started speculating that Ramaphosa was head-ed for the top job. Indeed, the ratings agency Fitch was so elated by his advancement that it said his election and the endorsement of the National Development Plan (NDP) offered 'some hope of more effec-tive leadership and a greater focus on structural reforms'.[14]

In KwaZulu-Natal, however, Ramaphosa has been viewed with deep suspicion, as he came in as Zuma's running partner just days before the actual elections in Mangaung. Indeed, Zuma supporters fanned out at the conference to shoot down all suggestions of a Zuma-Ramaphosa prenuptial agreement that would guarantee Ramaphosa the top job in 2017 at the next ANC national conference.

Which leaves Ramaphosa with a conundrum. He lacks a real base within the party, while KwaZulu-Natal has shown that it remains, at least in the run-up to December 2017, the most muscular – in numbers and organisational reach – and most important player in the race.[15]

If Ramaphosa really wants the top job, he will have to start mobilising serious players within the party. The ANC Youth League, for long a kingmaker (both Zuma and Mbeki benefited from its endorsement at a very early stage of their respective races), is a shadow of its former self. The ANC in the Eastern Cape and Limpopo, where Ramaphosa enjoyed huge support in the past, is divided and weak, with branches that cannot even form a quorum. The anti-Zuma Gauteng ANC, which Ramaphosa spurned in Mangaung, does not trust him.

However, if the KwaZulu-Natal ANC's initiatives and Zuma's comments are taken in tandem, the candidate who seems ahead right now is Dlamini-Zuma, who also happens to be Zuma's former wife. Her term at the AU Commission ends in 2016, just in time for her to come home, campaign for the top job and win at the ANC's December 2017 conference.[16]

The rise of a Zuma acolyte, chosen to continue to hobble and eunuch state institutions, would be a disaster for the country. It would mean that the dream that many have, that the ANC will wake from its slumber – that dream will be shattered. The hope is that a realisation will come that the party can no longer blame apartheid for its failures.

The ANC is in charge of the purse strings and it has received the people's votes. It has to govern, and govern decisively and well. When people see the fruit of such governance – jobs, schools that work, less corruption – then they will reinvest in the dream they bought into in 1994.

The pessimistic scenario, one that many prefer not to confront, is that the ANC remains in the grip of the predatory elite that is dragging it down. If the party stays on this trajectory, it opens the way for two types of new player to emerge. One would be a credible, ethical and believable opposition formation that can convince the electorate that the 1994 project of hope and prosperity can be continued.

The other new player would be a coalition of populists in the party. That coalition would make big promises without explaining how exactly these would be achieved. While it does this, with a thin margin of support, it would continue to lay waste to the Constitution, to install cronies at the top of state-owned companies and institutions of democracy so as to enable itself to loot without hindrance.

This brings me back to the idea of a Ramaphosa presidency. In 1996 I drove up to a very posh house in Bryanston, one of the formerly whites-only, top-end suburbs in Johannesburg. It was the home of the young ANC firebrand and the Deputy Minister of the Environment, Peter Mokaba.

Mokaba had been a hero of mine. In 1986, through the ANC's underground structures, he had led the formation of a youth organisation modelled on the ANC Youth League of Nelson Mandela in the late 1940s. It was called the South African Youth Congress and it brought together all progressive youth formations in South Africa together under one programme: to render South Africa ungovernable and make apartheid unworkable.[17]

A policy paper of the organisation was widely circulated, and it fired my imagination. For the first time in my life, someone spoke about the 'commanding heights of the economy' and how our free democracy would nationalise the mines and expropriate land and return it to the masses. My father had worked for Anglo American Corporation his whole life. He had started as a labourer underground, had risen to the position of a wages clerk and had then jumped over to the security division to earn more money. The policy paper's characterisation of that company, and its exploitative practices, struck a chord in me and many other young people across the country.

Mokaba had been arrested and detained by the apartheid government on numerous occasions. He struck fear into the hearts of many white South Africans as he chanted his fiery refrain: 'Shoot the boer! Shoot the farmer!'

He became the first president of the unbanned ANC Youth League, and served Mandela in the first democratic administration of the new South Africa.

Mokaba was powerful in the ANC by virtue of his presidency of the ANC Youth League and his massive and vocal constituency. With Winnie Madikizela-Mandela, Mokaba was the *enfant terrible* of the Mandela Cabinet. The President had to reprimand him several times to tone down his incendiary statements and his singing of 'Shoot the boer'.

And so, as I walked into his house in 1996, at his invitation, Mokaba took me by surprise. I had asked him about who should succeed Mandela, and who the youth league would back.

He tore into Ramaphosa.

'That man is weak and unprincipled,' he said. 'He is vain and would not be the right man to lead this great movement.'

He went on to say that Ramaphosa had failed to take the lead during the pre-democracy negotiations, that the man had sold out workers while he was secretary-general of the NUM, and that in his view the ANC would have 'sold out' to white capital if it elected him to lead.

These were extraordinary charges and did not accord with the Ramaphosa I knew. The man I knew was smart, courageous, principled and, above all, straight and true. There was no scandal attached to him. When a matter of principle came before him, he acted with courage and empathy.

One of the most painful, yet oddly great, moments of the internal struggle was when Ramaphosa and other United Democratic Front leaders chose to speak out against the actions of Winnie Mandela's football club, which at the time was accused of beating up and murdering a teenage activist suspected of being a spy. It was a hard and terrifying thing to do – to speak up against a woman known as the Mother of the Nation and whose power within the movement was enormous.

Yet, Ramphosa had the courage to do it.

Mokaba and the ANC Youth League endorsed Thabo Mbeki to succeed Nelson Mandela as president of the party. After that key forces within the tripartite alliance followed, and whatever ambitions for the top job Ramaphosa may have had were thwarted even before the party conference in Mafikeng in December 1997.

After he lost the race to succeed Mandela, the bruised Ramaphosa went into business. He quickly executed several deals that led to his becoming one of South Africa's richest people. In 2012 he threw his hat back in the ring by doing a deal, at the very last minute, to become Jacob Zuma's running mate. He won 75 per cent of the votes to become deputy president of the party. A large chunk of those votes were because of the iniquitous practice of slate voting; delegates to the party conference in Mangaung were given a list of names to vote for by the Zuma faction of the party. That faction now dominates 75 per cent of the powerful national executive committee.

And therein lies Ramaphosa's problem. As part of the Zuma faction, he has to defend every unprincipled decision taken by his current leader. Since he became the number two in government in May 2014, he has had to preside over the mess and reports of wanton corruption at Eskom and allegations of impropriety at almost every level. Virtually every week now an admired institution of our democracy is targeted for capture and destruction. Ramaphosa is part of that rot, at least by association if not by design.

And so the question must be asked: was Mokaba, all those years ago, right about Ramaphosa? Has Ramaphosa cast principle aside to become just another part of the predator state that is the Zuma administration? Should those who see in him a Messiah of sorts begin to ask themselves what he can do as Number 1 that he could not do as Number 2? What about his role in the Marikana Massacre, where 34 mineworkers were mowed down by the police after he had urged the police minister to take 'concomitant action' – although Judge Farlam has exonerated him of any wrongdoing?

Does it matter, though? The truth is that the debate is terribly skewed. How did we get to a stage where we are looking at one man as a possible saviour? In a country of 52 million, surely there are many others who can lead in the manner that we believe is the template – inclusive, unitary and visionary like Mandela?

It is a reflection of how sad things have become that we are now left scrabbling for a Messiah, and have given up on setting up structures that will throw up many good leaders instead of just one potentially compromised individual. The saddest part of looking to Ramaphosa as a potentially redemptive leader is that we have also lost agency as a people.

After walking away from township schools and settling for well-run private schools in towns; after abandoning the police to sign up with private security companies; after checking out of the state hospital system and signing up with the very expensive private healthcare companies – now we want to check out of our responsibilities as engaged citizens.

We want to hand over leadership of our society to Ramaphosa, or another 'great hope for South Africa', instead of retaining the capacity to 'rage against the dying of the light' – in the words of Dylan Thomas – that Mandela and other great men and women gifted us with.

What is dying or dead here is not just the ANC. What is corrupted here is not just the ANC.

What is truly terrible is that all of us have thrown our hands in the air and have given up on being leaders ourselves. We are hoping for some sort of religious father, a great man, to lead us. He is not there.

We are on our own now. We had better make it work, for no politician – certainly no politician from the ruling party – seems capable of displaying the sort of courage needed to break the logjam of corruption and stasis that grips our country. It is up to us now.

11

The Rise of the Opposition

'When President Mandela offered me a place in his cabinet,
I politely declined ... I believed then, as I do today, that a healthy
democracy needs an independent opposition.'
– Tony Leon, former leader of the
opposition Democratic Alliance, 12 December 2013

In May 2011, the then ANC Youth League president, Julius Malema, arrived at the temporary studios of the TV news station eNCA at the results centre of the Independent Electoral Commission (IEC) in Pretoria. Lindiwe Mazibuko, at the time the DA's spokesperson, had been waiting an hour for a televised debate with Malema.

Malema refused to take part, saying he was not asked to debate her.

'She's a nobody, she's a tea girl of the madam. I'm not debating with the service [sic] of the madam,' he said.[1] It was a deeply insulting slur that denigrated Mazibuko and cast aspersions on virtually all white people, even those who hold progressive views. Under apartheid, domestic workers were routinely referred to as 'tea girls' while white women were the 'madams' of their households. Malema was essentially saying that DA leader Helen Zille was a white manipulator who had sent a puppet to debate him.

The wheel has turned since then. Mazibuko is now a Harvard graduate with a Master's degree in Public Administration. Malema is now on the opposition benches in Parliament and represents his vociferous, volatile, energetic new party, the Economic Freedom Fighters, after being booted out of the ANC. After a year in Parliament the EFF is a force to be reckoned with: it sets some of the agenda in the chamber and has become a relentless, implacable thorn in the side of the ANC, where many of its MPs cut their political teeth.

Malema himself has mellowed somewhat. Although he still gives fiery speeches, he no longer insults as much as he used to and doesn't utter as many thoughtless remarks as he did in his ANC Youth League days. For a long time, from his ascension to the presidency of the ANC Youth League in 2008, Malema was Mr Apology and Mr Gaffe all rolled into one. Indeed, he seemed to have his foot in his mouth more than the gaffe-prone Zuma, the man he pledged in 2008 to kill and die for.[2]

When he launched his new party, Malema had to start by apologising to the numerous ANC leaders he had affronted. Soon after anointing himself 'commander-in-chief' of the Economic Freedom Fighters, Malema was saying sorry again. This time he was sitting next to Epainette Mbeki, mother of former president Thabo Mbeki, in the Eastern Cape. 'I am very happy that I got the opportunity to say to my grandmother here that whatever I could have said about her son, President Mbeki, at that time, if I offended her and her family in any way, I apologise. I am very sorry,' he said.[3]

Malema had been putting his foot in it and apologising since he crashed into our politics, and largely sullied them, in 2008 when a bum-flashing mob elected him to the top position in the ANC Youth League. In February 2009 he insulted his fellow comrade and then education minister Naledi Pandor, saying she must use her 'fake accent' to fix problems in education. The next day, Malema was apologising: 'I acknowledge that the remarks I made against you were uncalled for and might have disappointed and hurt you. I write this letter to unconditionally apologise for those remarks.'[4]

He went on to put his foot in it again and again, insulting and bullying journalists as he beat the drum in support of Zuma. No one was spared his insults. In March 2010 the Equality Court found him guilty of hate speech and discrimination after he claimed that Zuma's rape accuser had a 'nice time' with the man from Nkandla. Speaking at a gathering of Cape Peninsula University of Technology students in January 2009, Malema had said: 'Those who had a nice time will wait until the sun comes out, request breakfast and ask for taxi money. In the morning, that lady requested breakfast and taxi money ... You can't ask for money from somebody who raped you.' In June 2011, fifteen months after the Equality Court issued its verdict, Malema issued an apology and committed to paying the R50 000 fine imposed.[5]

This is the story of the 'commander-in-chief' of the EFF. We all remember the bullying and insulting of BBC correspondent Jonah Fisher, who Malema famously called a 'bloody agent',[6] and the savaging of opponents such as IFP leader Mangosuthu Buthelezi (he was called a 'factory fault').[7] In 2013 Malema even apologised to South Africans for his fervent support for Zuma: 'We once more sincerely apologise for having given you a president like Zuma.'[8]

It is this last apology that resonates most among voters, though. For when we hear that, under the current administration, a military ambulance carrying the ailing father of our democracy – Nelson Mandela – broke down by the side of the road, allegedly leading to a 40-minute wait for a replacement,[9] the heart lurches. It is a small incident, yet it carries intimations of the poor service delivery that we all now know comes with government and is dispensed to the poor every day. The heart does not lurch because the ambulance breakdown is a terrible thing in itself. These things happen. It lurches because the nation is uneasy. It lurches because there is just too much that should not go wrong that seems to go wrong.

Times are getting harder. Unemployment is on the rise. Every day, scores of communities are up in arms over service delivery. Eskom tells us we are using too much power and load shedding is threatened every night. Policemen are executed. Workers are mowed down by the police. The rand continues to weaken against other major currencies.

That was why the official launch of Agang in 2013, followed by the launch of the Economic Freedom Fighters, invigorated the political landscape. These new formations may not have much to offer in the long run (Agang imploded within months of launch), but their emergence offered a fresh new avenue for possible salvation.

The nation is uneasy. That is why, when former president Thabo Mbeki went on radio station PowerFM in June 2013 there was an outpouring of nostalgia, emotion and even regret that he is now lost to domestic politics.[10] This was startling, considering the man's extraordinary failure of leadership on HIV/Aids. The nation is uneasy, and it seeks answers, even in the past.

The nation is uneasy. It is uneasy because it is finally confronted with the enormity of the governing party's own problem. The ANC has a Jacob Zuma problem.

Nothing illustrates the enormity of the ANC's problem, and therefore our problem, like Zuma's defence in Parliament of his friendship with the notorious Gupta family. Asked by Independent Democrats MP Joe McGluwa if he would cut ties with the Guptas, Zuma responded: 'Every human being has a right to have friends ... We are not in the state that bans people because they have friends with others ...

'I don't think you can just say because there are these rumours around, can you therefore change what you are doing? Because you don't operate around rumours.'[11]

Rumours? Dear sir, these are people who have used your name to land planes in military establishments in your country in defiance of your own country's laws. These are the same people whom many in your organisation – and in your own intelligence services – have warned you against consorting with. And Zuma says these are rumours.

Perhaps the ANC does not see it, but the reason why it is more vulnerable than it has ever been since the 1994 election is because the man who leads it is so compromised. In many jurisdictions Zuma would be unelectable given the scandals his administration has swatted aside.

Even inside the ANC, many now regard Zuma with disdain. The main reason he remains in power is because he has sidelined potential challengers, and the leadership that now constitutes the party's national executive is largely made up of sycophants or those who are prepared to sugar-coat reality for him.

The nation is uneasy about all this. It is a time in which the new and old opposition parties should make hay. It does not seem likely that the ANC will ask Zuma to step down and that someone else will step forward to lead it. The party will be taking damaged goods to the battlefront in the 2016 local election campaign and in the 2019 national elections.

There has never been a better time for the opposition to thrive and grow. That is why, when the 34-year-old Mmusi Maimane was elected as the leader of the Democratic Alliance, on 10 May 2015, there was once again such a frisson in the political firmament.[12] Maimane, the DA's parliamentary leader, succeeded the combative Helen Zille, who had announced a month earlier that she would step down.

Maimane made history: 21 years after our democracy dawned, he became the first black leader of the party.[13] In his acceptance speech Maimane promised that the DA would be the next government of South Africa. He zoomed in on the ANC's biggest problems: that the young do not feel included in the democracy we enjoy and that Zuma is driving this wedge wider. 'President Zuma, if you are watching: we are still coming for you,' he vowed to loud applause.[14]

Can he do it, though? One of the most enduring fallacies of the new South Africa has been that the election of a black DA leader will bring about a windfall of black votes for the party.[15] This doesn't hold water.

Dr Mamphela Ramphele was a widely admired leader whose policies were pretty similar to those of the DA. Her short-lived entry into politics did not bring about the much-heralded windfall in black votes to her Agang.[16] The Pan Africanist Congress of Azania (PAC) under Clarence Makwetu and others was widely touted as a challenger to the ANC. Its policies were – except on race issues – broadly what the EFF represents today. It has not attracted more than 1 per cent of the vote in five successive national elections.[17] Neither has the party born of the activism of Steve Biko, the Azanian People's Organisation (Azapo).[18]

Mosiuoa Lekota and Mbhazima Shilowa attracted 7 per cent of the vote for the newly formed Cope in 2009, and then embarked on one of the most unseemly political suicides of recent times.[19] The admirable Bantu Holomisa's United Democratic Front (UDF) battles along with support of about 1 per cent after 16 years of hard graft. Mangosuthu Buthelezi's Inkatha Freedom Party (IFP) has been shedding support and votes consistently since 1994.[20] There is no doubt in my mind that it will cease to exist when Buthelezi retires or passes on.

All these parties are led by black people. Some of these leaders – Buthelezi, for instance, and Julius Malema – are blessed with powerful oratorical skills. Some of these parties have decent enough policies. Yet they have failed, over the past 21 years, to give the ANC sleepless nights.

What, therefore, leads so many to believe that a DA led by Mmusi Maimane will receive a windfall of black votes by dint of Maimane being black?[21] If Maimane and his fellow leaders are banking on race to unseat the ANC, they are on a hiding to nothing.

To my mind, Maimane will have to concentrate on a political programme that begins to speak to black constituents in a manner none of the parties mentioned in the previous paragraphs have done. He has to be revolutionary. The party of opposition that Tony Leon and Helen Zille have built assiduously over the past 21 years needs to begin a process of also becoming a party of belonging, of empathy, of trust, to attract the millions more black voters that it needs if it is to become a real contender for national government.

The way to do this is two-pronged. First, there is absolutely no reason to stop being tough on corruption and general malfeasance in the current government. So, like Leon and Zille and Lindiwe Mazibuko before him, Maimane must not let up on pointing out the rot that is creeping into state institutions and the frenzied feeding that high-powered and connected individuals are involved in at the moment.

In this sense Maimane has to be tough and relentless and ruthless. He cannot take his foot off the pedal. At the moment he is seen as slightly weaker on some of these issues than, say, Malema. There are important local elections taking place in 2016. If Maimane stops the pressure now he will see the DA lose – badly.

It cannot, however, be a one-track campaign. The second track is that the DA needs to fashion a message that begins to speak to the hearts of the massive number of South Africans who can see that the ANC, the party that delivered their freedom, the party that is hard-wired into their DNA, has lost its way. Yet they are sceptical of everyone else.

They are not sceptical because of race only. They have been sceptical of the PAC, Cope, IFP, UDM, EFF and everyone else before. If it was an issue of race, many would have gone for the PAC or Cope or someone else. They didn't.

The ANC's strength for the past 65 years – since it adopted its Programme of Action in 1949 and struck out on a more radical path than it had since its birth in 1912 – has been a political programme that speaks to the hearts and minds of South Africans. It has always had a plan to present to the people of South Africa. Read through South African political history of the past 65 years and you will find political parties who have vented their anger and frustration but have lacked a programme that connects with the hearts and minds of our people.

Say what you will about the ANC, it has been a master at offering hope and an associated programme to South Africa. Through this it has built up a huge store of trust among voters.[22] The DA will have to find a way to build that sort of trust among potential voters.

Mmusi Maimane's blackness may very well help when he knocks at the doors of black South Africans. Once in the house, though, he needs to speak to their hearts and show them a plan that the DA will continue to make their lives better, and that their children's lives will be better.

The ANC is increasingly failing to do this, but it doesn't mean that he will be handed the ball merely because he is black.

What is interesting, however, is that more and more black South Africans are 'coming out' and openly saying that they would vote for the DA.[23] This trend may accord with what happened in the May 2015 national elections in the UK.

Every pollster had predicted that the two main parties – the Conservatives and Labour – would pull about 33 per cent to 34 per cent of the vote each, leading to a long, exhausting battle by either side to form a coalition government.

The pollsters were wrong. David Cameron's Conservative Party streaked ahead and won 37 per cent of the vote. Crucially, the party managed to win the key seats it needed to form a majority in the House of Commons, where it commands a majority of 12 seats. Thanks to the first-past-the-post system, the Tories won 331 seats to Labour's 232, with the remainder being won by smaller parties.

What happened? Many ascribed the Conservative victory to the idea of 'shy Tories' – the vast, silent majority of people who are too shy and too intimidated to say out loud to pollsters that they would vote for the largely unsexy Conservatives. It's a phenomenon that goes back to the 1992 UK elections when pollsters said that the Labour Party would trounce the John Major-led Conservatives. They were wrong then, as the unsexy Major continued the Tory winning streak started by Margaret Thatcher.

In the May 2015 UK election, polling firm YouGov head Peter Kellner was quoted as saying the 'shy Tories' had returned: 'People said one thing and they did something else at the ballot box.'[24]

The DA elected Maimane partly in the belief that he could break through the ceiling many say it has reached in attracting white voters. Over the past 21 years it has been pretty tough to find anyone in black townships who would admit openly that they would vote for the DA. Again and again you find the refrain: 'It is a party of whites ...' or, even worse, that it is the party of apartheid.

I have often wondered why this view persists when the party that sits with the remnants of the National Party (NP), is the ANC. After the pact between the DA and the NP crumbled, Marthinus van Schalkwyk led a rump of what was left of the New National Party into the ANC in 2004. He was rewarded with a ministry and others were absorbed into various levels of the ANC.

The DA, however, was left with the toxic stink of the party of apartheid despite the fact that the NP had found its home in the warm bosom of the ANC. The DA has never been able to shake off this stink, hence the general perception that it was the party of privilege and of apartheid. Incredibly, survey respondents still express a fear that, if elected, the DA would 'bring back apartheid'. Even the powerful memory of Helen Suzman – for years the lone voice of opposition in the apartheid parliament – cannot wipe this perception away.[25]

In the run-up to the 2014 election, the ANC was faced with a massive problem. Its president, Zuma, was discredited and was and remains by all accounts a liability.[26] Its deployed cadres in government were mired in one scandal after another. Service delivery protests were spreading while Cosatu was imploding.

Yet the party had its 'shy voters'. It merely slipped from 65.9 per cent to 62 per cent of the vote. Given its problems and the bad press it received, the ANC fooled many among us. One London-based analyst had doggedly predicted that the ANC would fall to 55 per cent of the vote.[27] He was wrong.

The question now is whether there are some among us who are not overtly for the DA, but could enter the voting booth and vote for the party of Maimane. Are there 'shy DA' voters out there who still find it difficult to express their support for the party but could come out in support when they stand in the voting booth?

The corollary is that Zuma, the ANC leader, remains an embarrassment. Yet his party's brand is still powerful. Many exclaim in public that they find Zuma and his many scandals reprehensible, yet will still vote for the party of Mandela in the elections.

The actions of our 'shy voters' will be interesting over the next five years. My view is that the DA will become less 'toxic' in many townships and rural areas, that the ANC will continue to disappoint as long as Zuma and his cronies steer the ship, and that the ANC's shy voters will stay home rather than pitch up to endorse it. That opportunity is for the opposition to take.

What of Malema and his 30-strong group of MPs? Do they have a future? New parties have had a torrid time in the new South Africa. Only two parties have grown: the Democratic Party (now DA) started at 1.7 per cent in 1994 and now enjoys just over 22 per cent; while the ANC saw its fortunes soar from 62 per cent in 1994 to 69 per cent in 2004. Then it saw the reversal under Zuma in 2009 and 2014, taking it back to the 62 per cent where it now sits.

The rest have failed – dismally. Existing opposition parties have lost support or died. The NP ended up subsumed by the ANC. The UDM has languished at the bottom of the pile with support of about 1 per cent since 2004. Cope started off with a spectacular 7 per cent haul of the votes in 2009 but crashed and burned, ending up at below 1 per cent in 2014.

Is the EFF destined for the same fate? After he was kicked out of the ANC, Malema licked his wounds and formed the radical EFF with the express aim of running for Parliament on a platform of nationalising the mines and expropriating land without compensation. In essence, Malema's template is what Robert Mugabe has done since 2000 in Zimbabwe.

Despite the powerful example to the north of us, coupled with the hundreds of thousands, if not millions, of Zimbabweans working in South Africa, the EFF message has continued to resonate across South Africa. It certainly galvanised 1.1 million voters (6.35 per cent) in 2014.

After a year in Parliament the biggest threat facing the party was the possibility that Malema's tax troubles would lead to his sequestration by the South African Revenue Service (Sars). The case was strange, and raised the question of why exactly it had been brought in the first place. Was it political? Was there, as Malema alleged, a 'hidden hand' pulling the strings at the scandal-wracked Sars to ensure that he is kicked out of Parliament, where he has embarrassed Zuma?

The tax authority had obtained a provisional sequestration of Malema in February 2014 because he owed R18 million. Let me be clear: on this issue Malema comes across as extremely shady; he has never fully or convincingly explained how he managed to amass such wealth while earning a modest salary from the ANC Youth League. His explanations have been contradictory; he once claimed to live on handouts, while at the same time driving a massive Range Rover and building a multi-million-rand house in Sandton.[28] *City Press* has written extensively on allegations that Malema was receiving kickbacks from businessmen – but he has not been convicted of any crimes. This is now an issue for the state, which has failed dismally to deal with Malema's corruption – if there is any – or that of any other political heavyweight, for that matter.

In May 2014 Malema and Sars reached a compromise agreement whereby Malema agreed to pay R7.2 million of his outstanding tax bill. However, in March 2015 Sars totally reneged on the deal and applied to the court to have the provisional sequestration declared final. Extraordinarily, Sars said it now believed Malema had contravened the terms of the compromise agreement by, among other things, not disclosing the source of money used to settle the debt.

After the judge in the matter challenged Sars repeatedly about why it so desperately sought final sequestration of the man – meaning that he could not serve in Parliament as the law would bar him from doing so – its counsel informed the High Court that the revenue service had withdrawn its application.[29]

Malema walked out of court feeling buoyant and, just as Maimane had done a few weeks before when he became DA leader, promised the ANC a rough ride: 'An invisible hand is at play and it will be proven. As long as I'm alive, they are in for a high jump.'[30] Malema's confidence was further boosted when his fraud and corruption case was also struck off the court roll in Polokwane on 4 August 2015.

Between Maimane and Malema, it is clear that the ANC will see its dominance of South African politics constantly challenged. What will be interesting to see is how both opposition parties fare in the 2016 local government elections. These will be the most closely contested local elections in the democratic era.[31] In the national elections of 2014 the ANC lost its significant majorities in four major metropolitan areas (City of Johannesburg, City of Tshwane, Ekurhuleni and Nelson Mandela Bay).[32] These are major cities with massive budgets, and the opposition parties now have their eye on them.

The real opposition in South Africa may, however, lie elsewhere. The real opposition, to my mind, lies inside the tripartite alliance, and it is Cosatu. The union federation has been at the heart of our politics and economy since its formation on 1 December 1985. It helped bring apartheid to its knees. It has influenced the ANC significantly. It has fought against iniquitous labour laws and has been at the forefront of the introduction of a more humane labour rights framework in South Africa.

Cosatu has been a massive force for good. It has also been responsible for some negative outcomes. It has brought dignity and pride to many workers, but has also held our economy back. It has been a giant of our society and an important part of the consensual post-1994 dispensation.

Now this giant is in its death throes.[33] It is in turmoil and its leaders are at war with each other. Right now, Cosatu is living through a dark night and it is unclear if it will see the morning light. Cosatu may explode and die in the next few years. Should that take place, it will change the face of our political landscape significantly.

On the face of it, the union federation is divided between factions coalesced around its former secretary-general, Zwelinzima Vavi, and its president, the Zuma-supporting Sdumo Dlamini. Vavi – who was key to Zuma's comeback in the late 2000s, and who once also declared he would die for Zuma – has been a stern critic of the ANC's current government leadership and has lambasted its stance on corruption, famously referring to the 'hyenas' who are looting the state.

Dlamini, on the other hand, leads a faction that believes that Cosatu should not take an 'oppositional stance' to the government.[34] Dlamini is close to Zuma and also sits on the ANC's national executive committee.[35]

Cosatu and its alliance partners, the ANC and the SACP, have been living a lie for the past two decades. If any of the three parties were true to themselves, they would acknowledge that their relationship – save for their shared history of struggle against apartheid – is one huge contradiction.[36]

The ANC is a nationalist organisation whose roots, right from its foundation in 1912, are in the capitalist mould. It was formed by the elite and has largely fought to further the aspirations of the elite. The ANC of today, with affirmative action and black economic empowerment, continues to champion the black elite. It is what it is.

Such an organisation cannot function while it is in alliance with the SACP (whose leaders are leftist on public platforms by night but are fully and enthusiastically capitalist when they enter their ANC offices by day). Such an organisation cannot function while it is in alliance with Cosatu, which is dedicated to alleviating the plight of oppressed workers.

Yet these vastly different forces have been in an unhealthy, even toxic, embrace since the start of the democratic era. Cosatu has stopped the ANC from implementing its economic policies, while the ANC has caved in to its allies' sectarian whims. The youth wage subsidy that was crafted and put on the table by former Minister of Finance Pravin Gordhan was nearly stopped by Cosatu for partisan reasons.[37] Implementation of the National Development Plan (NDP) is stalled because of Cosatu's intransigence. Moves to stop teachers from striking and to up their performance are routinely throttled by Cosatu.[38]

These contradictions are really at the heart of what has happened to Cosatu over the past few years. Many inside the federation, save for those who have chosen to ensconce themselves firmly in Zuma's pocket, realise this. Vavi is among them, and so is Irvin Jim, general-secretary of the National Union of Metalworkers of South Africa (Numsa). Jim went so far as to threaten withdrawal of his union's funds from the ANC's 2014 election campaign if it did not change its ways.[39]

South Africa needed these three formations to stay together for us to achieve a post-apartheid stability. We live in a different world now, though.

The beginnings of a game-changer in our opposition politics lie in the fact that Cosatu is in a very public and very serious process of falling apart. Numsa has already served divorce papers on the federation, and is now only in the process of cat-and-mouse with Cosatu.[40]

Cosatu, after the departure of Numsa and about seven other trade unions aligned to it, as well as Vavi, will be left with what is essentially a federation of trade unions whose members are paid by the state: the South African Democratic Teachers' Union (Sadtu), the National, Education, Health and Allied Workers' Union (Nehawu) and the Police and Prisons' Civil Rights Union (Popcru). It is a cosy relationship. These trade unions will keep quiet so long as they get paid handsomely by the state, which explains why the public-sector wage bill has ballooned under Zuma.[41]

The Cosatu breakaway will form a left political party to contest the 2019 elections. Now, many have tried to do this. For example the Workers and Socialist Party (Wasp) tried to piggy-back on the Marikana turmoil.[42] The EFF is doing the same, but is hobbled because many of its leaders have a very public history of having their noses in the trough when they were in the ANC.[43]

The emergence of a well-funded, organised left party with Zwelinzima Vavi and some Numsa leaders at the helm may be the real game-changer in our politics. Two main events could be set off by such a development.

The first would be that the ANC veers towards populist left interventions: more social grants, higher pay for civil servants, and so forth. The second, more desirable, outcome would be that the ANC realises that the only correct response to criticism is to achieve something. Such a realisation would lead to an ANC that seeks to create jobs, grow the economy and reduce inequality. That ANC would adopt and implement the NDP and ramp up towards an efficient civil service that gives us 6 per cent GDP growth and gets young people into jobs.

163

This is the tough road, and it needs a tough ANC leadership corps to implement it. The emergence of such a group would be a game-changer in itself.

I am now unsure that such an outcome is possible in the ANC. This means that South Africa's hopes really lie in the hands of three opposition formations for now: Maimane's Democratic Alliance, Malema's Economic Freedom Fighters and a new left party supported by trade unions coalesced around Numsa.

Will they win in 2019? It doesn't matter. The key is that they need to do so well that the ruling party realises that if it does not up its game then it will be shouting from the opposition benches very soon. The bottom line is that we need competition in the system. We haven't had enough of it in more than 21 years of democracy, and that has led to the lethargy, and disrespect of voters, that we constantly see in our country.

12

And Along Came a Fearless Woman

'I was not a messiah, but an ordinary man who had become a leader because of
extraordinary circumstances.'
– Nelson Mandela, *Long Walk To Freedom*, 1994

There is always a panic at the beginning of my television interviews with South Africa's diminutive, soft-spoken Public Protector, Thuli Madonsela. The panic comes from the sound people on the show. 'No one,' I can usually hear them scream and shout in my ear from the technical gallery behind me and out of sight of viewers, 'can hear a word she is saying!' It is because Madonsela speaks extremely softly, extremely gently, and is quite shy, particularly at the beginning of her interaction with an interviewer or audience.

But then she warms up, the sound technicians adjust the volume levels slightly higher, and the deluge begins. From every corner of South Africa the messages, on social media and into our email inbox, begin to pour in. Almost every response that she gives is dissected, tweeted and immediately shared.

Thuli Madonsela surprises me every time she appears on my television show because she is that rarest of things: she is a South African hero. She is one of a few. There are the obvious ones, the struggle heroes: Mandela, Walter Sisulu, Oliver Tambo, Albertina Sisulu, Joe Slovo and others. Madonsela is a hero of the new South Africa, a beacon of hope as our public representatives falter and fall, as they imbibe the Kool-Aid of corruption and succumb to its fake nectar. She is straight and true and consistent – traits sadly lacking in our public life today.

And the man and woman in the street knows this. Even as ANC

leaders in the party, executive and in the legislatures bend over backwards to discredit, undermine and perhaps even physically harm her, ordinary people pour their admiration and adoration onto her. When she arrives at our television studios, hardened journalists gush and technical crews – bored with the endless parade of celebrities who pass through – suddenly whip out their phones for photographs and selfies with her. In the streets she is stopped and virtually mobbed.

Long after I have interviewed her, people will walk up to me asking what she is like, what drives her, what makes her so courageous. They want to know about her background, her current situation and her future plans. Will she become president? Will she run for office – any public office?[1] Usually, this line of inquiry is not even raised to get an answer. It is a hope, a prayer, a call for the caped Wonder Woman of South African public life to ride in and save the day.

In a country where political office is increasingly viewed with contempt and many believe that our political leaders are a bunch of untouchables feeding at the trough, Thuli Madonsela is the one South African whom they believe has stood up for the taxpayer, the small man and the ordinary woman who needs help. For this, she has faced relentless attack from the ruling party.[2]

While she was investigating the building of Zuma's Nkandla homestead, the State Attorney, the Chief State Law Adviser and several ministers demanded that she stop her investigation. It didn't work. She soldiered on.[3]

In November 2013 police minister Nathi Mthethwa threatened to have her arrested if she released her provisional report on the matter. It didn't intimidate her.

'We thought he was bluffing because there was absolutely no basis for doing that. If he ever tried that, it would have been handled by the judiciary. Anything that was going to be done through the judicial process, we were very confident of where we stood,' she told the *Times*.[4]

It didn't stop with just the threats, though. After the release of her report she said she believed that her communications were being tapped and that an opportunity was being created for the President to suspend her.[5]

Inside the ANC, powerful leaders did everything in their power to discredit her. Three cabinet ministers seemed to be working full time to besmirch her name and downplay her office's powers. These ministers popped up again and again as the defenders of the theft and looting that was taking place at Nkandla. These three stooges were the then police minister Nathi Mthethwa, state security minister Siyabonga Cwele and public works minister Thulas Nxesi.[6] After the 2014 election Mthethwa was replaced by Nathi Nhleko, who produced yet another report – the sixth from ministers, state bodies and Parliament following hers – seeking to undermine Madonsela's standing and findings.[7] Cwele was also moved from his job, but Nxesi continues to be a trusted defender of Zuma's cause. At every opportunity he seeks to deflect Madonsela's damning findings and recommendations that Zuma should in fact be held financially liable for at least some of the cost of the non-security upgrades to his house.

The attacks ranged from the sublime to the ridiculous. ANC North West chairman Supra Mahumapelo told the nation that 'working class people treat a president like a king'. He went on to tell *City Press* that ordinary people do not care for Madonsela's report: 'They [the working classes] say Zuma is our president ... we see him as our king. In the African tradition, a king must always be respected, regardless.'[8]

In the meantime, Zuma's protectors clutched at every straw to shield their leader, to the extent of telling the media not to publish pictures of Zuma's Nkandla home, built with taxpayers' money, because it was a national key point.[9]

Throughout the Nkandla matter ANC leaders and Zuma's Cabinet showed that they are in their positions merely as bodyguards for the President and nothing else.

The zenith of the attacks came when Madonsela appeared before Parliament's portfolio committee on justice in March 2015. Mathole

Motshekga, the chairman of the portfolio committee, showed in that appearance that he is truly an object to be gazed upon with wonder – and shame. Here is a man, said his actions, who has built nothing of substance and is in the process of destroying something of great significance to our nation.

Motshekga, with his Harvard degree and Unisa doctorate, was on that day and throughout his tenure as committee chairman clearly set upon the singular task of ensuring that Madonsela never again touches Zuma or brings him to account for his part in the blatant theft of taxpayers' money to build that monstrosity of a house in a sea of poverty in Zuma's home village. By his actions it was clear that Motshekga wants not just to destroy Madonsela but to neutralise the office she holds for generations to come. He wants to mould the Public Protector's office in his own and ANC MPs' image on this issue: a lapdog. He wants it to become brainless, acquiescent, toothless. He wants it to become a lackey of politicians.

When Madonsela appeared before the committee, Motshekga ruled that she must henceforth formally report to him four times a year. *Beeld* newspaper pointed out that this is 'two more times than other Chapter 9 institutions and entities which the committee oversees'.[10]

Watchers of Motshekga and his relentless assault on the Public Protector's office recalled that just two weeks before this extraordinary edict he repeatedly interrupted her in Parliament to refer to 'her supporters in the [opposition] Democratic Alliance'. His lackey, ANC MP Bongani Bongo, accused her of behaving 'like the DA'.[11]

Why is Madonsela being singled out for special treatment? What has she done to deserve it? *Beeld* pointed out that 'because Madonsela's office received an unqualified audit "with findings" during the last financial year, the committee during its budget speech said she had to submit an "audit action plan" to the committee and from now on do quarterly progress reports'.

Well, you would say, that's what Parliament does: it holds institutions to account. But then listen to this: 'The Public Protector is one of eight entities reporting to the justice committee. The Human Rights Commission and the Special Investigation Unit also received unqualified audits with findings, but still only [have] to report to the committee twice a year. Third Party Funds received a qualified audit, but no additional measures were taken against the fund.'[12]

Therein lies the rub. Motshekga is going after Madonsela because she dared to independently investigate and find against Zuma on the Nkandla matter. This is what it is all about.

All this happens despite numerous civil society voices explicitly agreeing with Madonsela that Zuma should pay back some of the money for Nkandla. The South African Catholic Bishops' Conference said in June 2015 that the expenditure on Zuma's house was 'morally unjustifiable'. 'We wish to remind our political leaders that, at a time when millions of our people are struggling to make ends meet, it is morally unjustifiable for the government to spend excessive amounts of money – R246 million – on one person and on non-security items highlighted by the public protector's report,' the organisation said. 'We therefore appeal to the president to show ethical leadership and take some responsibility for the runaway expenditure on the Nkandla project.'[13]

Even Zuma's former spokesman and long-time comrade and confidant, Mac Maharaj, said in July 2015 that Zuma should have prepared himself to pay back the money spent on the upgrades to his Nkandla residence. 'From the beginning I said to him, "President, prepare yourself for repayment." This was before the report came out. And I said, "If you have a problem, I'm sure that in your present position it won't be difficult to raise [the money]". He said, "No, I did not ask for those security enhancements. I'm not paying." We know how stubborn each of us can be. And we know each of us has a blind spot. But however this thing pans out, what is important is we create a culture of taking responsibility for our actions,' Maharaj told the *Financial Times*.[14]

This, however, is a message for those who still have the ability to follow their conscience and reason. Not, certainly, for the Motshekgas of this world.

What drives people like Motshekga, then? Like so many of Zuma's protectors, Motshekga has had a long and mediocre history in South African politics. He and his ilk are all too ready to stand on podiums to defend Zuma and denigrate institutions of accountability. In 1998 the ANC made Motshekga premier of Gauteng. President Thabo Mbeki did not pick him to continue in 1999. The ANC's secretary-general at the time, Kgalema Motlanthe, gamely tried to deny that the man had been fired and said his 'talents could be put to better use elsewhere'.

Motshekga then joined the Zuma grouping, the so-called coalition of the wounded. He was amply rewarded with the position of chief whip when the Zuma faction rose to power.

He didn't do such a great job. The *Sunday Times* reported in 2013 that his office had issued a directive to ANC MPs to 'go easy' on Cabinet members and not embarrass them with difficult questions.[15] Then he was fired as ANC chief whip as it became clear that the party's MPs had lost discipline and were essentially without meaningful leadership in Parliament.[16]

The truth is that Motshekga, now a political nonentity, probably feels unappreciated and neglected. Like a young child who cannot get a word in edgeways at the adults' dinner table, he is raising his hand to get Zuma's attention. The poor sod wants to be loved, and so has, since being bundled out of the chief whip's office, tried to make himself relevant to his boss. What is such a man likely to do? He is using every dirty trick in the book to bring Madonsela to heel. It is embarrassing and disgraceful.

In October 2014 Motshekga single-handedly absolved Zuma of any wrongdoing, saying: 'One should be upfront here and say the President has not violated any code of conduct. Even to begin to suggest payment by the President, of anything, begins to seem absurd.'[17]

Really?

Weak men are dangerous. Motshekga is politically weak (he did not make it onto the national executive committee of the ANC in 2012) and essentially survives at the whim of party bosses. He will do anything required of him to please.

He is a reflection of the Zuma Cabinet. Many of its members are political lightweights. They depend on being tapped by Zuma for high office – or else they are literally nothing. Many would struggle to find a meaningful job elsewhere in the economy.

Expect Motshekga, and about 75 per cent of the current ANC leadership, to continue this assault on the Public Protector and other institutions. They are, after all, weak men and women who depend on Zuma's blessing to continue to eat.

Unfortunately for them, it will not work. Madonsela is still standing and that is because her actions have been fair, clean and honest throughout the Nkandla matter.

The Public Protector's Nkandla report is an extraordinary thing. From it one can glean the depth of the rot, the malevolence and the Machiavellian scheming that has attended the Zuma administration from its inception. In the ANC's and Zuma's fight to discredit Madonsela you can see the extent to which such elements are prepared to go to continue looting the state. The attacks on Madonsela have chilled me, and I continue to worry that her life may be in danger.

The Nkandla saga started in November 2009 when the late journalist Mandy Rossouw, at the time with the *Mail & Guardian*, visited the village of Nkandla and wrote up what she saw: massive new buildings, plenty of workers and business as new money flowed into the village soon after Zuma's ascension to power.[18] A town was being built and a castle was springing up for the man whose conception of leadership was a feudal one, as explained earlier in this chapter by Supra Mahumapelo, the North West ANC leader.

Rossouw's report was the first to alert us to what was happening. Other journalists expanded on her work. Rossouw passed away before the full extent of the horror was revealed, but she would have been shocked as Madonsela slowly and patiently read out the litany of corruption ('a toxic concoction of a lack of leadership, a lack of control and focused self-interest,'[19] she said) that attended the building of that monstrous warren of houses for Zuma and his family at state

171

expense. That Zuma, as president, has official residences in Durban, Cape Town and Pretoria did not stop him from using taxpayers' money to build up this private home of his under the guise of 'security upgrades'. He just went ahead and did it. A budget of R38.9 million for the project was approved in 2010, and the expenditure on the house now stands at about R246 million. Police minister Nathi Nhleko has promised that further work will be done on the house despite the outcry from the public on the issue.

In brief, Madonsela's investigation into the building of Zuma's Nkandla house found that the President had unduly benefited from what she described as 'exorbitant' expenditure on his private home. She instructed that Zuma must pay back a reasonable portion of the costs to the state. The report, cheekily titled 'Secure in Comfort', went on to put the blame for the escalation of the house's costs squarely at Zuma's door: it said Zuma had contravened the executive ethics code because he failed to stop the spiralling costs of the upgrades, as is his duty as a member of the Cabinet.

The report requested the President to 'pay a reasonable percentage of the cost of the measures as determined with the assistance of National Treasury'.[20] Madonsela said she believed the President should have ideally asked questions regarding the scale, cost and affordability of the Nkandla project.[21]

She also recalled that Zuma had told a sitting of Parliament that his family had built its own houses at their own cost through a bond, that the state had not built any of it and that his family had not benefited from the improvements. Zuma had told Parliament in November 2012: 'Let me make one thing quite clear … my residence in Nkandla has been paid for by the Zuma family. All the buildings and every room we use in that residence was built by ourselves as a family, and not by government. I have never asked government to build a home for me and it has not done so, the government has not built a home for me.'[22]

Her response was short and sharp: 'This was not true. It is common cause that in the name of security, government built for the President and his family a visitors' centre, cattle kraal and chicken run, swimming pool and amphitheatre. The President and his family clearly benefited from this.'

Zuma was to later appoint several probes into this largesse, all of them designed to prove that these luxuries were part of the necessary security upgrades to his home. Unfortunately, this has not washed with the public.

Madonsela was, however, kind to Zuma in her report. She noted that Zuma did not 'wilfully' mislead Parliament when, in November 2012, he uttered the statement that 'all the buildings and every room we use in that residence was built by ourselves as family and not by government'.

Instead, she said: 'While his conduct could accordingly be legitimately construed as misleading Parliament, it appears to have been a bona fide mistake and I am accordingly unable to find that his conduct was in violation of … the Executive Ethics Code.'[23]

In this way, Zuma managed to avoid even greater censure than he received.

There was a deep cynicism that ran through the construction of the house in Nkandla. It is the sort of cynicism that grips nations that begin to believe that a president is akin to royalty in Victorian times, that every little person has to be squashed to ensure that the Big Man lives in opulence.

Madonsela found that at least one critical service delivery programme was shelved to divert cash to Zuma's house. 'Funds were reallocated from the Inner City Regeneration and the Dolomite Risk Management Programmes of the DPW [Department of Public Works],' the report said. 'Due to lack of proper demand management and planning service delivery programmes of the Department of Public Works were negatively affected.'[24]

Amazingly, Zuma did not dispute the fact that he had indeed asked for some of the upgrades and had promised to pay for them. In her report she writes: 'The President did not dispute during the investigation that he told me on 11 August 2013 that he requested the building of a larger kraal, and that he was willing to reimburse the state for the cost thereof.'[25]

So the assault on Madonsela has, largely, been led by people who want to shield Zuma from repaying – something even he knows is the right thing to do. Yet virtually every minister and ANC lackey who has spoken out on this matter has authoritatively stated that Zuma is not liable. The mind boggles: the guilty party is prepared to pay some reparations, but his retinue will not hear of it and are singing louder than the choirmaster.

Of all the corruption scandals that have attended the new South Africa, Nkandla is the most eagerly watched and commented upon. It is the scandal of our time, the defining load that could yet break the camel's back. Unlike the arms deal, which was much larger in terms of money and scale, this is a scandal that involves one individual seen to enrich himself personally at the expense of the many poor around him.

Did Zuma, the freedom fighter and man of the people, not know what was going on under his nose at his own home? Did he not see the escalating costs, the transformation of his home from humble homestead to palace, complete with swimming pool and amphitheatre?

He knew. Indeed, Madonsela found that the man constantly complained about the rate at which things were being done, demanding speedy completion. 'The fact that he complained on more than one occasion of the lack of progress made with the project and the impact that it had on his private life and that of his family clearly shows that he was aware of the measures taken and that status of its implementation,' she wrote in 'Secure in Comfort'.[26]

The President of the republic knew that he was getting massive and undue benefits from the so-called security upgrades to his Nkandla homestead. Yet he still sits in office, comfortable and unafraid. It tells us something about the power of the masses in the new South Africa. Powerless, they seek heroes. They hope the ANC can find itself again, that it can rekindle the flame that made its principles the template for all liberation struggles on the African continent. That movement, though, is busy with other things. It is engaged on a short- and long-term game. In the end, it wants to destroy one of its most beautiful creations, the Public Protector's office, while for now it is out to discredit and get rid of Thuli Madonsela. It is using methods we have seen before in the Zuma survival strategy.

It is worth remembering that it was our current sports minister, Fikile Mbalula, who was the key player in the rise and rise of Zuma between 2005 and 2009. Mbalula was integral to Zuma's 'Stalingrad' strategy: frustrate, stall and challenge every small move by the state, the judiciary and ANC internal processes to keep Zuma from facing corruption charges.[27]

With Mbalula at the helm of a then functional ANC Youth League, Zuma's nemeses within the ANC were frustrated at each and every point by the diminutive, energetic Mbalula. Decisions to suspend Zuma, for example, were nullified by Mbalula and a rising Nathi Mthethwa, who was later handsomely rewarded with Cabinet positions (first police, then arts and culture) he can neither handle nor deserves.

In 2007, when Zuma came closest to facing the music, the ANC extraordinarily decided at its conference to disband the Scorpions – the investigative unit that had amassed the evidence of corruption on Zuma – in a move led by Mbalula and others. The justice committees in Parliament moved with startling speed, and within a year the Scorpions were no more.[28]

Yunus Carrim and Maggie Sotyu, the two MPs who delivered this result – despite widespread condemnation of the move – were also handsomely rewarded with Cabinet seats when Zuma ascended to power in 2009. Mbalula was also rewarded with a deputy ministry in 2009 and full ministry thereafter.[29]

All this was done to protect Zuma and to ensure that he does not see the inside of a courtroom, let alone a cell. It worked.

The Stalingrad strategy has been hauled out again. Zuma's litany of scandals will not stop, so it is once again time to protect him. Every little detail, every little legal loophole, every political fissure, will be exploited to ensure that the ANC president does not face the music.

This time the strategy is firmly aimed at Madonsela.

Following the devastating findings by Madonsela on the Nkandla looting, both the ANC in Parliament and government entities have ratcheted up the noise around Madonsela. The trend has been similar to the noises we heard as the Scorpions' noose tightened around Zuma in the late 2000s. At the time the unit's leaders were investigated and followed by intelligence agents. Their telephones were tapped. ANC politicians jumped to stand on podiums and denounce the unit.[30]

Now it is happening to Madonsela. This is because she has been tough, fearless, straight and fair. She has endeared herself to a public that is tired of corruption in the public sector. At last, many have sighed, here is someone who stands up for the little guy.

The ANC does not like that one bit. More importantly, the ANC does not like it when state and other agencies start investigating one Jacob Zuma. The ANC gets out its guns for agencies that do that.

Hence the assault on Madonsela. Deputy Minister of Justice John Jeffery accused her of ignoring recommendations of the justice oversight committee, of failing to provide detailed reports on her work, and of overstepping her powers.[31]

In 2014, as the release of the Nkandla report loomed, ANC chief whip Stone Sizani accused Madonsela of trying to create the impression that the President and the ruling party were trying to evade accountability on Nkandla.[32] Madonsela had previously made recommendations to Parliament that it resolve where Public Protector reports involving the ethical conduct of the President should be submitted. Parliament had not done so.

Then ANC secretary-general Gwede Mantashe weighed in, saying 'the confusion [Madonsela] displayed when she said she did not know where to take the interim report worked on the psyche of the public in a way that reflected negatively on the President. She has handled it in a manner that suggests that she is an interested party.'[33]

And so it has been. Not a day goes by without an attack, a smear or a stratagem being advanced to discredit Madonsela both personally and professionally. The Stalingrad strategy is in motion, all in defence of one man: Jacob Gedleyihlekisa Zuma.

What is really shameful here is that the ANC is essentially turning its back on its own, poor, electorate. When Minister of Public Works Thulas Nxesi held a press conference in Pretoria on 27 January 2013 to explain away the Nkandlagate mess he, by all accounts, obfuscated and lied. Yet Nxesi ignored the one really huge scandal in front of him. He totally ignored it, though it was breaking wind in his face and begging for attention.

The scandal is line five of the findings section of Nxesi's press release. It says: 'The investigation has found that the amount paid by the state to date [for President Jacob Zuma's Nkandla home] is R206 420 644.37.'[34]

Read that again. In this country, where so many of our people are living in abject poverty and hunger visits schoolchildren and parents alike, the 'government of the people' spent R206 million on security upgrades for the presidential compound in his home village.

This is the scandal of our country: our leaders have forgotten that they lead a country of extreme poverty, and that it is obscene that so much money can be spent on just one man and his family. The real scandal is that there was no sense of shame, or even slight embarrassment, by the ministers assembled in Pretoria, or from Zuma himself.

The lack of shame, the belief by this administration and its acolytes that this is just fine – that is the scandal. It represents a fundamental loss of what makes us different from the kleptocratic leaders of this world. We are lost as long as this government, its ministers and all our people believe that it is right, that it is not to be questioned, when R206 million is spent on just one man. Nxesi probably does not realise it, but his failure to question why we need to spend R206 million on fortifying the house of a leader says more about him as a central committee member of the SACP and his loss of a moral and ethical compass.

Nxesi then added a fillip to the whole thing by suggesting that in fact the state was doing us all a favour by revealing the information it did. Then, incredibly, he asserted that Zuma did not know the gross escalation of costs to his own home. Firstly, what homeowner sits and watches his house grow, and grow, and grow and does not ask any questions about how and why this is being done? Either Zuma is a very incurious human being, who cares nothing for his own home or his finances, or we are being lied to.

In fact, the story of Nkandla is the story of how we ARE being lied to. Both *City Press* and the *Mail & Guardian* have in the past published documents showing that Zuma was informed of major aspects of the Nkandla homestead's progress.[35]

The story of Nkandla is the story of how low we have come as a people, as a country and as a government. It illustrates that we were lying to ourselves, all those years ago, when we South Africans would point at others and say we will never be like that. We are no better.

We are no better until one comes to the door of Thuli Madonsela, the soft-spoken woman who shows South Africa that it is possible to walk away from the herd, that it is possible and right to stand by principle, that those who make the loudest noises are not always right, that our Constitution is worth standing up for.

When she was selected as one of *Time* magazine's Most Influential People of 2014, former Central Bank of Nigeria governor Lamido Sanusi wrote in her citation: 'Thuli Madonsela is an inspirational example of what African public officers need to be. Her work on constitutional reform, land reform and the struggle for the protection of human rights and equality speaks for itself. As South Africa's public protector, with her ability to speak truth to power and to address corruption in high places, Madonsela has been outstanding.

'To speak about corruption in high places is often subversive and always embarrassing. The machinery of state can be called upon to intimidate or even destroy and eliminate whistle-blowers. It therefore requires extraordinary courage and patriotism to do what Thuli Madonsela has done. Yet in standing up for the truth as she sees it, she has assured herself a place in the history of modern South Africa and among the tiny but growing band of African public servants giving us hope for the future of our continent.'[36]

It is in this that I take heart. She is not alone. She is not the first, and she walks in the illustrious steps of Mandela and others. Even now, she continues to walk that principled road and believe in the goodness of all of us.

'The ones [politicians] that are attacking us are doing so because of fear, but it's fear of the unknown. I am a South African and I want South Africa to continue to be seen as a great country because despite our mistakes, I really think we're a great country and I am not just saying that for the cameras,' she told City Press in 2014.

'So if people see South Africa as a confused and dysfunctional democracy, I sink with South Africa, my children sink, my children's children sink.'[37]

This is really where the difference lies. Patriotism does not lie in covering up corruption. It does not lie in keeping quiet when bad men and women lay waste to your country. It does not lie in protecting a flawed leader as he hops from one scandal to the other. This is what many ANC leaders are doing. They have chosen to keep quiet, to hold their tongues and still their righteous hearts, as their movement and their country is stolen by one terrible leader.

Many of us, however, prefer the bravery and patriotism of Thuli Madonsela. We prefer men and women who speak out, who know that silence is the first step towards ruin. We prefer those who stand up for the small man and woman, the ordinary boy and girl, the poor and downtrodden, those who have no money and power to help them along in a cruelly unequal world.

My hope comes from the fact that she is not the only one. In many parts of South Africa, a Madonsela rises every day. They speak, without fear and without consideration of the odds they face, because they know they stand for what is right. There are many of them: whistle-blowers and civil servants and NGO workers and activists and lawyers and ordinary, uneducated men and women. They are the people who mob her in the streets, who ask her what she wants to do next.

They know what she is. She is a hero. Crucially, though, she is nourishing the seeds of heroism that lie deep inside all of us. She is awakening the giant that is the people of South Africa.

Thuli Madonsela. Hero. And she is just beginning.

13
The Fantastic Plan on the Shelf

'To achieve great things, two things are needed:
a plan, and not quite enough time.'
– attributed to Leonard Bernstein (quote origin unknown)

Flush from his election victory in the 2009 election, President Jacob Zuma called a press conference on 10 May and announced a major restructuring of the Cabinet. He said, in light of his commitments to the people of South Africa, he 'wanted a structure that would enable us to achieve visible and tangible socio-economic development within the next five years'.

First, he announced a bigger Cabinet. Under Nelson Mandela South Africa had 27 ministries. Mbeki had grown it to 28. Zuma then grew it to 34 and grew it again in 2014 to 35 ministerial portfolios, with an equal number of deputy ministers.

There was one new, key, announcement. The financial markets and political commentators had anticipated that he would retain Trevor Manuel, the revered finance minister under Mbeki, in some or other portfolio. Zuma did not disappoint. Although he appointed the former tax chief Pravin Gordhan to the finance portfolio, a move that was welcomed, he announced that Manuel would be moved to the Presidency in a new, strategic position.

'Following extensive research on international models on how governments in other parts of the world plan and monitor performance, we have decided to establish a National Planning Commission which will be based in the Presidency. The NPC will be responsible for strategic planning for the country to ensure one National Plan to which all spheres of government would adhere.

'This would enable us to take a more comprehensive view of socio-economic development in the country.'[1]

The idea of a national planning commission had been brewing for a long time. The proposal to launch it was presented by the SACP to the ANC around 2005.[2] At the time the SACP and Cosatu were incensed by the ANC's implementation of the Growth, Employment and Redistribution (Gear) macroeconomic policy.

The NPC was an attempt by the left to wrest control of macroeconomic policy from the Presidency under Mbeki and, crucially, from the National Treasury under Manuel at the time. The SACP's intention was that a permanent NPC would have oversight over the National Treasury and all other government ministries and would therefore steer policy towards a leftist agenda. At the time of Zuma's rise as ANC president at Polokwane, the most likely candidate touted for the new ministry of national planning was the SACP secretary-general, Dr Blade Nzimande. However, under pressure to show that the new NPC was not some communist attempt to bring back Big Government and central planning of the Soviet type, Zuma appointed Manuel to the post instead.[3]

This job was a big deal. The NPC that Manuel was tasked with guiding was made up of 26 people, drawn largely from outside government, with members being selected for their expertise in key areas. Manuel's number two on the commission was Cyril Ramaphosa.

The NPC's mandate was clear. In its diagnostic report, released in June 2011, it said that by 2030 the country needed to eliminate income poverty. 'In other words, it must reduce the proportion of households with a monthly income of below R419 (US$42.2) a person (in 2009 prices) from 39 per cent to 0 per cent. And secondly, it must reduce inequality – the Gini coefficient, a measure of income disparity, should fall from 0.69 to 0.6,' reported government website mediaclubsouthafrica.

'This will be achieved by increasing employment from 13 million in 2010 to 24 million in 2030; raising per capita income from R50 000

(US$5 000) in 2010 to R120 000 (US$12 100) by 2030; increasing the share of national income of the bottom 40 per cent from 6 per cent to 10 per cent; establishing a competitive base of infrastructure, human resources and regulatory frameworks; ensuring that skilled, technical, professional and managerial posts better reflect the country's racial, gender and disability makeup, and many other goals.

'An important focus of the NDP is to unite South Africans around a common programme that will enhance the Constitution's vision of a united, prosperous, non-racial and non-sexist society.'[4]

The National Development Plan (NDP) is a complex document that runs to some 484 pages, but key to it is the call for decisive policy moves from government leaders and a call for citizens to be encouraged to be active in their own development. The plan says that while the state 'must actively support and incentivise citizen engagement', citizens should actively seek opportunities for advancement, learning, experience and opportunity; work together with others in the community to advance development, resolve problems and raise the concerns of the voiceless and marginalised; and hold the government, business and all leaders in society accountable for their actions.

'The country we seek to build by 2030 is just, fair, prosperous and equitable. Most of all, it is a country that each and every South African can proudly call home. It is up to all South Africans to play a role in fixing the future,' it says.

'By 2030 we must be able to declare that no South African lives below a poverty line and we can fix that line,' said Manuel.[5]

By many accounts, this is a plan that is credible, embraced by virtually everyone in South Africa and viewed as most likely to lead to a better, more equitable and prosperous country. Of all the parties represented in Parliament, a staggering 93 per cent have backed the NDP, according to Mapungubwe Institute for Strategic Reflection head and ANC national executive committee member Joel Netshitenzhe. Only Julius Malema's EFF finds the plan totally unacceptable.

So why, then, since its release has South Africa seemed to prevaricate on its implementation? Why, if this is such a fabulous plan, aren't we growing at the rate we should be?

The NDP's goal is for GDP to grow by 5.4 per cent per annum, meaning that by 2030 the economy will be 2.7 times its size in 2010. By 2030 unemployment will decrease to 6 per cent while the labour force participation rate will increase from 54 per cent to 65 per cent.

Yet, three years later, many of the policies to achieve these goals have not been put in place. Why not? At its Mangaung elective conference, in December 2012, the ANC endorsed the NDP as its key policy for the transformation of the South African economy. The adoption of the plan was hailed by business and analysts as potentially the solution to South Africa's structural challenges. However, it has subsequently come under intense attack from Cosatu and the SACP.

Will the ANC continue to bow to pressure from its alliance partners, particularly ahead of the 2019 national elections, and abandon the plan outright or will it be diluted to such an extent that it becomes meaningless?

The NDP's key architect, former finance minister Trevor Manuel, has bowed out of government and has since 2012 not sat in the ANC's powerful national executive committee. His deputy, Cyril Ramaphosa, faces challenges from the KwaZulu-Natal faction of the party and is treated with suspicion by the party's alliance partners. The plan lacks strong political backing, as President Zuma is likely to seek a consensual, accommodationist way ahead.[6]

The sharpest differences between the ANC and its allies around the NDP lie in the proposals that envisage a high-growth economy, creation of medium-quality jobs, labour market deregulation and stimulation of SMMEs. Within the tripartite alliance, Cosatu wants the structure, and indeed the entire NDP, done away with. The SACP, on the other hand, wants a left-leaning (as opposed to the current technocratic entity) NPC that would be able to rewrite and refocus the NDP.[7]

For the ANC there are key considerations as it tries to implement a plan that is lauded by its business allies and railed against by its own comrades. The key drivers for the ANC's ability to move strongly ahead with the NDP's implementation are as follows:

Election 2016 and 2019: The ANC needs Cosatu on side for decisive victories in the 2016 and 2019 elections. Within Cosatu, attitudes towards the NDP are varied, with the now-expelled Numsa having been a vociferous critic while the embattled NUM – having undergone a traumatic leadership change – takes an accommodationist line that is slightly similar to that of its main policy influencer, the SACP. However, the increasingly strong public sector unions (notably Sadtu and Nehawu) see the NDP's call for a disciplined and professional civil service as a threat and are adamant about blocking the passage of such initiatives.[8]

The key question is how much the ANC will compromise on the NDP to secure full backing by Cosatu in the looming elections. Given that the ANC got reduced support in ALL provinces except KwaZulu-Natal in both the 2009 and May 2011 elections, the party needs Cosatu's continued support and is thus vulnerable to the union federation's pressure. To secure Cosatu support in vulnerable major metropoles such as Tshwane, Johannesburg, Port Elizabeth and Ekurhuleni, the ANC will most likely go easy on contentious aspects of the NDP, particularly on the call for a professionalised civil service – given the strength of public sector unions in Cosatu.

Ideological divide: The authors of the NDP tried to be as non-ideological as possible. However, the current battles inside the Cabinet – and in the tripartite alliance – are largely ideological. Inside Cabinet, the left is represented by economic planning minister Ebrahim Patel and trade and industry minister Rob Davies, while the more mainstream view is represented by finance minister Nhlanhla Nene and local government minister Pravin Gordhan. They represent very different worldviews, and the views of Cosatu and the SACP versus the mainstream ANC reflect this divide.[9]

Public sector unions: Public sector unions are set to clash with government in what may be the most high-profile noise around the plan. The NDP envisages a lean, professional and capable civil service. The unions (Nehawu, Sadtu and others) are determined to oppose these moves. That these unions have now become the nexus of Cosatu poses an even bigger problem for the ANC government.[10]

Investor sentiment: Given the negative publicity South Africa has received internationally in recent years, the ANC may try to push through reforms envisaged by the NDP in order to project itself as a capable government. This may yield positive results and may stave off negative sentiment and possible further negative action from the ratings agencies Fitch, S&P and Moody's.[11]

The NDP as a blueprint for South Africa is therefore on a knife-edge. Several scenarios present themselves, and whichever one our leaders choose will have a massive impact on where South Africa will be in 2030. There are four scenarios for the NDP today:

Scenario One (Positive): In this scenario, changes occur to the NDP proposals, but the changes are not substantial. The most important victory in this scenario would be the chapters on the economy and the proposals for a steep acceleration in job creation, with 11 million new jobs created through entrepreneurship and creation of small and medium-sized enterprises (SMMEs) by 2030. In this scenario, the political leadership, particularly President Zuma, becomes a champion of the plan and energetically throws its weight behind its implementation. Implementation begins immediately. This was the scenario envisaged by the markets and was echoed by Fitch Ratings in January 2013 after endorsement of the NDP by the ANC at its Mangaung conference and the election of Cyril Ramaphosa to the deputy presidency of the party.[12]

Chances for this outcome: 10 per cent

Scenario Two (Middling to Positive): Contestation around the NDP intensifies and the ANC makes crucial concessions to Cosatu and the SACP, particularly on the job creation, SMMEs, labour market regulation and economic policy proposals contained in the plan. Although some of the proposals are retained, the plan lacks the controlling ideas of high growth, job creation and entrepreneurship that guide the rest of the plan. In this scenario macroeconomic policy continues to be contested terrain (with the Industrial Policy Action Plan [Ipap], New Growth Path [NGP] and others coming to the fore) and economic growth stutters along at less than 2.5 per cent per annum as it is already doing. This is not enough to stimulate job creation, and leaves South Africa a stable but structurally flawed country. This scenario holds for at least nine years, when I project a more coherent and decisive leadership may emerge to lead South Africa after the 2024 election.

Chances for this outcome: 55 per cent

Scenario Three (Middling to Negative): In this scenario, the NDP becomes mired in factional battles inside the ANC and among its allies. Leaders fail to take action, and summit after summit vows to rejig the plan. The ANC and government will establish task teams to review its clauses, and it will lose momentum except for the implementation of a few of its proposals. In this scenario, macroeconomic policy is dominated by bureaucratic, left-leaning interventions such as the NGP and Ipap. Job creation and economic growth stall steadily, business struggles and the civil service and a bloated and corrupt government become the main source of new jobs. South Africa slides slowly in most indicators.

Chances for this outcome: 25 per cent

Scenario Four (Negative): The NPC is centralised with a permanent office dominated by the ANC's leftist allies. The original intent of the NPC as envisaged by the SACP (that National Treasury is marginalised) materialises and this entity becomes a central planning tool.

187

Macroeconomic policy becomes statist and driven from the NPC and its ministry and leads to a state-led, bureaucratic path that becomes mired in socialist politics. In this scenario, the NDP becomes a total shadow of its present self and South Africa follows a route that may not be dissimilar to many socialist countries. This is the absolute down scenario and accords with the scenario of a failing state.

Chances for this outcome: 10 per cent

My view is that we are now firmly set on Scenario Three. The greatest challenge for the ANC in implementing the proposals in the NDP is that the glaring ideological contradictions within the party and in its alliance with the SACP and Cosatu will continue to hobble any policy it puts on the table. The NDP's boldness is a threat to large chunks of this alliance, and without a decisive break from these elements it is unlikely to be implemented.

The only way, therefore, to get the NDP back on track lies in decisive leadership. What is needed is an ANC leadership that will boldly say that it is implementing all aspects of the NDP and that it is doing so vigorously. With a clear mandate of 62 per cent of the vote, and overwhelming parliamentary endorsement of the NDP, clearly what is needed is a leadership corps that can take the bull by the horns.

That, unfortunately, is not happening at the moment. President Zuma has, instead of fully backing the NDP, allowed two new and divergent plans, the NGP by Ebrahim Patel and the Ipap by Rob Davies, to flourish. Ann Bernstein, executive director of the Centre for Development and Enterprise, and David Kaplan, Professor of Business Government Relations at the University of Cape Town, have written that 'it is in the national interest for the government to resolve the differences (between the NDP, Ipap and the NGP) and make clear policy choices'.

Bernstein and Kaplan point out that the three plans are not compatible with each other. 'Consider, for example, the objectives of the three policies,' they wrote in *Business Day* following research by the CDE. 'Ipap's goals are reasonably standard fare for an industrial policy – expand and diversify exports, improve the economy's technological base and so on. But the only aggregate quantified target set in the document (unusual for industrial policies in that it relates to employment creation) is that, according to Trade and Industry Minister Rob Davies, Ipap will create 2.45 million jobs, directly and indirectly, by 2020.

'The NGP also emphasises jobs but, because of its wider ambit, it promises a lot more of them – nearly 5 million by 2020. Like Ipap, the NGP offers no other metrics against which its success is to be judged, suggesting that employment creation is its overriding objective.

'Like the other documents, the NDP emphasises that employment growth is key to resolving the country's challenges, and it also sets goals – 5.9 million new jobs by 2020 and another 5 million by 2030.

'Unlike the other documents, however, the NDP suggests that growing employment depends critically on securing other economic objectives – especially more rapid economic growth.

'Accordingly, the NDP sets a range of quantitative goals that, it says, must be achieved: between 2011 and 2030 it would like to see investment grow at a rate of 15 per cent a year, exports grow at 6 per cent a year and output growth of 5.4 per cent a year. The different economic goals and their time frames are not insignificant.'[13]

The list of contradictions between the three plans continues in the same vein. In the meantime, ordinary men and women wait for leadership from Zuma and his Cabinet. However, pretty much like the tripartite alliance, these leaders are engaged in petty point-scoring, pussyfooting around the real issues, and no real progress is made.

The writing of the NDP is one of the most significant achievements of the Zuma administration. For decades he will be remembered for setting up this institution of great men and women, who gave us a clear, implacable plan for us to make our country great for our children and their children.[14]

If he does not show leadership and begin following its recommendations, though, it will also be known down the ages as the great plan that never saw the light of day. It is not the NDP's fine words that our children's children will want to admire. They will want lights, water, comfort and dignity.

We have a chance to give it to them in just a decade. Let's do it.

14

Damascus

'Immediately, something like scales fell from Saul's eyes,
and he could see again.'
– Acts 9:18

Pessimism is a dead-end street. Analysis of our current malaise must lay the basis for the opposite of pessimism, and that means finding solutions for our deep and seemingly intractable problems. Proper and rigorous analysis lays the foundation for positive action. Positive action can happen only when there is optimism: optimism for the future; optimism for my beloved country; optimism in the ability of my people to once again make fools of the doomsayers.

Every country needs a vision. From that vision a plan must be developed and then implemented. It must be implemented implacably, resolutely, with a clear-headedness and ruthlessness that illustrates to all across the globe our hunger for the eradication of the poverty, inequality and corruption that stalks our land.

Before all this, though, there must come a realisation that the great, hulking plane called South Africa has begun its approach to the emergency runway. There must be a realisation that the landing mechanism does not work. There must be a realisation that we need more 'lift' before the craft ploughs into the ground. And we are coming in fast. If nothing is done, we shall all perish.

What is to be done? This formulation by Vladimir Ilyich Lenin in 1901 now confronts South Africa. What is to be done?

The story of the new South Africa is the story of leadership: courageous, values-based, implacable, authentic, resolute and humane leadership. We would not be where we are today if it were not for the great displays of leadership of the founding fathers of the new South Africa: a flawed, impossible-to-love FW de Klerk on the one hand, and a visionary Nelson Mandela on the other. Both men had to strip themselves naked and become servants of the greater good to show the leadership that was needed to take South Africa from the horror it was in 1990 to the democracy it is today.

Their leadership would have been for nothing if South Africans had not been willing to make some tough compromises – to give something of themselves for all of us to succeed. There were no happy negotiators in the 1990s in South Africa, no happy supporters. ANC supporters felt short-changed. National Party members felt powerless, that they had lost everything.

The first of our solutions therefore has to start here: with the voters. They have to find their voice again. They have to find the courage to send a powerful message to their leaders that they are not to be taken for granted. They need to send a message.

What does South Africa need to do now, urgently, to give South Africa the 'lift' it needs to avoid disaster? I have some suggestions. They are not exhaustive, but perhaps we can begin that journey back to greatness by debating, and implementing, some of them.

1. After Two Decades, it is Time to Vote for Delivery, not History

ANC deputy president Cyril Ramaphosa kicked off the party's 2014 election campaign by declaring: 'The time for talking is over. We want action, and action man Jacob Zuma will ensure that this country moves forward.'[1]

What if the 'Action Man' continues on the same inactive and uninspired path he has trod since 2009?

The greatest act of love anyone who cherishes the ANC can perform for the party in the upcoming elections is to reduce its electoral majority. They should vote for an opposition party, any opposition party.

They should not do so because they have fallen out of love with the ANC. For many, such a thing is near impossible. The ANC is not just in their blood; it is their blood.

They should do so because what the ANC has built, the ANC seems hell-bent on destroying. To protect the ANC from tarnishing, stamping on and destroying its own glorious achievement, they should send the party a love letter. It should be a love letter that the party's leaders can understand. It is a love letter that says 'If you continue to treat us, the voters, and our party in this manner, then we shall kick you out of power'.

These South Africans can remind the party that they are servants of the people, not traditional leaders. They should reduce the ANC's majority to just over 50 per cent.

Most of the opposition can be unlovable, and some are so downright objectionable it is impossible to conceive of being drawn to vote for them. Why would you vote for a party as right-wing and intolerant as the African Christian Democratic Party? Why would you vote for a party with such a predilection for infighting as the Congress of the People?

Then there are the parties that are merely irrelevant. Can the Pan Africanist Congress of Azania – or its numerous offshoots – say why they still exist? What about Azapo, a party that comes with so much admirable history and intellectual rigour, and yet is so feeble and facile today?

The ANC's grip on the psyche of many South Africans – black and white – is loosening, but its hold on many hearts remains so tight that it is anathema even to think about putting a cross anywhere else but near the ANC's colours on the ballot paper.

South Africans vote ANC despite the horrific education system the ANC has perpetuated for the past two decades. In our heads we know that this is wrong. Many of us vote ANC despite the looting in Nkandla and the cynicism at the heart of our parliamentary politics.[2]

It was therefore interesting to see Zackie Achmat, a long-standing ANC member, founder of the Treatment Action Campaign (TAC) and a hero of the HIV/Aids struggle, saying that he will give up his ANC membership.

'If Zuma is elected, I don't want to be a member of the ANC any more,' Achmat was quoted as saying in 2013. 'The party needs a leader with integrity, someone above reproach, who doesn't hesitate to take action against corruption … the President is indefensible, and the ANC is no longer the party I joined in 1990.'[3]

To show his displeasure, Achmat and those who hold his view should vote – for anyone else. However, many will stay at home at election time instead of exercising their right to vote – the single most important time in which to register their displeasure.

They will stay at home because they cannot imagine themselves voting for any other party. Then they will wonder why the ANC can be so arrogant as to build one man a house for R246 million while children learn under trees. It will be because they did not vote, and if those who are unhappy about the ANC leaders' shenanigans do not vote then they will get the leaders they deserve.

It is time for South Africans, particularly those who harbour a deep love for the ANC, to be educated in tactical voting. According to Wikipedia, 'tactical voting (or strategic voting or sophisticated voting or insincere voting) occurs, in elections with more than two candidates, when a voter supports a candidate other than his or her sincere preference in order to prevent an undesirable outcome … For example, in a simple plurality election a voter might sometimes gain a "better" outcome by voting for a less preferred but more generally popular candidate.'[4]

A better outcome than what we have today, for the ANC as a party and for the country, is one whereby our leaders know that they can lose power. It is an outcome whereby our leaders lose the arrogance of a huge majority and start enjoying the humility – and pride – that comes with knowing that they have been asked to serve for five years only. Not, as Zuma believes and has said out loud, until Jesus comes.[5]

2. A Capable, Merit-Based State Led by
Visionary Political Leadership

Some countries walk along nonchalantly. Others crawl along like snails, while still others run like the wind. China is the perfect example of a sprinter. In just 30 years it has transformed itself from global non-entity to an economic and political giant. Today its economic growth is pedalling along at an incredible 7 per cent – and that's called a weak performance by the country's leaders. Of course, the world's second largest economy is currently facing its own problems as factory activity shrinks and concerns rise that losses on the Shanghai stock exchange mean that China's hitherto runaway growth is faltering.

Still, imagine if South Africa's economy grew at 7 per cent!

Alas, we are a snail. South Africa's economy grew at a mere 1.5 per cent in 2014, and in 2015 we will be lucky if we get to the 2 per cent projected by finance minister Nhlanhla Nene.[6] We are crawling.

There was a time when we were walking very fast and even breaking into a jog. The economy grew strongly between 2001 and 2008. We started making a dent in unemployment. The black (and white) middle class grew. The tills were ringing in shopping malls across the country. The good times were here.[7]

We were jogging along nicely. By 2006 our economic growth was nearly 6 per cent. What we needed to do was keep jogging at the same pace. Unfortunately we didn't.

In 2009 we stopped jogging. We started crawling. We started losing jobs. Confidence in our economy waned. Manufacturing slowed down. Our workers are striking more and more frequently. Something is going wrong.

We could spend the next five years blaming our government, the global crisis, South Africa's poor education system and a whole range of other factors. The blame game is, however, ultimately useless. We need solutions, and we need them fast.

Perhaps we should look to another country in Asia for answers. In March 2015 one of the world's most admired leaders, Lee Kuan Yew of

195

Singapore, died. When Lee took over the country of 1 million people in 1965 it was 'impoverished and disease-ridden'.

By the early 2000s, writes *Global* magazine, 'Singapore continues to sit on top of the global economic pile. This tiny state, with a population of just over five million, has once again been acknowledged by the World Bank as the best place in the world in which to do business (for the seventh consecutive year). With a per capita income of around US$61 000, it is also the world's richest non-resource based country,' the magazine said in 2013.[8]

What did Lee Kuan Yew do? It was not rocket science. First, he set out to build a merit-based government staffed by highly educated and capable technocrats. Political connections did not cut it. You got a job in government only if you had the education, the skill, the drive and the ability.

Second, he opened the country's arms to foreigners. Lee purposely went out of his way to teach Singaporeans to welcome skilled foreigners because only in that way would the country grow. The idea, he told his fellow countrymen, was that high-calibre people would create employment and pass on their skills.

Third, he made sure that the institutions of government worked. He was a stickler for the rule of law. No one was too high or too low – the law applied equally to everyone. Corruption was fought and defeated at every level.

Finally, his greatest push was to build a world-class public education system. Singapore had no mineral resources. It was a poor piece of sand. Its only wealth was its people – so he ensured that they were the best educated in the world.

The result is that Singapore today ranks top in the world in virtually every measurable category (income, health, education, quality of life).[9] It is a country that has sprinted up the rankings from being a nonentity to being one of the top three in the world.

We should learn from these sprinters.

3. Protect Our Great Constitution and its Institutions

Sometimes, too rarely perhaps, someone – maybe a thinker, a politician or a businessperson – puts their finger on it. They just say it, once, and the weight of their words just spreads, and spreads, and spreads and shakes everyone and everything around them.

In March 2015, US President Barack Obama spoke to a crowd gathered in Selma, Alabama, to commemorate the march 50 years ago in that town when blacks were brutalised by police in what came to be known as 'Bloody Sunday'. They were not demanding much: they wanted the right to vote. Obama gave a wonderful, moving speech, but the 'aha' moment of that speech was when he said that the most powerful word in the US Constitution is the word 'we'.

'We' is also the first word of the American Constitution. Obama went on to say that the Constitution is a document that all Americans strive to fulfil, to live up to its vision.[10]

I was struck by that. What Obama was saying, in wonder and awe, was that the American Constitution is a beautiful thing, an achievement so high that all of the US has spent the past 228 years trying to match it.

Our Constitution is, I venture, more beautiful and sets a higher bar for humanity than even the American Constitution does. It also starts with the word 'we' and it is magnificent. Read this out loud and be proud:

> We, the people of South Africa, recognise the injustices of our past;
> Honour those who suffered for justice and freedom in our land;
> Respect those who have worked to build and develop our country; and
> Believe that South Africa belongs to all who live in it, united in our diversity.[11]

Thus begins a document that constitutional lawyers across the globe read with awe. Many international experts say it is one of the best constitutions in the whole world, if not the best.

Here is where we differ with Obama, though. You see, the US President believes in lifting himself and his people up to meet the expectations of the country's Constitution. He does not want to change the Constitution. He wants his people to become as noble as it demands them to be.

Here in South Africa, every politician who sees a microphone complains about how the Constitution stops them from achieving something or the other. They never put themselves in the shoes of people like the late ANC constitutional expert Kader Asmal or retired Constitutional Court judge Albie Sachs, two of the key authors of the words quoted above. In my view, our founding fathers saw that we are capable of far greater things than we comprehend. They knew we are capable of far more than we perceive.

Our country is a mere baby compared to the US. We will face many more problems in the future than we have in the past 21 years. Destroying our Constitution, as so many of our politicians want, is not the answer.[12] The answer lies in a totally different path. It is in strengthening the Constitution we have adopted, hard as that may be to do. No one said it would be easy, but the South African Constitution is one of the keys to getting over our problems and building the kind of society we dreamt of 21 years ago, and can still build.

It is the society Nelson Mandela spoke of in his famous speech from the dock in 1964: 'I have cherished the ideal of a democratic and free society in which all persons live together in harmony and with equal opportunities. It is an ideal which I hope to live for and to achieve. But if needs be, it is an ideal for which I am prepared to die.'[13]

Yes, we can. And the Constitution is still our road map to that good society. We must defend it.

4. Take Proactive, Pro-Growth Measures to Tackle Inequality

I am my brother's keeper. I was reminded of this old saying while driving through Alexandra township in Johannesburg. I remembered

198

that Nelson Mandela once lived in that township. My uncles travelled to Johannesburg, like Mandela, in the 1950s and 1960s and lived in 'Township', as it was known, as they worked in the mines and factories around Johannesburg.

If there is anything that sums up South Africa's wide Gini coefficient (the measure of inequality in a country), it is Alexandra township and the rich suburb across the highway from it. Sandton is the wealthiest square mile on the African continent. Alexandra township can count itself among the poorest. Alexandra is certainly among the most squalid.

There is no need to feel guilty about being wealthy or comfortably off, dear reader. There is something, however, that always niggles: can we do more to make the lives of the poor better? This is where I think politicians need to think beyond asking us to be more charitable. To defeat poverty and inequality we need more than just handouts to the poor. We need a systematic assault on inequality itself.

One of the big debates that gripped South Africa in the mid-1990s was whether South Africa needed a 'reconstruction tax', or 'wealth tax'. This would have been a higher tax on the wealthy (at the time mainly white) that would have gone directly towards the rebuilding of the country after the inequality and poverty caused by apartheid. At the time, President Nelson Mandela chose not to impose such a tax. Instead, the government raised value-added tax (VAT) from 10 per cent to 14 per cent, thereby raising the money that would see South Africa reduce its huge apartheid debt. So successful was this move that by the late 2000s our country was hailed worldwide as a model of how a country can reduce its debt and set itself on the path to prudent fiscal management and prosperity.

Today, South Africa faces a new set of challenges. Following the global financial crisis, South Africa's extremes of inequality, unemployment and poverty are becoming increasingly stark. Should we now aggressively target the wealthy through taxes to raise the money to help the poor? Should, metaphorically speaking, Sandton be taxed to make Alexandra a better place?

In the 1990s I was one of the few who urged our leaders to impose a wealth tax. As a middle-class worker then, I was prepared to pay higher taxes because I sincerely believed that I am my brother's keeper. I believe many South Africans hold the same view.

Life is a give-and-take, though. Today our media are full of stories of corruption, of public officials caught with their grubby hands in the till. There are many stories of the same corrupt individuals not going to jail but being rewarded with even more powerful posts.

This is the key obstacle to why many rich people don't feel that 'I am my brother's keeper'. If government showed a greater commitment to fighting corruption, and actually using the massive amounts it collects from taxpayers every month, there would be a feeling that our money was well used. Nowhere in the world do taxpayers want to feel that they are taken for fools and that their money is used wastefully and to line the pockets of politicians.

That is the bargain South Africans have to strike. Government needs to be seen to have a vision, a plan (the National Development Plan already exists and needs to be implemented) and a commitment to implementing that plan.

If all those elements exist many individuals would feel confident in calling for a tax on the wealthy. My humble view is that many wealthy South Africans do want to make a contribution and would not mind a higher tax if it was seen to be used prudently.

I am my brother's keeper. We are all our brothers' and sisters' keepers. Government needs to come to the party and we can raise some serious cash for South Africa.

5. Stop Obsessing About Mineral Wealth. Obsess About Values-Based Leadership

One of the most popular theories of international politics is that of the 'resource curse': the more a country is blessed with mineral wealth, the more likely it is to do badly in terms of democracy and economic growth. Economists refer to it as the 'paradox of plenty'.[14]

200

On our continent, Nigeria was for many decades a poster child for the paradox of plenty. Blessed with an abundance of oil, it was also cursed with coups, military dictators and kleptocrats. Its people never saw the wealth of their country. Instead, the wealth disappeared into the pockets of dictators.

In August 2014, for example, the United States government took control of more than US$450 million looted by former Nigerian dictator Sani Abacha and his associates after a court ruling directed that the money be returned to Lagos.[15] Between US$3 billion and US$5 billion of public money was looted during Abacha's regime between 1993 and 1998, according to Transparency International.

Is it, however, the presence of mineral wealth in a country that leads to the resource curse? Or is it something else? Some economists have tried to debunk the resource curse narrative, saying instead that it is the volatility in commodity prices, rather than abundance of resources, that has led to poor governance, corruption, low economic growth and general misery in many countries.

I think there is some credence to both theories, but they ignore a more powerful curse: the leadership curse. In my view, a visionary leadership can lift a country out of its misery whether that country is blessed with abundant resources or not. A visionary leadership can lead a country through the booms and busts of commodity prices and into steady economic growth.

Take Botswana, for example. This is a country that is abundantly blessed with diamonds. It doesn't have much else. Most of Botswana is just desert. However, it was also blessed with leadership. The diamond exploration and mining deal that Botswana's first post-colonial leader, Sir Seretse Khama, struck with De Beers ensured that the nation enjoyed the fruits of their mineral wealth. Botswana sent its young people across the globe to learn, built up its infrastructure, and oversaw an economy that grew consistently for more than 30 years. They had no wars, no dictatorships and no looting of the government purse.[16]

That is what leadership gives you. Singapore has never had any minerals. Yet, from the 1950s, it emphasised the education of its people beyond anything else. Today, its people enjoy one of the highest stand-ards of living in the world. This is a country that does not have a drop of oil or an ounce of gold. Yet it is one of the great successes of the world. It is all thanks to the visionary leadership of Lee Kuan Yew.[17]

You know by now where I am going with this. I was struck by the wailing of leaders from many oil-rich countries at the beginning of 2015 when the price of oil plummeted to record levels. Just a year before, these countries were swimming in cash while the world paid high prices for oil. They never stopped to ask: what happens when the oil price collapses?[18]

The challenge for the world, and for South Africa, today is to pro-duce and nurture the kind of leaders who can help us build prosperity without relying on our mineral wealth. South Africa, for example, has for decades been blessed with gold, diamonds, coal, platinum and other minerals. Yet, because of the absolutely shocking leadership of the apartheid regime, we live in the most unequal country in the world today.

Many obsess about our mineral wealth in South Africa. Of course they should. There is little or no equity in current ownership patterns. A quick glance at the world, however, amply illustrates that the bigger challenge is the one we don't talk about enough. It is the leadership curse. That is what we need to avoid.

6. It's the Economy, Stupid

One of the key problems we South Africans face is that we are still ruled by the heat and the emotion, the noise and the theatre, of poli-tics. We rate our politicians on their ability to deliver a speech and a quick put-down, instead of on just how much detail there is in their policies. We reward the loud and the showy while we ignore, and some-times even punish, the cerebral and analytical.

It is time to break with tradition. We are into our third decade of democracy. We are grown now. We need less noise from ourselves and our politicians. What is needed now is a more rigorous analysis of the cold, hard numbers.

It is in the numbers that we will know whether we are moving forwards or backwards. It is in a clear analysis of the numbers that we will be able to chart a way forward and build a vibrant democracy and economy to take us to 2050 and beyond.

So how are we doing, South Africa? Are we the country of our dreams or are we the nightmare that so many say we have become? What are the numbers that South Africans should consider as they prepare to vote in this great country's fifth democratic elections?

Neva Seidman Makgetla, the deputy director-general in the Department of Economic Development, wrote in the *Sunday Times*: 'The South African economy has grown since 1994 almost exactly at the average for middle-income economies excluding China – and three times as fast as in the 1980s. The *Financial Times* named South Africa the "African Country of the Future" for 2013–14. Given these indisputable successes, why is everyone so miserable?'[19]

It is a good question. Yet if we were to read political commentator Songezo Zibi in the *Financial Mail* of the same week, we would have to pause and reflect on where we are going. Writing ahead of then finance minister Pravin Gordhan's Medium-Term Budget Policy Statement in late 2013, Zibi said: 'By almost every significant economic measure, the Zuma administration has failed: far from the millions of jobs Zuma promised, unemployment has grown. Economic growth targets have been cut, and cut, and cut again. SA sustained its first credit rating downgrade since democracy, public debt has almost doubled, more government institutions have received poor audits, delivery protests have increased, crime is up and SA has broken another record this year for strike duration. It's been a government performance record from hell.'[20]

Both commentators are absolutely right. The numbers that Makgetla quotes can be empirically proven. So can Zibi's. The problem is that we, as voters, treat the numbers that they have put in front of us the way politicians handle them. Imagine Makgetla's numbers in the hands of a gifted ANC politician who wants his party to be re-elected. Imagine Zibi's numbers in the hands of a DA politician who wants to wrest power from the ANC.

The beauty of numbers, though, is that they put power in the hands of the voter. If we, the voters, were to consider these two statements fully, we would realise that two time periods are at play. Makgetla wants us to consider the ANC's record since 1994 – and it speaks of success, no? Zibi is judging President Jacob Zuma's administration on its record since 2009 – and it is dismal, no?

Now, many shall come begging at your door over the next few elections. They want your vote. Don't give it to them because you like them, or your mother likes them, or they give a good speech, or they are so sexy. This is the noise of politics. It is of no use to you.

Instead, ask them about their record of delivery. Ask them to give you examples of where and how nationalisation has worked. Ask them about the numbers. Tell them the days of emotions, speeches and oratory are over.

Tell them it is about what is in your, and your children's, pockets. Tell them: show me the numbers.

7. Back to School

It's not rocket science. It really is not. We might be tempted to look back on the past five years and think of the deep problems we face and conclude that they cannot be solved. We might be tempted to think that the economy will remain moribund, that unemployment will stay as high as it is and that inequality will worsen.

None of that is true. The beauty of South Africa is that our problems may be deep but the solution is not as far off as many may think. What we need to turn the tide is leadership that is committed to implementing the solution.

Let me start with this solution. It is simple. We need to give our children and our young quality education right from primary school all the way to technical colleges and universities. We cannot continue, more than two decades after we tasted democracy, to avert our eyes from the truth. The quality of our education is terrible. A Centre for Development and Enterprise report, for example, points out that only 25 per cent of South African schools are 'mostly functional', and those that are – even in the private education sector – lag behind international standard norms for developing nations. Grade 6 mathematics teachers in poor and rural areas are often unable to answer the test questions set for their pupils. Heartbreakingly, fewer than 50 per cent of students who start primary school reach matriculation exams.[21]

This is the great hole at the heart of our country. Without the plumbers, artisans, welders, engineers, social workers, nurses, doctors and many others, South Africa is going nowhere. We can shout as much as we like about the National Development Plan, but without these educated people there will be no new infrastructure, no new health system and no revival of the manufacturing sector.

'The evidence is unequivocal: education saves lives and transforms lives, it is the bedrock of sustainability,' Unesco director-general Irina Bokova said in September 2014. 'This is why we must work together across all development areas to make it a universal right.'[22]

For South Africa the issue is clear: it is not the resources under our soil that will make us free. It is our ability to exploit the wealth under us – be it gold, platinum, diamonds, shale gas or oil. To do that best, we need education. Quality education.

To get that, we have to make some tough calls. Key among these tough calls is to make sure that our teachers are the best in the world. To do that, we have to introduce standards, and by that I mean teachers have to pass the exams that children sit.

It is not rocket science. What it needs are leaders who are prepared to fight this battle and win it.

The truth is that our leaders are not dealing with the key issues facing us: unemployment and poverty. Our parliamentarians are not administering the one key, long-term solution available to us: quality education.

So for the next two decades I am not asking for much from each and every one of us. Let's give some money, or some time, to an education initiative in an impoverished area or school. Let's get involved. There are no silver bullets in life, but education seems to me to be the closest we can get to one.

8. Our Chance, Every Day, to Say No to Corruption

Step back for one moment and ask yourself two questions. When you die, what kind of country do you want your children to inherit? What kind of South Africa will our kids have to navigate in 2030?

You could be anyone. Say you are a small construction company owner in the capital city, Tshwane. You make relatively small deals – a few so-called RDP houses here, a hospital renovation there, and perhaps even a new office complex for a government department.

The government complex stretches you. It's a big contract. But you go through your address book and you call university mates and comrades and even your mother-in-law and finally put together technical partners and other skills and you pull it off.

There is a problem, though. In virtually every deal you have made you have been asked for a bribe. Remember the clerk at the municipality who called up out of the blue and told you that 'We have your invoice in front of us'? What, she asked, will you do to expedite payment?

You know the stories of companies going out of business because payments from municipalities and government departments arrived months, even years, late. Did you give a little gift? Did you give a 'cold drink'?

The interesting thing about the South African narrative is how we write and talk about issues, particularly corruption. Corruption is written up as if it is a government problem only. When we talk corruption, we talk about politicians who ask for and receive bribes.

We are never part of the narrative.

Yet we undoubtedly are. You see, we pay the bribes and we give the gifts. As we do it – and many of us do it, by the way – corruption becomes a culture. Every service, every transaction, has a premium. The government tender is inflated by 20 per cent to 50 per cent. It becomes more expensive. It becomes the norm. That is why we enthuse about good service and are shocked when we are not asked for a bribe. These things are no longer the culture.

So, what kind of country do you want your children to inherit? Do you want them to inherit a country where they – remember, you will be dead, senile or running around the retirement home – have to pay bribes for every service they get? Do you want them to have to battle for what is considered normal in many jurisdictions around the world?

The country I would like my – and your – children to inherit is a country of laws, a country of fairness and a country where they will not have to shell out 'a little gift' for everything they do. I have travelled in too many countries where everything is a hustle, where everything is predicated upon a 'gift' or a bribe. I do not want my children to wait in the queue while the child of the 'Big Man' is rushed to the front.

How will your children get a job? Will they get a job because of their education and what Martin Luther King, Jr, called 'the content of their character' or will they have to pay a bribe? Which country do you want your children to inherit from you in 2030?

So there is something we can do about this. If we want our children to inherit a country unlike the ones I have spoken about, then we have to stop doing things that turn bad practice into a culture. We can start by saying no when a traffic cop asks for a bribe. We should ask for the fine instead.

Many of us look to politicians to solve our problems, but, if we are to face the truth, the solutions lie with each and every one of us. So, next time you pay that bribe, ask yourself: what kind of country are you bequeathing your children, and their children after them?

9. Say This Again, and Again: Jobs, Jobs and More Jobs

I am sitting at a swanky new Sandton hotel, across the table from one of South Africa's most successful black entrepreneurs, and he says: 'I have been travelling across the country, meeting ordinary people. I am interested in one thing: Are they happy?'

The entrepreneur says that if the poor are unhappy, then he is unhappy. 'If they don't smile, then I cannot smile. No matter how much money I have stuffed in the bank, the truth is that if they become restless, if they riot, then we don't have a country and none of us can enjoy our wealth. The poor must have jobs, and that will make them happy.'

This is one of the key habits of successful countries: people have the dignity of jobs, and that leads to stability.

How are we doing on this score? The entrepreneur will not be happy. Unemployment is unsustainably high in South Africa. It has been getting worse since 2009.

Yes, there is a lot of noise about scandals such as Nkandla and the numerous Gupta family issues, but the real measure of the stability of South Africa will be whether the poor feel that their lives are getting better. In light of the staggering unemployment figures, my millionaire entrepreneur and the poor will realise that things are certainly not getting better.

In future South African elections, history will still remain a powerful force. For example, in 2014 the DA fired off its 'Know Your DA' campaign in which it told the electorate that it, too, or at least its leaders past and present, fought against apartheid. This was an attempt to wrest some of the 'liberation dividend' away from the ANC. Interestingly, the party released a picture of its icon, Helen Suzman, in an affectionate embrace with Nelson Mandela.[23] The ANC responded with its own attacks on the campaign and its controversial release of photographs and footage of President Zuma and other party leaders with a mute, ailing Mandela.[24]

The message is clear: the past matters in order to win elections, and these two formations are going to continue to battle over who owns the past – and they will use it to get your vote. It is worth saying to our politicians on both sides that those who cling to the past are generally those who have no plan, and no strategy or tactics, to forge forward into the future.

The second trend is about the young, employment and how both fit into a future for our country. Facing the future means dealing with the massive unemployment problem we have. This is something at which the ANC is failing significantly.

Coupled with the drip-drip of corruption scandals and those that seem to follow President Zuma and his private arrangements, it is a fair bet to say that the ANC will see its electoral support slipping from the 62 per cent the party received in 2014.

The key question for all of us, however, is the one that troubles our entrepreneur. Will the people continue to have a smile on their faces? We know that Tunisia, Egypt, Libya and many other countries that have imploded in recent times were plagued by one big problem: unemployment among the young. This too is our problem now.

We cannot sleep easy so long as this problem persists.

10. Implement the Plan You Have

We specialise in economic plans here in South Africa. From the RDP to Gear and the NGP, we love writing them and we love giving them names. The latest is the National Development Plan, which was crafted by Trevor Manuel and a panel of experts to give us a blueprint for the future.

It is an excellent piece of work and, if implemented, holds the key for a bright and prosperous South Africa. The NDP is an easy win: whoever is in power merely needs to implement it, not spend years and years talking about it. There is no opposition to it.

So why hasn't this glorious piece of work been implemented? We need to implement the plan we have.

11. A New Leadership Ethos

Every April, many across South Africa cast their minds back and remember Chris Hani, the fiery ANC and SACP leader who was murdered on 10 April 1993 by a right-wing assassin, Janusz Walus.

I remember that day with an extraordinary clarity. It was a Saturday morning when we got the news. A few of my colleagues at the *Star* and I went to Hani's East Rand home that afternoon. Fear and anger were in the air. What South Africa was building, and was on the verge of consummating – a consensual agreement to start a new democracy and a new country – was in peril. Across the country, young people said: this is war.

An eye for an eye, many said. Arm us and let us fight the apartheid government, others said. You could not blame them. Hani was the most militant, most hardline and most eloquent of the young cohort of leaders – including Cyril Ramaphosa and Thabo Mbeki – behind Nelson Mandela at the negotiating table. An attack on him was felt sorely, but his assassination? This was war.

An extraordinary thing happened, though. It is called leadership. President FW de Klerk knew that he was a powerless man. Nelson Mandela was the key to restoring calm and peace to the angry populace. And so it was agreed that Mandela would essentially do the deed that needed to be performed by a president.

Mandela went on television instead of De Klerk. He said: 'To the youth of South Africa we have a special message: you have lost a great hero. You have repeatedly shown that your love of freedom is greater than that most precious gift, life itself. But you are the leaders of tomorrow. Your country, your people, your organisation need you to act with wisdom. A particular responsibility rests on your shoulders.'[25]

Violence was averted. Exactly a year later South Africa went to the polls. More than 20 years later, we are here.

Hani was not a saint, but every year he is extolled as an exemplar of the most noble of ANC values. The same people who praise him will mostly likely, in their daily execution of their duties, be trampling on much of what he fought and died for.

Take the extraordinary deaths of 13 SANDF soldiers in the Central African Republic on 23 March 2013. They died far from home, in pain and without proper medical care, for a cause we don't know. We surely know they did not die for peace, or democracy, or some noble ideal. Depending on which minister you listen to, they died training a tinpot dictator's army or they died protecting our military equipment. They had only one medic. They had no air support, with the Rooivalk helicopter idling at home in a hangar while they were under attack.

We did not even provide them with the intelligence to at least take precautionary measures.[26]

Rubbing salt into the wound, President Jacob Zuma, responding to calls for a thorough investigation of the whole fiasco, told us: 'The problem in South Africa is that everyone wants to run the country ... There must also be an appreciation that military matters and decisions are not matters that are discussed in public, other than to share broader policy.'[27]

The name of Chris Hani is often hauled out to defend such drivel. We are told that we must 'defend the revolution' that he fought for, yet there will be no mention of the sheer contempt for openness, for constitutional democracy, that the President's utterances display.

In his television address to the nation in 1993, Mandela quoted Hani's words on his return to South Africa after 30 years of exile. Hani said: 'I have lived with death most of my life. I want to live in a free South Africa even if I have to lay down my life for it.'[28]

A free South Africa is a South Africa of accountability. It is certainly not enough to be told that soldiers die; the how matters to all of us. It is not enough to tell us that they fought heroically; the why is crucial for our continued belief in the system of democracy.

These are concepts that seem to be beyond our leaders in the presidency or in some of the ministries. Indeed, they seem to have forgotten that our struggle, the struggle of Chris Hani, was exactly about the preservation of the life of that young soldier dying a lonely death in the CAR – and the right of the citizenry to demand answers about it.

What am I calling for when I recall Hani and the leadership that saved our country after his brutal, senseless murder? I am calling for South Africans to find in themselves the courage to know when it is time to change their leaders. If the new ones don't work out, they can always bring back the devil they know.

Epilogue

On a Thursday afternoon in August 2012 a lone man carrying a plastic bag calmly walked up to the shiny glass doors of the headquarters of the ANC in central Johannesburg. He pulled a thick piece of wood out of the bag and began pounding the doors. The man, reportedly in his early thirties, raved that he could not find a job despite having a university degree.[1]

He was not the first, and certainly not the last, to rage at South Africa and its ruling party, which turned 100 that year. The unemployment rate in South Africa increased to 26.4 per cent in the first quarter of 2015 from 24.3 per cent in the fourth quarter of 2014, the highest rate since 2005.[2] Every day now we add one more angry young man, similar to that lone protestor in 2012, to the deep well of anger and frustration that is growing in South Africa.

Statistics South Africa says there are 8.7 million jobless men and women in the country. Why haven't they risen up like that young man? What makes them believe tomorrow will be better than today?

In February 2011 Moeletsi Mbeki, the well-known political economist, author and businessman, made a chilling call about our future. 'I can predict when South Africa's "Tunisia Day" will arrive. Tunisia Day is when the masses rise against the powers that be, as happened recently in Tunisia. The year will be 2020, give or take a couple of years. The year 2020 is when China estimates that its current minerals-intensive industrialisation phase will be concluded,' he wrote.

'For South Africa, this will mean the ANC government will have to cut back on social grants, which it uses to placate the black poor and to get their votes. China's current industrialisation phase has forced up the prices of South Africa's minerals, which has enabled the government to finance social welfare programmes.'[3]

We are now fast approaching 2020. It is mid-2015 as I write this, and the prospects of this country being able to stand on its own by 2020 are looking bleak. The *Financial Mail* reports that for the past two years South Africa has experienced growth of 2.2 per cent. The Reuters consensus is that the economy will fail to break out of this low-growth trap over the next three years, growing at just 2.4 per cent in 2016 and 2.6 per cent in 2017.[4]

This means that the prospects of millions of unemployed young black people out there will stay exactly the same: hopeless (remember that, according to the South African Institute of Race Relations, 70.4 per cent of black youth between the age of 15 and 24 are neither working nor in training, compared to 21.7 per cent of whites).[5]

This low-growth trap means that the 16 million who draw some or other form of government grant will keep doing so, if we are lucky, or their number will increase. It is likely that the 14 700 protests reported by police in 2014–2015 will persist, or increase.

The new South Africa, hailed as a miracle by so many, remains a nightmare for millions of poor black people. Moreover, it will remain so, or become even more hopeless, for a while longer.

It is time to stop and reassess our political and economic trajectory. It is time for courage in leadership and policy. It is time to change gear. For we have now begun our descent.

It is not the first time that we find ourselves here. In 1990, when Nelson Mandela walked out of prison, many said the end was nigh. The country was in dire straits as the peace talks started, stuttered and stopped.

Even patriots such as writer and author Shaun Johnson found themselves worried about the direction our country was taking. Johnson wrote in his popular *Saturday Star* column in 1992: 'People are talking about leaving again. This time around there are many middle-class blacks among them. The hope that blossomed in 1990 has wilted.'[6]

Two years later, when violence engulfed the nation on the eve of our first democratic election, many said the end was staring us in the face. The *New York Times'* Bill Keller – a friend of South Africa – wrote from Johannesburg on 26 April 1994: 'Bombs exploded across South Africa today, hitting mainly black taxi terminals and polling places in a crescendo intended to demoralize the new South African electorate on the eve of its first vote.

'A few hours after the worst attack, a horrific morning blast that killed 10 and sprayed human body parts and mangled minivans across a taxi park in suburban Germiston, the police said they were questioning a suspect and hoped for a breakthrough. More than a dozen explosions were reported today, including one in a restaurant that killed two people. On Sunday, a car-bomb in downtown Johannesburg killed nine people.

'The explosions today, most minor but ominous in their message, led some panicky residents to stockpile household goods but seemed only to harden the resolve of black voters to exercise their first franchise.'[7]

We came through, though. Indeed, in the years between 1994 and 2009 we thrived, defying the doomsday scenarios. South Africa's unemployment rate was 30 per cent when Mbeki took over from Mandela in 1999. It reached 37 per cent in 2003, and then declined to 22.8 per cent when he was fired in 2008. South Africa's debt-to-GDP ratio was 50 per cent in 1994. Mbeki pushed it down to 27 per cent by 2009.[8]

There were many mistakes made, of course, but the trajectory was upwards rather than the other way. Why? What did we get right then?

It is leadership. On 6 August 1990 I remember my friends and I cursing Nelson Mandela's name because he had travelled to Pretoria and met with State President FW de Klerk. They emerged afterwards and declared that the ANC had suspended the armed struggle.

My friends and I thought Mandela was a sellout, that he had drunk too much of apartheid's propaganda and was now giving up the one thing that the ANC and the black masses still held over the De Klerk government's head. Mandela sent out his fellow leaders across the country to calm angry young people who were threatening to walk across to the militant Pan Africanist Congress of Azania. He sold his message to his followers and organisation in meetings across the country in the weeks following the signing of what was called the Pretoria Minute.

It was not a popular decision. Yet it was necessary. And Mandela, like a true leader, knew that he had to take it and bring his followers along with him.

We need Mandela's kind of leadership now. We need leaders who know that time is finite, that our people's needs are urgent, and that we need to act. They need to know none of the decisions will be easy: long-standing trade union allies will have to swallow hard and take the medicine, business will have to give a little bit.

Department of Economic Development deputy director-general Neva Makgetla has said that apartheid was a system designed to prevent black South Africans from accumulating wealth. 'It is a long, difficult process to overcome this and get rid of the barriers to accumulating wealth,' she said.

Makgetla's point presents a double challenge to all of us: continually rolling back the legacy of apartheid, and constantly ensuring that all of us – particularly the black poor whose lives are still defined, every day, by apartheid's heinous policies – continue to grow more prosperous.

The problem with our current situation is that we are doing neither. We are moving so slowly now that we are in danger of stopping. We are stopping because we have poor leadership. That is the first problem we have to resolve, that the ANC has to resolve. President Jacob Zuma has proven that he is not the man for the job.[9]

A leadership moment now stares Zuma in the face: he has to choose to step down. He has to raise his hand and tell his comrades that it is time for someone else to continue. This is his only challenge now. After more than six years in power, he can achieve nothing and has failed at everything he has attempted. Jobs, education, crime, housing, economic growth: he has lost them all.

If he does not take this leadership moment and use it to regain his dignity then we continue on Moeletsi Mbeki's trajectory towards a Tunisia moment. Why, you may ask, haven't we had one already when the International Labour Organization says South Africa will have the eighth-worst unemployment rate in the world for 2015?[10]

This, after all, gives us exactly the same conditions that prevailed in countries where the Arab Spring erupted: young populations faced with extremely high unemployment. We have not got there because we have the government grants that Mbeki referred to, and we do not live in the sort of dictatorships that prevailed in Tunisia, Libya and Egypt. The people's frustrations are aired in regular elections and in the ability to protest peacefully, although there has been violence in recent times.

The coffers are, however, running dry. This year government handed public sector workers a 7 per cent increase, only to realise later that the deal will cost R66.2 billion more than has been budgeted for over the medium term. This will wipe out government's R65 billion contingency reserve.[11] This means that, down the line, money may have to be diverted from other necessary expenditure areas – education, social grants – to plug some other hole that may appear.

All this means one thing, and one thing only. It is time to act, to do rather than talk. It is time to smell the coffee and take decisive action. Our country has great resources and amazing people. We should be leading the world in many aspects of governance and delivery of services. We still can.

We cannot afford to fritter our chances away. It is time to act. In this regard we need to remember why the South African government caved in and rolled out the provision of anti-retroviral drugs to HIV-positive patients in the 2000s despite President Thabo Mbeki's Aids denialism. It was because civil society stood up and said 'this far and no further'.

It is time for South Africans, from all walks of life, to show the same courage again.

Acknowledgements

Many people have made this book possible. My heartfelt thanks to Jonathan Ball, who convinced me that we could make this book come together, despite my skepticism, and to Jeremy Boraine, who encouraged and brought the idea to fruition despite many missed deadlines. Alfred LeMaitre, the editor, was assiduous and a pleasure to work with. The entire Jonathan Ball Publishers family endured my idiosyncrasies for six months, and for this I am grateful.

Brad Latilla-Campbell pulled several all-nighters to work on the notes and bibliography and to offer some fantastic contributions on the text. I am grateful for his help and dedication. Many thanks to Michelle Leon and her library team at Times Media Group for allowing me to trawl their archives. My sister Gloria made me endless cups of tea over a frenzied deadline weekend in Hammanskraal, and thus pulled me through.

My lovely wife, Justine, has been a pillar of strength and encouragement every step of the way. Without her, this book, and much else, would not be possible.

Parts of this book have been published in various forms – as standalone pieces of commentary or columns – in *The Times*, *Sunday Times*, *Destiny Man* and *The Guardian*. I am grateful to these publications for the chance to continue to contribute to them regularly as a columnist and commentator.

Notes

PROLOGUE

1   National Public Radio (NPR), 'ANC, From "terrorist" label to liberation movement', NPR News, 9 January 2012. Available at www.npr.org. Accessed on 21 August 2015.

2   Joshua Keating, 'Why does Ruth Bader Ginsburg like the South African Constitution so much?', Foreign Policy, 6 February 2012. Available at foreignpolicy.com. Accessed on 21 August 2015.

3   Amogelang Mbatha, 'Zuma speech is sideshow as South Africa's Malema plots chaos', Bloomberg Business, 11 February 2015. Available at www.bloomberg.com. Accessed on 25 August 2015.

4   Public Protector of South Africa. 'Secure in Comfort: Report on an investigation into allegations of impropriety and unethical conduct relating to the installation and implementation of security measures by the Department of Public Works at and in respect of the private residence of President Jacob Zuma at Nkandla in the KwaZulu-Natal province', 19 March 2014. Available at www.publicprotector.org. Accessed on 4 August 2015.

5   Nazmeera Moola, 'Voters in Nkandla can't be bothered to participate in elections', Rand Daily Mail, 5 June 2015. Available at www.rdm.co.za. Accessed on 25 August 2015.

6   David Smith, 'Where Concorde once flew: the story of President Mobutu's "African Versailles"', The Guardian, 10 February 2015. Available at www.theguardian.com. Accessed on 25 August 2015.

7   Sapa, 'Zuma to deliver #SONA2015 amid tight security, disruption threats', Times Live, 11 February 2015. Available at www.timeslive.co.za. Accessed on 25 August 2015.

8   Amy Musgrave, 'SONA: "Bring back the signal" chants', Independent Online, 12 February 2015. Available at www.iol.co.za. Accessed on 25 August 2015.

9   ITWeb, 'SONA jamming declared a mistake', 19 February 2015. Available at www.itweb.co.za. Accessed on 25 August 2015.

10   Diane Hawker, 'I was kicked in the face: EFF MP injured at SONA', eNCA, 16 February 2015. Available at www.enca.com. Accessed on 25 August 2015.

11   'Speech by Cyril Ramaphosa at the signing of the Constitution'. Available at www.polity.org.za. Accessed on 25 August 2015.

12   Fitch Ratings, 'South African MTBPS highlights growth, fiscal challenges', 28 October 2014. Available at www.fitchratings.com. Accessed on 25 August 2015.

13   Mathew le Cordeur, 'SA's unemployment rate hits 12-year high', Fin24, 26 May 2015. Available at www.fin24.com. Accessed on 25 August 2015.

14   Joanna Taborda, 'South Africa GDP Growth Rate', Trading Economics, 27 May 2015. Available at www.tradingeconomics.com. Accessed on 25 August 2015.

15   Linda Ensor, 'Protests continue to strain SAPS resources, says police minister', *Business Day*, 15 May 2015. Available at www.bdlive.co.za. Accessed on 25 August 2015.

16   National Planning Commission, *National Development Plan 2030: Our future – make it work*, National Planning Commission and Department of the Presidency, 2013. Available at www.poa.gov.za. Accessed on 25 August 2015.

17   'State of the nation address by the President of South Africa, Nelson Mandela', Houses of Parliament, Cape Town, 24 May 1994. Available at www.sahistory.org.za. Accessed on 25 August 2015.

18   Lizel Steenkamp, 'Political hyenas in feeding frenzy – Vavi', *Beeld*, 26 August 2010. Available at www.news24.com. Accessed on 25 August 2015.

CHAPTER 1

1   African National Congress, 'The Freedom Charter', 26 June 1955. Available at www.anc.org.za. Accessed on 5 August 2015.

2   Albie Sachs, 'Preparing ourselves for freedom', paper prepared for an ANC in-house seminar on culture, in Ingrid de Kok and Karen Press, *Spring is Rebellious: Arguments About Cultural Freedom*, Cape Town, 1990.

3   21 Sharda Naidoo, 'ANC high-rollers spare no expense', *Mail & Guardian* 13 January 2012. Available at mg.co.za. Accessed on 25 August 2015.

4   IOL news, 'A closer look at Jacob Gedleyihlekisa Zuma', Independent Online, 6 May 2009. Available at www.iol.co.za. Accessed on 25 August 2015.

5   Jenna Etheridge, 'Zuma does not read: analyst', Independent Online, 26 September 2013. Available at www.iol.co.za. Accessed on 25 August 2015.

6   Barry Bearak, 'South Africa drops charges against leading presidential contender', *The New York Times*, 6 April 2009. Available at www.nytimes.com. Accessed on 25 August 2015.

7   James-Brent Styan, 'Pictures of Zuma's Nkandla home illegal', Fin24, 21 November 2013. Available at www.news24.com. Accessed on 25 August 2015.

8   News24, 'Gupta jet at Waterkloof an "invasion"', 2 May 2013. Available at www.news24.com. Accessed on 25 August 2015.

9   Thulani Gqirana, 'EFF appeals fall on deaf ears as Parly passes new rules', *Mail & Guardian*, 30 July 2015. Available at mg.co.za. Accessed on 25 August 2015.

10   BBC News, 'S Africa's Zuma cleared of rape', 8 May 2006. Available at news.bbc.co.uk. Accessed on 25 August 2015.

11   Sapa, 'Zuma confirms "love child"', *Mail & Guardian*, 3 February 2010. Available at mg.co.za. Accessed on 25 August 2015.

12   AmaBhungane team and Matuma Letsoalo, 'Jacob Zuma links to "untouchable" SAA boss', *Mail & Guardian*, 7 November 2014. Available at mg.co.za. Accessed on 25 August 2015.

13   Amanda Khoza, '"I sold my Zuma name for R10m house"', Independent Online, 17 November 2013. Available at www.iol.co.za. Accessed on 25 August 2015.

14   Sapa, 'Ramaphosa warns against the return of "boers"', *Mail & Guardian*, 11 November 2013. Available at mg.co.za. Accessed on 25 August 2015.

15   'Statement of Nelson Mandela at his inauguration as President', 10 May 1994. Available at www.anc.org.za. Accessed on 25 August 2015.

16   Mmanaledi Mataboge and Qaanitah Hunter, 'Gwede Mantashe admits ANC could lose power', *Mail & Guardian*, 19 December 2014. Available at mg.co.za. Accessed on 25 August 2015.

17   David Smith, 'Grace Mugabe's super-speedy PhD raises eyebrows around the world', *The Guardian*, 15 September 2014. Available at www.theguardian.com. Accessed on 25 August 2015.

18   Moloko Moloto, 'Boy dies after falling into pit toilet', Independent Online, 22 January 2014. Available at iol.co.za. Accessed on 25 August 2015.

19   *City Press*, 'Sadtu's trail of sex and bribery', news24.com, 10 August 2015. Available at news24.com. Accessed on 25 August 2015.

20   Alec Hogg, 'Police Minister battles to defend Zuma in Nkandla "pay back money" grilling, BizNews.com, 30 July 2015. Available at www.biznews.com. Accessed on 25 August 2015.

21 *City Press*, 'Zuma: Nkandla is like PW's George airport', news24.com, 20 October 2014. Available at news24.com. Accessed on 25 August 2015.

22 Xolela Mangcu, 'They're laughing at you out there, President Zuma', Rand Daily Mail, 18 November 2014. Available at www.rdm.co.za. Accessed on 25 August 2015.

23 Verashni Pillay and Mmanaledi Mataboge, 'Zuma's daughter gets top state job', *Mail & Guardian*, 25 July 2014. Available at mg.co.za. Accessed on 25 August 2015.

24 BBC News, 'Mbeki digs in on Aids', 20 September 2000. Available at news. bbc.co.uk. Accessed on 25 August 2015.

25 Tony Karon, 'Why South Africa questions the link between HIV and AIDS', *Time*, 21 April 2000. Available at content.time.com. Accessed on 25 August 2015.

26 Sarah Boseley, 'Mbeki Aids policy "led to 330,000 deaths"', *The Guardian*, 27 November 2008. Available at www.theguardian.com. Accessed on 25 August 2015.

27 Times Live, 'Listen to exactly what King Goodwill Zwelithini said about foreigners', 16 April 2015. Available at www.timeslive.co.za. Accessed on 25 August 2015.

28 Nabeelah Shaikh, 'Seven Mercs for Zulu King's wives', Independent Online, 5 April 2015. Available at iol.co.za. Accessed on 25 August 2015.

CHAPTER 2

1 Anna Cox, Shaun Smillie, Charlotte Chipangura and Lesego Makgatho, 'Joburg crippled by power sabotage', Independent Online, 6 September 2013. Available at www.iol.co.za. Accessed on 25 August 2015.

2 Dele Olojede, 'Ask nothing of God: the good society and its discontents', speech at NLNG Grand Award Night, Lagos, 8 October 2005. Available at www.aspeninstitute.org. Accessed on 25 August 2015.

3 Mia Malan, 'Motsoaledi: Why I use government hospitals', *Mail & Guardian*, 6 September 2013. Available at mg.co.za. Accessed on 25 August 2015.

4 Verashni Pillay and Mmanaledi Mataboge, 'Zuma's daughter gets top state job', *Mail & Guardian*, 25 July 2014. Available at mg.co.za. Accessed on 25 August 2015.

5 *City Press*, '19 Cabinet members still have private business interests', news24.com, 27 July 2014. Available at www.news24.com. Accessed on 25 August 2015.

6   Beauregard Tromp, 'Little Taegrin's horrific journey to death', Times Live, 27 July 2014. Available at www.timeslive.co.za. Accessed on 25 August 2015.

7   Africa Check, 'Factsheet: South Africa's official crime statistics for 2013/14'. Available at africacheck.org. Accessed on 25 August 2015.

8   China.org, 'S Africa cracks down on illegal initiation schools', 10 July 2015. Available at www.china.org.cn. Accessed on 25 August 2015.

9   Government of South Africa, 'Deputy Minister Obed Bapela condemns illegal initiation schools', media statement, 6 July 2015. Available at www.gov. za. Accessed on 25 August 2015.

10   City Press, 'Tjatjarag: How my free SA was corrupted', news24.com, 8 September 2013. Available at www.news24.com. Accessed on 25 August 2015.

11   Sapa, 'Cops admit Mzilikazi wa Afrika arrest was wrongful', Times Live, 18 November 2012. Available at www.timeslive.co.za. Accessed on 25 August 2015.

CHAPTER 3

1   South African History Online, 'Pretoria the segregated city', no date. Available at www.sahistory.org.za. Accessed on 25 August 2015.

2   African Studies Center, University of Michigan, 'Bantu education', South Africa: Overcoming Apartheid, Building Democracy, no date. Available at overcomingapartheid.msu.edu. Accessed on 25 August 2015.

3   Edward F Fiske and Helen B Ladd, Racial Equality in Education: How Far has South African Come? Terry Sanford Institute of Public Policy, Duke University, Working Papers Series 05-03, January 2005. Available at files. eric.ed.gov/fulltext/ED493386.pdf. Accessed on 25 August 2015.

4   Staff Reporter, 'Education system worse than under apartheid: Ramphele', Mail & Guardian, 23 March 2012. Available at mg.co.za. Accessed on 25 August 2015.

5   Faranaaz Veriava, 'Our courts are schooling the state', Mail & Guardian, 14 March 2014. Available at mg.co.za. Accessed on 25 August 2015.

6   News24, '18 Limpopo schools to get flush loos', news24.com, 24 January 2014. Available at www.news24.com. Accessed on 25 August 2015.

7   The Citizen, 'Flush toilets for Limpopo school', 24 January 2014. Available at citizen.co.za. Accessed on 25 August 2015.

8   Babalo Ndenze, 'Textbook saga: Manuel slams government', Independent Online, 1 September 2012. Available at www.iol.co.za. Accessed on 25 August 2015.

9   Sipho Masombuka, Pertunia Ratsatsi and Amukelani Chauke, 'Textbooks crisis a national shame', Times Live, 28 June 2012. Available at timeslive. co.za. Accessed on 25 August 2015.

10   Vusi Xaba, 'Zuma: Officials in hot water over delayed textbooks', Sowetan Live, 2 July 2012. Available at www.sowetanlive.co.za. Accessed on 25 August 2015.

11   Sapa, 'Declare crisis in education: Jonathan Jansen', Moneyweb, 3 October 2012. Available at www.moneyweb.co.za. Accessed on 25 August 2015.

12   Bekezela Phakathi, 'State takes over Eastern Cape's schools', Business Day, 4 March 2011. Available at www.bdlive.co.za. Accessed on 25 August 2015.

13   Eastern Cape Socio Economic Consultative Council, 'A perspective on the Eastern Cape 2013 matric results', ECSECC, 2014. Available at www. ecsecc.org. Accessed on 25 August 2015.

14   News24, 'E Cape teachers' strike affects pupils', 8 January 2012. Available at www.news24.com. Accessed on 25 August 2015.

15   Staff Reporter, 'ANC furious at Zille for refugee comment', Mail & Guardian, 21 March 2012. Available at mg.co.za. Accessed on 25 August 2015.

16   Africa Check, 'Why the matric pass rate is not a reliable benchmark of education quality', 7 January 2014. Available at africacheck.org. Accessed on 25 August 2015.

17   Klaus Schwab (ed), Global Competitiveness Report 2012–2013, World Economic Forum, Geneva, 2012. Available at nmi.is. Accessed on 25 August 2015.

18   The Presidency, Republic of South Africa, Twenty Year Review: South Africa, 1994–2014. Available at www.thepresidency-dpme.gov.za/news/Pages/20-Year-Review.aspx. Accessed on 25 August 2015.

19   Mark Gevisser, Thabo Mbeki: the Dream Deferred, Jonathan Ball Publishers, Johannesburg, 2007.

20   Unesco, 'Apartheid: its effects on education, science, culture and information', report, 1967. Available at unesdoc.unesco.org. Accessed on 25 August 2015.

21   Jonathan Jansen, 'Seven costly mistakes', 5 April 2012. Available at www. ufs.ac.za. Accessed on 25 August 2015.

22   City Press, 'Sadtu's trail of sex and bribery', news24.com, 10 August 2015. Available at www.news24.com. Accessed on 25 August 2015.

23   Nickolaus Bauer, 'ANC and Cosatu square off at Mangaung', Mail & Guardian, 20 December 2012. Available at mg.co.za. Accessed on 25 August 2015.

24   Nickolaus Bauer, 'ANC moves to make education an essential service',

Mail & Guardian, 4 February 2013. Available at mg.co.za. Accessed on 25 August 2015.

25   Andile Makholwa, 'Private schools: What is the attraction?', *Financial Mail*, 22 January 2015. Available at www.financialmail.co.za. Accessed on 25 August 2015.

26   Centre for Development and Enterprise, 'South Africa can achieve quality schooling for many more people if bold choices are made', press release, 20 September 2011. Available at www.cde.org.za. Accessed on 25 August 2015.

CHAPTER 4

1   Ra'eesa Pather, 'Eating out in Cape Town: a starter of racism, anyone?', The Daily Vox, 6 January 2015. Available at www.thedailyvox.co.za. Accessed on 25 August 2015.

2   News24, 'Hofmeyr faces Twitter backlash after apartheid post', 28 October 2014. Available at www.news24.com. Accessed on 25 August 2015.

3   Mia Lindeque, 'Steve Hofmeyr tried to make money out of racism', Eyewitness News, October 2014. Available at ewn.co.za. Accessed on 25 August 2015.

4   Sapa, 'Chester Missing questions sponsorship of "apartheid denialist"', *Mail & Guardian*, 30 October 2014. Available at mg.co.za. Accessed on 25 August 2015.

5   SABC, 'Anti-racism campaign will work if there's support: De Lille', 22 March 2015. Available at www.sabc.co.za. Accessed on 25 August 2015.

6   Matthew Burbidge, 'Gallery refuses to remove "spear of the nation" artwork', *Mail & Guardian*, 17 May 2012. Available at mg.co.za. Accessed on 25 August 2015.

7   Jackson Mthembu, 'ANC outraged by Brett Murray's depiction of Zuma', Politicsweb, 17 May 2012. Available at www.politicsweb.co.za. Accessed on 25 August 2015.

8   Daniel Howden, 'Jacob Zuma's lawyer weeps in court case against artist', *The Independent*, 25 May 2012. Available at www.independent.co.uk. Accessed on 25 August 2015.

9   Donna Bryson, 'History behind Zuma's lawyer's sobs', Independent Online, 26 May 2012. Available at www.iol.co.za. Accessed on 25 August 2015.

10   Zanele Sabela, 'De Klerk speaks out', Destinyman.com, 15 May 2012. Available at www.destinyman.com. Accessed on 25 August 2015.

11   Michael Wines, 'A highly charged rape trial tests South Africa's ideals', *The*

New York Times, 10 April 2006. Available at www.nytimes.com. Accessed on 25 August 2015.

12   Carolin Gomulia, 'From subject to citizens through social cohesion in SA', comment, SABC News, 10 May 2012. Available at www.sabc.co.za. Accessed on 25 August 2015.

13   Shanti Aboobaker, 'Zille sparks new twitter war with "professional black" jibe', *Cape Times*, 29 December 2011. Available at www.iol.co.za. Accessed on 25 August 2015.

14   Thabo Mbeki, 'I am an African', speech at the adoption of the The Republic of South Africa Constitution Bill, 8 May 1996. Available at www.anc. org.za. Accessed on 25 August 2015.

15   *The Observer*, 'Slovo widow "racist" smear', 18 July 1999. Available at www. theguardian.com. Accessed on 25 August 2015.

CHAPTER 5

1   Angelo Ragaza, 'Using star power to repair Nigeria's image', *The New York Times*, 10 July 2008. Available at www.nytimes.com. Accessed on 25 August 2015.

2   Lee-Anne Alfreds, 'The real cost of the arms deal', Corruption Watch, 27 March 2014. Available at www.corruptionwatch.org.za. Accessed on 24 August 2015.

3   Sahara Reporters, '234Next newspaper to shut down print edition this weekend', 23 September 2011. Available at saharareporters.com. Accessed on 26 August 2015.

4   Politicsweb, 'Threat to withdraw govt adverts "unacceptable" – Sanef', 10 September 2007. Available at www.politicsweb.co.za. Accessed on 26 August 2015.

5   Sibusiso Ngalwa, 'Pahad may cancel adverts in *Sunday Times*', Independent Online, 7 September 2007. Available at www.iol.co.za. Accessed on 26 August 2015.

6   Mmanaledi Mataboge and Matuma Letsolao, 'State poised to wield advertising axe', *Mail & Guardian*, 12 December 2014. Available at mg.co.za. Accessed on 26 August 2015.

7   Staff Reporter, 'Young South Africans: Media', *Mail & Guardian*, 26 June 2008. Available at mg.co.za. Accessed on 26 August 2015.

8   Gavin Davis, 'Dept of Communications spends R10m on *New Age* advertising', Politicsweb, 29 January 2015. Available at www.politicsweb.co.za. Accessed on 26 August 2015.

9   Staff Reporter and Sapa, 'Guptas want apology or R1 billion from *Sunday Times, M&G'*, Times Live, 3 October 2013. Available at www.timeslive.co.za. Accessed on 26 August 2015.

10   Staff Reporter, 'The beginners' guide to the Guptas', *Mail & Guardian*, 7 May 2013. Available at mg.co.za. Accessed on 30 August 2015.

11   Pierre de Vos, 'Zuma and the Guptas: the "symbiosis" continues', Daily Maverick, 3 May 2013. Available at www.dailymaverick.co.za. Accessed on 24 August 2015.

12   *City Press*, 'Zuma's cunning paranoia', News24, 10 December 2012. Available at www.news24.com. Accessed on 26 August 2015.

13   Julius Baumann, 'Transnet CEO: Gupta attacks smack of xenophobia', *Business Day*, 3 March 2011. Available at www.bdlive.co.za. Accessed on 26 August 2015.

14   Maureen Isaacson, 'Guptas give Ace royal treatment', Independent Online, 22 March 2011. Available at www.iol.co.za. Accessed on 26 August 2015.

15   Craig McKune and Stefaans Brümmer, 'Guptas "bankroll" Mrs Zuma's bond', *Mail & Guardian*, 30 November 2012. Available at mg.co.za. Accessed on 24 August 2015.

16   Craig Dodds, 'Hlaudi's pals "appointed for loyalty"', Independent Online, 20 June 2015. Available at www.iol.co.za. Accessed on 26 August 2015.

17   Sapa, 'SABC bans Zuma booing: *City Press'*, Independent Online, 11 December 2013. Available at www.iol.co.za. Accessed on 26 August 2015.

18   Media Workers Association of South Africa (Mwasa), 'How INM "harvested" Independent Newspapers in SA', submission to National Treasury, Politicsweb, 26 February 2013. Available at www.politicsweb.co.za. Accessed on 26 August 2015.

19   Mandy de Waal, 'Interview: Iqbal Survé, Indy's new boss and SA's latest media mogul', Daily Maverick, 19 February 2013. Available at www.dailymaverick.co.za. Accessed on 26 August 2015.

20   Paul Vecchiatto, 'Firing of *Cape Times'* editor raises eyebrows', *Business Day*, 9 December 2013. Available at www.bdlive.co.za. Accessed on 26 August 2015.

21   Marianne Thamm, 'True colours shining through: Should journalists be draping themselves in party political colours?', Daily Maverick, 13 January 2015. Available at www.dailymaverick.co.za. Accessed on 26 August 2015.

22   Nelson Mandela, 'Address to the International Press Institute Congress', 14 February 1994. Available at www.anc.org.za. Accessed on 26 August 2015.

23   Marcel Golding, 'I'm being railroaded for rejecting political instructions to

e.tv', BizNews.com, 23 October 2014. Available at www.biznews.com. Accessed on 26 August 2015.

24 Mandy de Waal, '*City Press* buckles to ANC demands – and threats', Daily Maverick, 29 May 2012. Available at www.dailymaverick.co.za. Accessed on 26 December 2015.

25 Sapa, 'ANC: Media is the main opposition', Independent Online, 12 April 2011. Available at www.iol.co.za. Accessed on 26 August 2015.

CHAPTER 6

1 Chris Hedges, 'Cornel West and the fight to save the black prophetic tradition', 9 September 2013. Available at www.truth-out.org. Accessed on 6 August 2015.

2 Baldwin Ndaba, 'Thuli a CIA spy, says deputy minister', Independent Online, 8 September 2014. Available at www.iol.co.za. Accessed on 6 August 2015.

3 Mzilikazi wa Afrika and Piet Rampedi, 'Kebby admits he ran away from MK camp', Times Live, 14 September 2014. Available at www.timeslive. co.za. Accessed on 26 August 2015.

4 Wyndham Hartley, 'Administration of veterans is in a shambles', *Business Day*, 2 October 2014. Available at www.bdlive.co.za. Accessed on 26 August 2015.

5 Charles Molele, Matuma Letsaolo and Khuthala Nandipha, 'Vavi reveals secret report used to "assassinate" him', *Mail & Guardian*, 16 August 2013. Available at mg.co.za. Accessed on 26 August 2015.

6 **Peter Ramothwala**, 'Kebby tells prof "to leave"', *The New Age*, 15 September 2014. Available at thenewage.co.za. Accessed on 26 August 2015.

7 Anthony Butler, 'Ambassador post at stake in media exchange', *Business Day*, 15 October 2010. Available at www.bdlive.co.za. Accessed on 26 August 2015.

8 Stephen Ellis, 'Mbokodo: security in the ANC camps, 1961–1990', *African Affairs* 93(371), April 1994. Available at libcom.org. Accessed on 26 August 2015.

9 United Press International, 'Mbeki says CIA had role in HIV/AIDS conspiracy', 6 October 2000. Available at www.nelsonmandela.org. Accessed on 26 August 2015.

10 News24, 'Sexwale, Phosa angry over Mbeki conspiracy claims', 25 April 2001. Available at www.news24.com. Accessed on 26 August 2015.

11 Eric Conway-Smith, 'Jacob Zuma: Leaked KPMG report shows S. Africa

president was a "kept politician"', *The Telegraph*, 7 December 2012. Available at www.telegraph.co.uk. Accessed on 26 August 2015.

12 News24, 'Mac, Mo and journo "conspired"', 18 December 2003. Available at www.news24.com. Accessed on 26 August 2015.

13 Rapule Tabane, 'It all went horribly wrong', *Mail & Guardian*, 21 November 2003. Available at mg.co.za. Accessed on 26 August 2015.

14 Mzilikazi wa Afrika, 'Zuma revealed as hidden hand in spy scandal', Times Live, 7 August 2014. Available at www.timeslive.co.za. Accessed on 26 August 2015.

15 Report of the Hefer Commission of Inquiry, 7 January 2004. Available at www.justice.gov.za/commissions/comm_hefer/2004%2001%2020_hefer_report.pdf. Accessed on 26 August 2015.

16 Alan Cowell, 'Fiery "necklace" becomes emblem of deepening South African violence', *The New York Times*, 29 June 1985. Available at www.nytimes.com. Accessed on 6 August 2015.

17 Paul Trewhela, 'The ANC prison camps: an audit of three years, 1990–1993'. Available at www.disa.ukzn.ac.za/webpages/DC/slapr93.3/slapr93.3.pdf. Accessed on 24 August 2015.

CHAPTER 7

1 BBC News, 'South Africa's Lonmin Marikana mine clashes killed 34', 17 August 2012. Available at www.bbc.com. Accessed on 26 August 2015.

2 Jonisayi Maromo, 'Marikana commission: Strikers used muti, believed they were invincible', *Mail & Guardian*, 26 November 2013. Available at mg.co.za. Accessed on 26 August 2015.

3 Sapa, 'Marikana: Mortuary vans called before shooting', *Mail & Guardian*, 14 October 2013. Available at mg.co.za. Accessed on 26 August 2015.

4 Greg Nicolson, 'Marikana report: Key findings and recommendations', Daily Maverick, 26 June 2015. Available at www.dailymaverick.co.za. Accessed on 26 August 2015.

5 Jonisayi Maromo and Sapa, 'Some Marikana victims shot in head', Independent Online, 4 December 2013. Available at www.iol.co.za. Accessed on 26 August 2015.

6 Report of the Marikana Commission of Inquiry, 31 March 2015. *Government Gazette*, 10 July 2015. Available at http://www.justice.gov.za/legislation/notices/2015/20150710-gg38978_gen699_3-marikana.pdf. Accessed on 26 August 2015.

7 Greg Marinovich, 'The murder fields of Marikana. The cold murder fields

of Marikana', Daily Maverick, 8 September 2012. Available at www.daily-maverick.co.za. Accessed on 6 August 2015.

8   South African Civil Society Information Service (SACSIS), 'Socio-economic rights still eluding Marikana communities', 9 May 2013. Available at sacsis.org.za. Accessed on 6 August 2015.

9   Desné Masie, 'We need to talk about Cyril: South Africa's Ramaphosa should face greater scrutiny over business and tax affairs', African Arguments, 23 November 2014. Available at africanarguments.org. Accessed on 26 August 2015.

10   Greg Nicolson, 'NUM: The end of the age of Frans Baleni', Daily Maverick, 7 June 2015. Available at www.dailymaverick.co.za. Accessed on 26 August 2015.

11   **Luyolo Mkentane**, 'NUM is "not a sweetheart union"', *The New Age*, 13 September 2012. Available at thenewage.co.za. Accessed on 26 August 2015.

12   Matuma Letsoalo, 'NUM plans disciplinary action over Baleni salary leak', *Mail & Guardian*, 31 May 2012. Available at mg.co.za. Accessed on 26 August 2015.

13   Greg Marinovich, 'Beyond the chaos at Marikana: The search for the real issues', Daily Maverick, 17 August 2012. Available at www.dailymaverick. co.za. Accessed on 26 August 2015.

14   Niren Tolsi, 'SAPS rot runs deep in Marikana cover-up', *Mail & Guardian*, 2 July 2015. Available at mg.co.za. Accessed on 26 August 2015.

15   Times Live, 'Judge throws book at cops who murdered Mido Macia', 25 August 2015. Available at www.timeslive.co.za. Accessed on 26 August 2015.

16   David Smith, 'Police shoot dead three-year-old in South Africa', *The Guardian*, 10 November 2009. Available at www.theguardian.com. Accessed on 26 August 2015.

17   Sapa, 'Cops acquitted of Andries Tatane's murder', *Mail & Guardian*, 28 March 2013. Available at mg.co.za. Accessed on 26 August 2015.

18   Sapa, 'Cops "shouldn't be sorry" about Marikana shooting', *Mail & Guardian*, 20 August 2012. Available at mg.co.za. Accessed on 26 August 2015.

19   Sapa, '"Shoot the bastards" – Fikile Mbalula', 12 November 2009. Available at www.csvr.org.za. Accessed on 26 August 2015.

20   Sebastien Berger, '"Kill the bastards" South African police advised', *The Telegraph*, 10 April 2008. Available at www.telegraph.co.uk. Accessed on 26 August 2015.

21   Kwanele Sosibo, 'Violence on tape confirms police tactics', *Mail & Guardian*, 25 March 2011. Available at mg.co.za. Accessed on 26 August 2015.

22   *City Press*, 'Senseless death of a kind family man', News24.com, 3, February 2013. Available at www.news24.com. Accessed on 26 August 2015.

23   Africa Check, 'Will 74,400 women be raped this August in South Africa?', 28 August 2014. Available at africacheck.org. Accessed on 26 August 2015.

24   Staff Reporter, 'Lekota defends Umshini Wami remarks', *Mail & Guardian*, 5 September 2007. Available at mg.co.za. Accessed on 26 August 2015.

25   Mandy de Waal, 'Jane Duncan on the ever-increasing power of SA's security cabal', Daily Maverick, 16 June 2011. Available at www.dailymaverick. co.za. Accessed on 26 August 2015.

26   Jeremy Gordin, 'The Zuma alumni', Politicsweb, 12 June 2009. Available at www.politicsweb.co.za. Accessed on 26 August 2015.

27   Sello S Alcock, 'Billy's off the hook', *Mail & Guardian*, 17 January 2009. Available at mg.co.za. Accessed on 26 August 2015.

28   Staff Reporter, '"Mbeki must account to Luthuli House", says Masetlha', *Mail & Guardian*, 28 December 2007. Available at mg.co.za. Accessed on 26 August 2015.

29   SouthAfrica.info, 'Black economic empowerment', 19 April 2013. Available at www.southafrica.info. Accessed on 26 August 2015.

30   Sapa, 'Despite challenges, Davies views B-BBEE as a success', *Mail & Guardian*, 3 October 2013. Available at mg.co.za. Accessed on 26 August 2015.

31   *The Economist*, 'The president says it has failed', 31 March 2010. Available at www.economist.com. Accessed on 26 August 2015.

32   MiningMx, 'Shanduka seizes control of Incwala', 2009. Available at www. miningmx.com. Accessed on 26 August 2015.

33   BizNews.com, 'The Ramaphosa billions: How *Forbes* calculates his wealth at $700m', 28 May 2014. Available at www.biznews.com. Accessed on 26 August 2015.

34   Nompumelelo Magwaza, 'Ramaphosa gives boards a headache', *Business Report*, 11 January 2013. Available at www.iol.co.za. Accessed on 26 August 2015.

35   News24, 'Ramaphosa wanted "concomitant action"', 23 October 2013. Available at www.news24.com. Accessed on 6 August 2015.

36   Khadija Patel, 'Marikana massacre: Ramaphosa's statement, revisited', Daily Maverick, 25 October 2013. Available at www.dailymaverick.co.za. Accessed on 6 August 2015.

37   Jonisayi Maromo and Sapa, 'Ramaphosa is Marikana accused No 1: Mpofu', Independent Online, 12 November 2014. Available at http://www.iol.co.za. Accessed on 26 August 2015.

38   Khadija Patel, 'Marikana massacre: Ramaphosa's statement, revisited'.

39   Report of the Marikana Commission of Inquiry, p. 437.

40   Craig McKune, 'Lonmin gives Ramaphosa priority over workers', M&G Centre for Investigative Journalism, 3 October 2014. Available at amabhungane.co.za. Accessed on 26 August 2015.

41   Mahathir Mohamad, 'The New Malay Dilemma', speech to the Harvard Club of Malaysia, 29 July 2002. Available at www.mahathir.com. Accessed on 26 August 2015.

42   Thabo Mbeki, 'Address at the Freedom Day celebrations, Bisho Stadium, Eastern Cape', 27 April 2007. Available at www.dfa.gov.za. Accessed on 26 August 2015.

43   Kwanele Sosibo, 'Marikana: NUM commends and condemns striking miners', *Mail & Guardian*, 31 January 2013. Available at mg.co.za. Accessed on 26 August 2015.

CHAPTER 8

1   BBC News, 'South African leader sacks deputy', 14 June 2005. Available at news.bbc.co.uk. Accessed on 26 August 2015.

2   Political Bureau, 'Mbeki booed by hostile Polokwane delegates', Independent Online, 17 December 2007. Available at www.iol.co.za. Accessed on 26 August 2015.

3   Jovial Rantao, 'It's crunch time for the ANC and the nation', Independent Online', 16 December 2007. Available at www.iol.co.za. Accessed on 26 August 2015.

4   News24, 'Delegates fear vote rigging', 16 December 2007. Available at www.news24.com. Accessed on 26 August 2015.

5   Jeremy Michaels, Moshoeshoe Monare and Moipone Malefane, 'ANC council restores Zuma to party activities', Independent Online, 1 July 2005. Available at www.iol.co.za. Accessed on 26 August 2015.

6   Conversation with ANC leader, now in business.

7   Anso Thom, 'Fired for "doing my job" – Madlala-Routledge', Health-e News, 13 August 2007. Available at www.health-e.org.za. Accessed on 27 August 2015.

8   Caiphus Kgosana, 'We gave Mbeki too much power', *City Press*, 19 November 2007. Available at m24arg02.naspers.com/argief/berigte/citypress/2007/11/19/CP/4/ckMagashu.html. Accessed on 27 August 2015.

9   Staff Reporter, 'A potential for crisis', *Mail & Guardian*, 11 December 2007. Available at mg.co.za. Accessed on 27 August 2015.

10   Sapa, 'Party in Polokwane as Zuma sweeps to victory', Independent Online, 18 December 2007. Available at www.iol.co.za. Accessed on 27 August 2015.

11   Sam Sole and Stefaans Brümmer, 'The kept politician: Zuma's willing benefactors', *Mail & Guardian*, 7 December 2007. Available at mg.co.za. Accessed on 27 August 2015.

12   Christi van der Westhuizen, 'Zuma's coalition a mish mash of views', *The Final Call*, 15 May 2009. Available at www.finalcall.com. Accessed on 27 August 2015.

13   Staff Reporter, 'ANC dumps Mbeki, moves to "heal rift"', *Mail & Guardian*, 20 September 2008. Available at mg.co.za. Accessed on 27 August 2015.

14   Andiswe Makinana, 'Mbeki "not behind formation of Cope"', Independent Online, 14 January 2011. Available at www.iol.co.za. Accessed on 27 August 2015.

15   Pierre de Vos, 'Zuma and the Guptas: the "symbiosis" continues', Daily Maverick, 3 May 2013. Available at www.dailymaverick.co.za. Accessed on 27 August 2015.

16   Nickolaus Bauer, 'Motlanthe's challenge on Zuma is "about principle"', *Mail & Guardian*, 10 December 2012. Available at mg.co.za. Accessed on 27 August 2015.

17   Roger Southall, 'Thabo Mbeki's fall: the ANC and South Africa's democracy', Open Democracy, 14 October 2008. Available at www.opendemocracy.net. Accessed on 27 August 2015.

18   Jonny Steinberg, 'Zuma has vision, but it excludes ordinary people', *Business Day*, 10 July 2015. Available at www.bdlive.co.za. Accessed on 27 August 2015.

CHAPTER 9

1   Charles Onyango-Obbo, 'Back to 1999: A bearded general, Obasanjo, Mbeki and the African horses that bolted from the stable', *Mail & Guardian*, 27 March 2015. Available at mg.co.za. Accessed on 27 August 2015.

2   International Criminal Court (ICC), 'ICC Prosecutor presents case against Sudanese President, Hassan Ahmad AL BASHIR, for genocide, crimes against humanity and war crimes in Darfur', press release ICC-OTP-20080714-PR341, no date. Available at www.icc-cpi.int. Accessed on 27 August 2015.

3   Wendell Roelf, 'South African president defends failure to arrest Sudan's Bashir', Reuters, 6 August 2015. Available at www.reuters.com. Accessed on 27 August 2015.

4   Palesa Vuyolwethu and Tshandu Lutho Mtongana, 'South Africa court says state broke law in al-Bashir escape', Bloomberg Business, 24 June 2015. Available at www.bloomberg.com. Accessed on 27 August 2015.

5   Thomas Hartleb, 'Laughter as court told al-Bashir has left', News24, 15 June 2015. Available at www.news24.com. Accessed on 27 August 2015.

6   ANA, 'Zuma would not allow Bashir's arrest', Independent Online, 16 June 2015. Accessed on 27 August 2015.

7   Mzilikazi wa Afrika, Piet Rampedi and Stephan Hofstatter, 'The truth behind Bashir's great escape, *Sunday Times*, 21 June 2015. Available at www. timeslive.co.za. Accessed on 27 August 2015.

8   Wyndham Hartley, 'Zuma under pressure over al-Bashir', *Business Day*, 16 July 2015. Available at www.bdlive.co.za. Accessed on 27 August 2015.

9   AFP, 'Ugandan president calls for mass Africa pullout of ICC court', *Daily Mail*, 12 December 2014. Available at www.dailymail.co.uk. Accessed on 27 August 2015.

10   News24, 'Rwanda's Kagame slams "selective" ICC justice', 16 October 2014. Available at www.news24.com. Accessed on 27 August 2015.

11   Anthony Kariuki, 'War crimes and punishment: why is the ICC targeting Africa?', *Brown Political Review*, 12 March 2015. Available at www.brown-politicalreview.org. Accessed on 27 August 2015.

12   eNCA, 'ANC on Bashir: "ICC is no longer useful"', 14 June 2015. Available at www.enca.com. Accessed on 7 August 2015.

13   AFP, 'Nobel peace summit cancelled after South Africa refuses visa for Dalai Lama', *The Guardian*, 2 October 2014. Available at www.theguardian. com. Accessed on 7 August 2015.

14   South Africa.info, 'South Africa, China strengthen ties', 8 December 2014. Available at www.southafrica.info. Accessed on 7 August 2015.

15   Jasmine Nelson, 'Zuma's growing relationship with Russia's Putin raises questions about nuclear deal', *Atlanta Black Star*, 13 May 2015. Available at atlantablackstar.com. Accessed on 7 August 2015.

16   Laurie Nathan, 'Explaining South Africa's position on Sudan and Darfur', transcript of lecture, Chatham House, 12 February 2008. Available at www.cmi.no. Accessed on 7 August 2015.

17   Thomas Hartleb, 'Laughter as court told al-Bashir has left'.

CHAPTER 10

1   Setumo Stone, 'Mathews Phosa: Looking for scapegoats creates culture of impunity', News24, 9 August 2015. Available at m.news24.com. Accessed on 27 August 2015.

2   Goldman Sachs, 'Two Decades of Freedom: What South Africa is doing with it, and what now needs to be done', report, 4 November 2013. Available at cdn.bdlive.co.za/images/pdf/20yearsofFreedom.pdf. Accessed on 27 August 2015.

3   Research on Socio-Economic Policy, 'The emergent South African middle class', Stellenbosch University, 2013. Available at resep.sun.ac.za/wp-content/uploads/2013/10/The-emergent-SA-middle-class_.pdf. Accessed on 7 August 2015.

4   *City Press*, 'Helen Zille sets her sights on 2016 municipal elections, News24, 10 May 2014. Available at www.news24.com. Accessed on 27 August 2015.

5   Siphe Macanda, 'DA's Fort Hare coup riles ANC', *The Times*, 4 May 2015. Available at www.timeslive.co.za. Accessed 7 August 2015.

6   Zwelinzima Vavi, 'Address to the Sactwu National Congress, Cape Town', 23 September 2010. Cosatu Today, no date. Available at www.cosatu.org.za. Accessed on 7 August 2015.

7   Lizel Steenkamp, 'Political hyenas in feeding frenzy – Vavi', *Beeld*, 26 August 2010. Available at www.news24.com. Accessed on 25 August 2015.

8   Busi Chimombe, 'Crime agencies losing public confidence: experts', SABC News, 28 January 2015. Available at www.sabc.co.za. Accessed on 27 August 2015.

9   Thabo Mbeki, 'Address at the Freedom Day celebrations, Bisho Stadium, Eastern Cape', 27 April 2007. Available at www.dfa.gov.za. Accessed on 26 August 2015.

10   Songezo Zibi, 'Mini budget and the NDP: Action Man wanted', *Financial Mail*, 17 October 2013. Available at www.financialmail.co.za. Accessed on 27 August 2015.

11   Natasha Marrian, 'New ANC Women's League leader dashes Ramaphosa hopes', *Business Day*, 10 August 2015. Available at www.bdlive.co.za. Accessed on 27 August 2015.

12   S'Thembiso Msomi, 'Ramaphosa has one hand on the crown', Rand Daily Mail, 26 November 2014. Available at www.rdm.co.za. Accessed on 27 August 2015.

13   Matuma Letsaolo, 'Zuma: SA ready for a woman president', *Mail & Guardian*, 6 May 2014. Available at mg.co.za. Accessed on 27 August 2015.

14　Fitch Ratings, 'SA downgraded from BBB+ to BBB, outlook stable – Fitch', Politicsweb, 10 January 2013. Available at www.politicsweb.co.za. Accessed on 27 August 2015.

15　Natasha Marrian, 'New ANC Women's League leader dashes Ramaphosa hopes'.

16　*City Press*, 'Speculation abounds over AU future of Dlamini-Zuma, News24, 1 February 2015. Available at www.news24.com. Accessed on 27 August 2015.

17　Padraig O'Malley, 'South African Youth Congress (SAYCO)', O'Malley – The Heart of Hope, no date. Available at www.nelsonmandela.org. Accessed on 27 August 2015.

CHAPTER 11

1　Staff Reporter, '"Terrified" Juju bails on debate with "Zille's tea girl"', *Mail & Guardian*, 20 May 2011. Available at mg.co.za. Accessed on 27 August 2015.

2　IOL News, '"We will kill for Zuma"', Independent Online, 17 June 2008. Available at www.iol.co.za. Accessed on 27 August 2015.

3　*City Press*, 'Juju: I'm very sorry, MaMbeki', News24, 12 April 2014. Available at www.news24.com. Accessed on 27 August 2015.

4　Staff Reporter, 'Malema apologises for Pandor comment', *Mail & Guardian*, 12 February 2009. Available at mg.co.za. Accessed on 27 August 2015.

5　Sapa, 'Malema pays R50 000 fine for rape remark', News24, 8 August 2011. Available at www.news24.com. Accessed on 27 August 2015.

6　David Smith, 'ANC's Julius Malema lashes out at "misbehaving" BBC journalist', *The Guardian*, 6 April 2010. Available at www.theguardian.com. Accessed on 27 August 2015.

7　Bheki Mbanjwa, 'Buthelezi is a factory fault: Malema', Independent Online, 13 October 2009. Available at www.iol.co.za. Accessed on 27 August 2015.

8　Sapa, 'Malema apologises for giving SA "a president like Zuma"', *Mail & Guardian*, 2 July 2013. Available at mg.co.za. Accessed on 27 August 2015.

9　BBC News, 'Nelson Mandela ambulance broke down on way to hospital, 22 June 2013. Available at www.bbc.com. Accessed on 27 August 2015.

10　Greg Nicolson, 'Mr Mbeki goes to Power FM', Daily Maverick, 21 June 2013. Available at www.dailymaverick.co.za. Accessed on 27 August 2015.

11　Craig Dodds, 'Zuma: Guptas are my friends', Independent Online, 20 June 2013. Available at www.iol.co.za. Accessed on 27 August 2015.

12   BBC News, 'South Africa opposition elects Maimane first black leader', 10 May 2015. Available at www.bbc.com. Accessed on 27 August 2015.

13   Sibusiso Tshabalala, 'The first black leader of South Africa's opposition party is inspired by Obama', Quartz, 11 May 2015. Available at qz.com. Accessed on 27 August 2015.

14   ANA Reporter, 'Zuma's days are numbered – Maimane', Independent Online, 26 May 2015. Available at www.iol.co.za. Accessed on 27 August 2015.

15   BizNews, 'Future SA president? Tim Modise interviews new DA leader Mmusi Maimane', transcript, 10 May 2015. Available at www.biznews. com. Accessed on 27 August 2015.

16   Qaanitah Hunter, 'Six things you need to know if you still care about Agang', *Mail & Guardian*, 11 March 2015. Available at mg.co.za. Accessed on 27 August 2015.

17   Sapa, 'Election results an embarrassment to PAC', Times Live, 8 May 2014. Available at www.timeslive.co.za. Accessed on 27 August 2015.

18   eNCA, 'Azapo youth wing laments poor election results', 10 May 2014. Available at www.enca.com. Accessed on 27 August 2015.

19   *The Citizen*, 'Lekota will have to eat his words', editorial, 1 May 2014. Available at citizen.co.za. Accessed on 27 August 2015.

20   Sapa, 'Elections 2014: Vote counting completed, ANC wins with reduced majority', *Mail & Guardian*, 10 May 2014. Available at mg.co.za. Accessed on 27 August 2015.

21   Allister Sparks, 'At Home and Abroad: A victorious Maimane could ease way to coalition politics', *Business Day*, 6 May 2015. Available at www. bdlive.co.za. Accessed on 27 August 2015.

22   Mara Kardas-Nelson and Benjamin Fogel, 'Why South Africans keep voting for the ANC', *The Nation*, 13 May 2014. Available at www.thenation. com. Accessed on 27 August 2015.

23   Herman Mashaba, 'Why I'm joining the DA', statement, Politicsweb, 27 May 2014. Available at www.politicsweb.co.za. Accessed on 27 August 2015.

24   Peter Kellner, 'We got it wrong. Why?', YouGov UK, 11 May 2015. Available at yougov.co.uk. Accessed on 27 August 2015.

25   Staff Reporter, 'Sample survey of young blacks believe DA would bring back apartheid', *Mail & Guardian*, 23 April 2013. Available at mg.co.za. Accessed on 27 August 2015.

26   Futurefact, 'Is Jacob Zuma becoming too much of a liability for the ANC?',

15 January 2014. Available at www.futurefact.co.za. Accessed on 27 August 2015.

27   Thalia Holmes, 'Analyst: No rosy elections outlook for ANC', *Mail & Guardian*, 7 August 2013. Available at mg.co.za. Accessed on 27 August 2015.

28   News24, 'Sars accuses Malema of lying, hits him with R14m bill – report', 12 April 2015. Available at www.news24.com. Accessed on 27 August 2015.

29   Qaanitah Hunter, 'Julius Malema: sequestration withdrawn', *Mail & Guardian*, 1 June 2013. Available at mg.co.za. Accessed on 27 August 2015.

30   Hlengiwe Nhlabathi, '"I have SARS by the balls": Malema', *Sowetan*, 6 June 2015. Available at sowetanlive.co.za. Accessed on 27 August 2015.

31   Qaanitah Hunter, Mmanaledi Mataboge and Thulani Gqirana, 'Even ANC voters say the ruling party is performing badly', *Mail & Guardian*, 22 May 2015. Available at mg.co.za. Accessed on 27 August 2015.

32   Setumo Stone, 'ANC has work to do in metros for 2016 local polls', *Business Day*, 12 May 2014. Available at www.bdlive.co.za. Accessed on 27 August 2015.

33   *Business Day*, 'Editorial: Perils of Cosatu's implosion', 1 April 2015. Available at www.bdlive.co.za. Accessed on 27 August 2015.

34   Natasha Marrian, 'The rise and fall of Vavi', *Financial Mail*, 15 August 2013. Available at www.financialmail.co.za. Accessed on 27 August 2015.

35   Natasha Marrian, 'Vavi's backing of Zuma polarises Cosatu', *Financial Mail*, 8 May 2014. Available at www.financialmail.co.za. Accessed on 27 August 2015.

36   Staff Reporter, 'The Tripartite Alliance is an anachronism', Daily Maverick, 11 July 2013. Available at www.dailymaverick.co.za. Accessed on 27 August 2015.

37   Donwald Pressly, 'Cosatu continues to block youth wage subsidy', *Business Report*, 9 July 2013. Available at www.iol.co.za. Accessed on 27 August 2015.

38   Patrick Craven, 'Cosatu opposed to making education an "essential service"', Politicsweb, 5 February 2013. Available at www.politicsweb.co.za. Accessed on 27 August 2015.

39   Reuters, 'Numsa's ANC boycott a serious blow – analyst', News24, 21 December 2013. Available at www.news24.com. Accessed on 27 August 2015.

40   Mpho Raborife, 'Numsa ready to build new trade union federation', Fin24, 23 July 2015. Available at www.fin24.com. Accessed on 27 August 2015.

41   Prega Govender, '"Overpaid" army of civil servants sucking SA dry',

Sunday Times, 3 May 2015. Available at www.timeslive.co.za. Accessed on 27 August 2015.

42   Workers & Socialist Party (WASP), 'WASP to be re-founded as a revolutionary party', 18 February 2015. Available at workerssocialistparty.co.za. Accessed on 27 August 2015.

43   Isaac Mahlangu and Sibongakonke Shoba, '"Sushi King" opens up about Julius Malema', Times Live, 18 February 2015. Available at timeslive.co.za. Accessed on 27 August 2015.

CHAPTER 12

1   Jan-Jan Joubert, 'Madonsela for president? Madonsela says "not interested"', Times Live, 12 April 2015. Available at www.timeslive.co.za. Accessed on 27 August 2015.

2   ANA, 'Madonsela saddened by "spiteful attacks"', *Cape Times*, 3 August 2015. Available at www.iol.co.za. Accessed on 27 August 2015.

3   Sapa, 'Ministers "tried to stop Nkandla probe" – court papers', *The Citizen*, 13 November 2013. Available at citizen.co.za. Accessed on 27 August 2015.

4   Chris Barron, 'I feared a hit – Thuli', Times Live, 23 March 2014. Available at www.timeslive.co.za. Accessed on 27 August 2015.

5   Stephen Grootes, 'Thuli Madonsela: State Security Agency lied to the nation', Daily Maverick, 17 March 2015. Available at www.dailymaverick.co.za. Accessed on 27 August 2015.

6   SABC News, 'Security Cluster ministers release task team report on Nkandla', 19 December 2013. Available at www.sabc.co.za. Accessed on 27 August 2015.

7   Jan-Jan Joubert and Bianca Capazorio, 'Nkandla report adopted', Times Live, 19 August 2015. Available at www.timeslive.co.za. Accessed on 30 August 2015.

8   *City Press*, 'Untouchable Jacob Zuma', 23 March 2014. Available at www.news24.com. Accessed on 27 August 2015.

9   Andrew England, 'S Africa orders media ban over pictures of Zuma's house', *Financial Times*, 21 November 2013. Available at www.ft.com. Accessed on 27 August 2015.

10   Maryna Lamprecht, 'Parliament trying to keep Madonsela under its thumb', News24, 13 May 2015. Available at www.news24.com. Accessed on 27 August 2015.

11   Marianne Merten, 'Feathers fly at protector sitting', *Daily News*, 30 April 2015. Available at www.iol.co.za. Accessed on 27 August 2015.

12   Maryna Lamprecht, 'Parliament trying to keep Madonsela under its thumb'.

13   RDM News Wire, 'Nkandla expenditure is "morally unjustifiable", Catholic bishops say', *Sowetan*, 2 June 2015. Available at www.sowetanlive.co.za. Accessed on 27 August 2015.

14   Alec Russell, 'Full transcript: Mac Maharaj on Mandela, Zuma and South Africa', *Financial Times*, 26 July 2015. Available at www.ft.com. Accessed on 27 August 2015.

15   Thabo Mokone and Caiphus Kgosana, 'ANC calls MPs to heel', Times Live, 3 February 2011. Available at www.timeslive.co.za. Accessed on 27 August 2015.

16   Sapa, 'Mathole Motshekga to be replaced as ANC chief whip', Times Live, 20 June 2013. Available at www.timeslive.co.za. Accessed on 27 August 2015.

17   *City Press*, 'Absurd to say Zuma must pay for Nkandla – ANC', News24, 30 September 2014. Available at www.news24.com. Accessed on 27 August 2015.

18   Chris Roper, 'The day we broke Nkandla', *Mail & Guardian*, 4 December 2013. Available at mg.co.za. Accessed on 27 August 2015.

19   Public Protector of South Africa, 'Secure in Comfort', p. 422.

20   Public Protector of South Africa, 'Secure in Comfort', p. 68.

21   Ranjeni Munusamy, 'Blurred lines: Zuma's non-response to Nkandla report', Daily Maverick, 15 August 2014. Available at www.dailymaverick. co.za. Accessed on 27 August 2015.

22   Sapa, 'Zuma, family benefited from Nkandla: Madonsela', Times Live, 19 March 2014. Available at www.timeslive.co.za. Accessed on 27 August 2015.

23   Paul Vecchiatto and Natasha Marrian, 'Pay back Nkandla spending, public protector tells Zuma', *Business Day*, 19 March 2014. Available at www. bdlive.co.za. Accessed on 27 August 2015.

24   Public Protector of South Africa, 'Secure in Comfort', p. 62.

25   Public Protector of South Africa, 'Secure in Comfort', p. 63.

26   Public Protector of South Africa, 'Secure in Comfort', p. 423.

27   Drew Forrest, 'Who's who in the Zu(ma) NWC', *Mail & Guardian*, 10 January 2008. Available at mg.co.za. Accessed on 27 August 2015.

28   Reuters, 'S Africa parliament votes to disband elite crime unit', 23 October 2008. Available at www.reuters.com. Accessed on 27 August 2015.

29 The Presidency, 'Jacob Zuma announces cabinet choices', Politicsweb, 10 May 2009. Available at www.politicsweb.co.za. Accessed on 27 August 2015.

30 Deon de Lange, 'Fresh ANC broadside for Scorpions', Independent Online, 24 April 2008. Available at www.iol.co.za. Accessed on 27 August 2015.

31 Craig Dodds, 'ANC MP hits back at Madonsela', *Daily News*, 30 May 2013. Available at www.iol.co.za. Accessed on 27 August 2015.

32 Sapa, 'Madonsela can take Nkandla report to Parliament, says Jeffery', *Mail & Guardian*, 3 November 2013. Available at mg.co.za. Accessed on 27 August 2015.

33 Sapa, 'Handling of Nkandla report worries ANC, Independent Online, 4 November 2013. Available at www.iol.co.za. Accessed on 27 August 2015.

34 *City Press*, 'No evidence public money spent on Nkandla – Nxesi', News24, 27 January 2013. Available at www.news24.com. Accessed on 27 August 2015.

35 Gareth van Onselen, 'Proof that Zuma did intervene on Nkandla', *Business Day*, 19 November 2014. Available at www.bdlive.co.za. Accessed on 27 August 2015.

36 Lamido Sanusi, 'Thuli Madonsela: South Africa's fearless public advocate', The 100 Most Influential People, *Time*, 23 April 2014. Available at time. com. Accessed on 11 August 2015.

37 *City Press*, 'What's next for Thuli Madonsela?', News24, 31 August, 2014'. Available at www.news24.com. Accessed on 27 August 2015.

CHAPTER 13

1 The Presidency, 'Jacob Zuma announces cabinet choices', Politicsweb, 10 May 2009. Available at www.politicsweb.co.za. Accessed on 27 August 2015.

2 Natasha Marrian, 'SA Communist Party: Red sunset looming?', *Financial Mail*, 16 July 2015. Available at www.financialmail.co.za. Accessed on 27 August 2015.

3 South African Communist Party (SACP), 'SACP Statement on the National Planning Commission', Cosatu Today, no date. Available at www.cosatu. org.za. Accessed on 27 August 2015.

4 National Planning Commission, 'Diagnostic Overview', The Presidency, 9 June 2011. Available at www.gov.za/sites/www.gov.za/files/npc_diagnostic_overview_1.pdf. Accessed on 27 August 2015.

5   National Planning Commission, *National Development Plan 2030: Our future – make it work*, Executive Summary, The Presidency, 2013. Available at www.gov.za. Accessed on 27 August 2015.

6   Karl Gernetzky, 'Government can't bow to specific interests on National Development Plan', *Business Day*, 30 April 2015. Available at www.bdlive. co.za. Accessed on 27 August 2015.

7   Sipho Hlongwane, 'SACP on the NDP: We do need a plan, just not this one', Daily Maverick, 17 May 2013. Available at www.dailymaverick.co.za. Accessed on 27 August 2015.

8   Sadtu Political Education Forum, 'The National Planning Commission: Draft National Development Plan. *Chapter 9 on Education*', Google Groups, 13 June 2013. Available at groups.google.com/forum/#!topic/sadtu-political-education-forum/BkSXctH-1OM. Accessed on 27 August 2015.

9   Natasha Marrian, 'SA Communist Party: Red sunset looming?'

10   *City Press*, 'Cosatu will never accept "DA-inspired" NDP', News24, 25 July 2013. Available at www.news24.com. Accessed on 27 August 2015.

11   Stephanie Johnson, 'Why ratings agencies are downgrading South Africa', Market Realist, 17 December 2014. Available at marketrealist.com. Accessed on 27 August 2015.

12   Fitch Ratings, 'SA downgraded from BBB+ to BBB, outlook stable – Fitch', Politicsweb, 10 January 2013. Available at www.politicsweb.co.za. Accessed on 27 August 2015.

13   Ann Bernstein and David Kaplan, 'Clear policy choices are needed, not conflicting plans', *Business Day*, 30 October 2013. Available at www. bdlive.co.za. Accessed on 10 August 2015.

14   PWC, 'The NDP – The right plan for private sector participation', Price-waterhouseCoopers, no date. Available at www.pwc.co.za. Accessed on 27 August 2015.

CHAPTER 14

1   Sapa, '"Action man" Zuma will help SA – Ramaphosa', Independent On-line, 11 January 2013. Available at www.iol.co.za. Accessed on 28 August 2015.

2   Mara Kardas-Nelson and Benjamin Fogel, 'Why South Africans keep voting for the ANC', *The Nation*, 13 May 2014. Available at www.thenation. com. Accessed on 27 August 2013.

3 Sapa, 'Choose Zuma and I'll leave the ANC, says Achmat', *Mail & Guardian*, 28 November 2012. Available at mg.co.za. Accessed on 28 August 2015.

4 Wikipedia, 'Tactical voting', Available at en.wikipedia.org. Accessed on 11 August 2015.

5 Paul Vecchiatto, 'Déjà vu as Zuma says ANC will rule until Jesus comes again', *Business Day*, 7 January 2015. Available at www.bdlive.co.za. Accessed on 28 August 2015.

6 Sechaba ka'Nkosi, 'SA's outlook for growth cut to 2.5%', *Business Report*, 14 April 2015. Available at www.iol.co.za. Accessed on 28 August 2015.

7 Marius Strydom, 'Did you know Thabo Mbeki presided over SA's highest economic growth rate in the past 35 years?', South Africa – The Good News, 6 May 2015. Available at www.sagoodnews.co.za. Accessed on 28 August 2015.

8 Anver Versi, 'Singapore: SEA's economic miracle', *Global: the international briefing*, no date. Available at www.global-briefing.org. Accessed on 11 August 2015.

9 Kishore Mahbubani, 'Why Singapore is the world's most successful society', The World Post, 4 August 2015. Available at www.huffingtonpost.com. Accessed on 28 August 2015.

10 Barack Obama, 'Remarks by the President at the 50th Anniversary of the Selma to Montgomery Marches', 7 March 2015. Available at www.whitehouse.gov. Accessed on 28 August 2015.

11 Republic of South Africa, The Constitution of the Republic of South Africa, 1996, as adopted on 8 May 1996 and amended on 11 October 1996 by the Constitutional Assembly. Available at www.justice.gov.za. Accessed on 28 August 2015.

12 Pierre de Vos, 'On changing the Constitution', blog post, Constitutionally Speaking, 23 May 2012. Available at constitutionallyspeaking.co.za. Accessed on 28 August 2015.

13 Nelson Mandela, 'I am prepared to die', speech from the dock, 20 April 1964. Available at www.nelsonmandela.org. Accessed on 28 August 2015.

14 Isaac Arnsdorf, 'The resource curse', Bloomberg QuickTake, 12 September 2014. Available at www.bloombergview.com. Accessed on 28 August 2015.

15 Transparency International, 'Transparency International calls on the Nigerian government to rescind its Centenary Award to the late president Sani

Abacha', press release, 12 March 2014. Available at www.transparency.org. Accessed on 28 August 2015.

16   World Bank, 'Botswana: Overview', 16 October 2014. Available at www.worldbank.org. Accessed on 28 August 2015.

17   Kishore Mahbubani, 'Why Singapore is the world's most successful society'.

18   Roy Mathew, 'Effect of declining oil prices on oil exporting countries', no date. Available at web.stanford.edu. Accessed on 28 August 2015.

19   Lucille Davies, 'South Africa is "Country of the Future"', Media Club South Africa, 22 October 2013. Available at www.mediaclubsouthafrica.com. Accessed on 28 August 2015.

20   Songezo Zibi, 'Mini budget and the NDP: Action Man wanted', *Financial Mail*, 17 October 2013. Available at www.financialmail.co.za. Accessed on 28 August 2015.

21   Nicholas Spaull, 'South Africa's Education Crisis: The quality of education in South Africa 1994–2011', Centre for Development and Enterprise, October 2013. Available at www.section27.org.za. Accessed on 28 August 2015.

22   Unesco, 'UNESCO: Sustainable development begins with education', Unesco Media Services, 18 September 2014. Available at www.unesco.org. Accessed on 28 August 2015.

23   Rebecca Davis, 'Know your DA (A Tale of Two Helens)', Daily Maverick, 14 May 2013. Available at www.dailymaverick.co.za. Accessed on 28 August 2015.

24   Wyndham Hartley, 'ANC, DA battle over struggle legacy rages on', *Business Day*, 29 April 2013. Available at www.bdlive.co.za. Accessed on 28 August 2015.

25   Nelson Mandela, 'Television address to the nation by ANC President Nelson Mandela on the assassination of Chris Hani', 13 April 1993. Available at www.anc.org.za. Accessed on 28 August 2015.

26   DefenceWeb, 'Lack of intelligence contributed to SANDF deaths in CAR – Claim', 5 April 2013. Available at www.defenceweb.co.za. Accessed on 28 August 2015.

27   Philip de Wet, 'Zuma: Questions on CAR endanger South Africa', *Mail & Guardian*, 2 April 2013. Available at mg.co.za. Accessed on 28 August 2015.

28   Nelson Mandela, 'Television address to the nation by ANC President Nelson Mandela on the assassination of Chris Hani'.

EPILOGUE

1   Staff Reporter, 'Angry man attacks ANC's HQ', *The Star*, 24 August 2012. Available at www.iol.co.za. Accessed on 28 August 2015.

2   Trading Economics, 'South Africa Unemployment Rate', 29 July 2015. Available at www.tradingeconomics.com. Accessed on 28 August 2015.

3   Moeletsi Mbeki, 'Wealth creation', *Business Day*, 10 February 2011. Available at www.bdlive.co.za. Accessed on 28 August 2015.

4   Claire Bisseker, 'Economic growth outlook: The 2% economy', *Financial Mail*, 4 June 2015. Available at www.financialmail.co.za. Accessed on 28 August 2015.

5   Finweek Staff, 'Young, black and angry – little hope for millions', *Finweek*, 7 May 2015. Available at finweek.com. Accessed on 28 August 2015.

6   Shaun Johnson, 'Our Noble Compromise', in *Strange Days Indeed*, Transworld Publishers, London, 1993, p. 199.

7   Bill Keller, 'More bombings rattle South Africans', *The New York Times*, 26 April 1994. Available at www.nytimes.com. Accessed on 11 August 2015.

8   Marius Strydom, 'Did you know Thabo Mbeki presided over SA's highest economic growth rate in the past 35 years?', South Africa – The Good News, 6 May 2015. Available at www.sagoodnews.co.za. Accessed on 28 August 2015.

9   Peter Bruce, 'Thick End of the Wedge: Zuma is a failure but we'll survive him', *Business Day*, 7 August 2015. Available at ww.bdlive.co.za. Accessed on 28 August 2015.

10 *City Press*, 'SA ranks 8th on worst unemployment rate list', News24, 20 January 2015. Available at www.news24.com. Accessed on 28 August 2015.

11 Claire Bisseker, 'Public sector wage bill: A really tight corner', *Financial Mail*, 4 June 2015. Available at www.financialmail.co.za. Accessed on 28 August 2015.

Index